Makers at Work

Folks Reinventing the World One Object or Idea at a Time

Steven Osborn

Apress·

Makers at Work: Folks Reinventing the World One Object or Idea at a Time

ISBN-13 (pbk): 978-1-4302-5992-3

ISBN-13 (electronic): 978-1-4302-5993-0

President and Publisher: Paul Manning
Acquisitions Editors: Jeff Olson, Michelle Lowman
Developmental Editor: Jeff Olson
Editorial Board: Steve Anglin, Mark Beckner, Ewan Buckingham, Gary Cornell,
    Louise Corrigan, Jonathan Gennick, Jonathan Hassell, Robert Hutchinson,
    Michelle Lowman, James Markham, Matthew Moodie, Jeff Olson, Jeffrey Pepper,
    Douglas Pundick, Ben Renow-Clarke, Dominic Shakeshaft, Gwenan Spearing,
    Matt Wade, Tom Welsh
Coordinating Editor: Rita Fernando
Copy Editor: Kim Burton-Weisman
Compositor: SPi Global
Indexer: SPi Global
Cover Designer: Anna Ishchenko
Transcriptionist: Kristen Ng

Distributed to the book trade worldwide by Springer Science+Business Media New York, 233 Spring Street, 6th Floor, New York, NY 10013. Phone 1-800-SPRINGER, fax (201) 348-4505, e-mail orders-ny@springer-sbm.com, or visit www.springeronline.com. Apress Media, LLC is a California LLC and the sole member (owner) is Springer Science + Business Media Finance Inc (SSBM Finance Inc). SSBM Finance Inc is a Delaware corporation.

For information on translations, please e-mail rights@apress.com, or visit www.apress.com.

Apress and friends of ED books may be purchased in bulk for academic, corporate, or promotional use. eBook versions and licenses are also available for most titles. For more information, reference our Special Bulk Sales–eBook Licensing web page at www.apress.com/bulk-sales.

Any source code or other supplementary materials referenced by the author in this text is available to readers at www.apress.com. For detailed information about how to locate your book's source code, go to www.apress.com/source-code/.

Apress Business: The Unbiased Source of Business Information

Apress business books provide essential information and practical advice, each written for practitioners by recognized experts. Busy managers and professionals in all areas of the business world—and at all levels of technical sophistication—look to our books for the actionable ideas and tools they need to solve problems, update and enhance their professional skills, make their work lives easier, and capitalize on opportunity.

Whatever the topic on the business spectrum—entrepreneurship, finance, sales, marketing, management, regulation, information technology, among others—Apress has been praised for providing the objective information and unbiased advice you need to excel in your daily work life. Our authors have no axes to grind; they understand they have one job only—to deliver up-to-date, accurate information simply, concisely, and with deep insight that addresses the real needs of our readers.

It is increasingly hard to find information—whether in the news media, on the Internet, and now all too often in books—that is even-handed and has your best interests at heart. We therefore hope that you enjoy this book, which has been carefully crafted to meet our standards of quality and unbiased coverage.

We are always interested in your feedback or ideas for new titles. Perhaps you'd even like to write a book yourself. Whatever the case, reach out to us at editorial@apress.com and an editor will respond swiftly. Incidentally, at the back of this book, you will find a list of useful related titles. Please visit us at www.apress.com to sign up for newsletters and discounts on future purchases.

The Apress Business Team

For Noah (2007–2012), whose favorite thing in the world was building projects with me at The Home Depot Kids Workshops.

Contents

Foreword

During the past few years, a remarkable phenomenon—the Maker Movement—has emerged. For two decades, humans have been immersed in creating new things based on bits. The Internet has woven itself into the fabric of everything we do. The radical evolution of how humans and computers interact has been profound, and as we get closer to a world where humans and machines are intrinsically linked, our minds—and innovative energy—has started to shift back to the physical world.

I'm 47. When I was in high school over 30 years ago, we had three "labs"—shop class, home economics, and a computer lab. Shop class was a function of the industrial revolution—an effort to teach teenagers how to use the tools in our parents' garages to make things. Home economics was an artifact of history that put women as "makers in the home." And computer lab was a hint of the future.

To really understand the future, it's important to look at the past. Before the industrial revolution, the world had an incredible maker culture. Not surprisingly, the phrase "cottage industry" came from makers who created things in their cottages, before the industrial revolution led to the rise of the factory. The industrial revolution, in a quest for massively scaling production, led to the consolidation and centralization of maker activities into factories. For 100 years, we operated under this model, using bizarre phrases like "mass production" and "mass customization" to describe what was going on.

In the mid-1990s, the commercial Internet appeared on the scene. Suddenly, we had a "platform" (the Web) for creating endless customization. Today, in 2013, the "web" is different for everyone—we all have whatever experience we want, because of the incredible flexibility of software to be customized, configured, tinkered with, changed, and distributed. We've learned just how cool and powerful bits really are.

But that's the past. And while the trajectory we started with computers—and bits—will continue ferociously over the next two decades, a new movement has resurfaced. Once again, humans are messing around with physical stuff. It's as though, as individuals, we've rediscovered the beauty and joy of playing around with atoms.

The maker movement has arisen from this. Suddenly, all over the world, maker spaces, the contemporary version of our parents' garages, are appearing. Unlike old factories, they are spaces available to do whatever you want in them. They are endlessly configurable and broadly distributed. 3D printers are suddenly appearing in homes and offices—just like their 2D grandparents of 30 years ago—ready to change the way we work with things, in the same way that 2D printers changed the way we work with text, words, and pictures.

New consumer products of all sorts are being created by brand-new start-ups, rather than giant industrial companies. It's no longer surprising as a venture capitalist to see a steady stream of consumer hardware companies looking for financing in areas ranging from human instrumentation to home automation to robotics. Conversations have shifted from the number of daily active users and K-factors to supply chains, bills of materials, gross margins, and distribution channels.

Five years ago, my partners and I at Foundry Group became completely obsessed with the maker movement. Our interest was framed by our human computer interaction (HCI) theme, where we believe that the way humans and computers interact over the next 20 years will be radically different than today. Some of the companies around HCI that we invested in were software companies, but a number of them, like Fitbit and MakerBot, were companies that had a significant hardware component. We initially viewed them as "software wrapped in plastic" and loved new products like those from Orbotix (the Sphero) and Sifteo.

But as we dug in more, we realized something broader was going on. Software is once again disrupting society—this time by transforming the way we think about making things. When we invested in Craftsy, we knew there was something primal about crafts, but we didn't realize it was an education site for an entire category of makers. And, by having the core of the education generated by the makers themselves via video, we were creating a wonderfully self-referential maker community of makers.

As I've gotten to know and work with some of these makers, such as Bre Pettis at MakerBot or David Merrill at Sifteo, I've learned that their minds and work habits are amazing things to observe. I have been rooted in software for a long time, so hanging out with Eric Schweikardt in his factory in Boulder, watching him tune his assembly line and work closely with his "elves" who make the actual product, is stunningly cool.

I believe we are at the dawn of an era where an entirely new vector of innovation emerges. It's as profound as the industrial revolution, the impact of electricity on society, or the Internet. No longer is the means of production of physical products limited to a small number of large organizations. Once again, anyone can, and everyone should, be a maker.

Vive la Revolution!

Brad Feld

Foundry Group, Managing Director

Boulder, CO

August 2013

www.feld.com

About the Author

Steven Osborn is a serial start-up entrepreneur, software hacker, and hardware enthusiast. In 2009 he co-founded a mobile messaging company called Urban Airship (urbanairship.com) that powers thousands of mobile applications on iPhone and Android for companies like Starbucks, Redbox, and ESPN. More recently he co-founded Smart Mocha (smartmocha.com), a company combining cloud services and digital sensor network technology. In his spare time, he enjoys participating in triathlons, baking bread, traveling, and spending time with his family. Steven lives in Portland, Oregon, with his wife, Jenny, and son, Theo. He is also an accomplished Guitar Hero rock star and Army veteran.

Acknowledgments

There are a seemingly endless number of individuals whose contributions brought this book together and I feel fortunate to have played my small part in its birth. It seems like a ruse for me to take credit as the author of this work, considering the amount of time the individuals mentioned below have put into making this a reality. I simply stood on the shoulders of giants and learned along the way.

First and foremost, I am in debt to all of the subjects who put aside their busy schedules to answer my questions and tell me their stories. Their vast knowledge provided me personally with an amazing education and a great amount of inspiration.

I'm honored to have had the privilege of working with all of the amazing individuals at Apress on this project. I am especially grateful to Michelle Lowman and Jeff Olson, whose guidance was invaluable. And special thanks to Kim Burton-Weisman for fixing my innumerable errors and to Rita Fernando for keeping me on schedule and ensuring everything went as planned. I would also like to extend a special thank you to Kristen Ng, my transcriptionist, who went out of her way to help me out on numerous occasions.

Most importantly, I would like to thank my wife, Jennifer, who has put up with me through three software start-up companies, one of which was launched while writing this book. Her continual encouragement and unwavering support is an endless blessing when deadlines are closing in and stress levels are high.

Introduction

I am a big fan of the original book in this series, *Founders at Work*. One thing that stuck with me about the stories in *Founders at Work* is the fact that CEOs of massive, successful Internet companies are just regular people who have overcome many obstacles and failures. Great projects, great companies, and great products don't just happen. These things start with one or more people who have the enthusiasm and desire to challenge what everyone else has done before them. These folks also have stories—not just about triumph and achievement—but also about failure, overcoming adversity, and persistence. Failures and challenges are a part of anything we do as humans, and how those failures and challenges are overcome is where the best stories are tucked away.

Stories are things we can all learn from and draw inspiration. I started this project because I have a passion for making things and I wanted to hear and share the stories behind the scenes, from inside the workshops and garages of people leading the way and building interesting projects that inspire other people to catch the maker bug.

What is so great about the stories in this book is the incredible amount of diversity in the projects and passions people have. Remote-controlled submarines, 3D printers, pinball machines, conductive ink, blinking suspenders—these are all projects created by makers whose stories are contained in these pages. As you'll see, the maker movement is vast and diverse. Electrical engineers, software developers, designers, schoolteachers, chefs, hipsters, and hackers—anyone can make things. It's one of the most accessible movements in modern history. The tools and knowledge needed to create objects married with technology is more readily available than ever. Although it may sound like a cliché, the saying, "You are limited only by your imagination"—considering the tools available to the average Joe—takes a heightened meaning.

The concept of the maker movement or maker culture is very simple at a low level. It is just people manipulating everyday things in their own environments. A maker's motivation is often to improve the way they interact with the objects and the world around them. The nature and motivation of the projects aren't any different from the DIY culture of yesteryear. The maker movement is just an acceleration of that culture, thanks to modern manufacturing technologies along with the availability and sharing of information via the Internet.

The availability of this information has given anyone with a little curiosity a way of removing the mysteries and magic of the things around us through learning and exploration.

The long-term impact of the maker movement can't be measured solely by the acceleration in the number of people choosing to create things as a hobby. This acceleration is a product of the movement; it's not the key that will drive great social and technological impact. The wide availability of information through sharing is the cornerstone of the maker movement. The conversation about how things work and how to improve them has an exponential effect on the rate at which technology is explored and advanced.

A better measure of the maker movement would be the rate at which this conversation is unfolding. The open-hardware movement is a good example of a subset of the maker culture that is driven by the availability of information. The same way open software has changed the software landscape forever, open hardware designs will enable a new level of collaboration and experimentation at a global scale.

Another important element that has enabled the explosive growth of maker culture is the availability of components at a drastically reduced cost. The era of the smartphone has fueled cheap components, making technology exceedingly accessible. High demands on smartphone manufacturing have drastically dropped the prices of "embeddable" processors and various electronics components like accelerometers and GPS modules. The availability of new and more powerful microchips and the sinking price of components have made new types of projects viable for the first time. All of the things in our world are rapidly becoming more intelligent, more seamless, more connected.

It's hard to think of the maker movement without mentioning digital manufacturing technologies like 3D printing, CNC milling, and laser cutting. Although these technologies are not extremely recent—the first 3D printer was developed in 1984, the first laser cutter in 1965—the availability of 3D printing and other digital manufacturing methods are becoming more affordable, easier to use, and more accessible to designers, engineers, and hobbyists.

The advances in these technologies, along with the broader availability and adoption, are key for makers. These technologies enable individuals to produce extremely detailed and precise objects that would be difficult or impossible to produce by hand. A CNC mill can turn a moderately creative person into an artisan wood carver in a matter of hours. Technologies that were reserved for extremely well-funded projects are now widely used.

The wide availability of digital manufacturing tools is allowing us to explore, for the first time, the world of 3D printing as a global community and share our experiences and designs with the rest of the world. 3D printing is being used in almost every job field imaginable, from culinary masterpieces 3D-printed in chocolate to 3D-printed prosthetics and custom-fitted transplants for medical patients, these tools are changing the way the world itself is prototyped and designed.

For individuals without the capital to buy these tools, maker spaces are popping up in droves all over the world to provide makers with the tools they need, as well as provide an environment of collaboration and information sharing. Fablab, Hackerspace, Techshop, Makerspace—whatever you call it, there is likely one nearby filled full of amazing individuals building an endless list of creative projects. Many of these spaces are run as nonprofit organizations and operate simply for the creative good of their local community.

The maker community is not only changing the way products are designed and developed, it is changing the way products are sold. With the rise in popularity of crowdfunding via Kickstarter, projects that may have been considered risky to bring to market are finding their way into people's homes. Crowdfunding is a way for makers to ask their existing community to support their projects or causes financially. This removes the risk of having to predict future demand of the product before investing in materials and manufacturing.

In addition, social commerce sites like Etsy and Tindie make it possible to sell custom-made, short-run products to niche markets. This provides makers with a way to engage global communities for specialty products.

We are living in a time akin to the birth of the personal computer era during the early days of the homebrew computer club. One day in the near future, we will look back on this time as a pivotal moment in technology history when the way products are designed and developed changed and the objects around us became smarter and more dynamic.

This book will introduce you to people at the forefront of this movement, who are inventing these new technologies, building things, sharing processes, and changing the way we think and interact with the physical world.

Most projects start out as a need for the maker to scratch an itch or to materialize the vision of an object they wish to exist in their world. Sharing their creation and the story behind it is where the project ends and the maker movement begins. For me, the itch was simply a desire to read the stories contained in these pages. The object I wished to exist was this book. Hopefully, it will serve in some small way as my contribution to the maker community.

Erik Kettenburg

Founder

Digistump

As a boy, **Erik Kettenburg** taught himself electronics and programming. His natural curiosity for hardware electronics has led him to build some impressive projects, even at a young age.

His recent Kickstarter project, the Digispark, was a big hit for providing a cheap, easily embeddable Arduino-compatible board for hackers and hobbyists. What started out as a way to scratch a personal itch turned into a wildly successful project. Erik continues to contribute to the open-hardware community through his website and online store at Digistump.com, as well as exploring small-scale manufacturing methods, and performing contract work.

Steven Osborn: It's always good to hear from folks doing interesting things here in the Northwest. I've only been here for a few years, but the maker community is really strong and growing. Anyway, tell me a bit about your background prior to Digistump.

Erik Kettenburg: Currently, my day job is the CTO of a company in Portland called Vacasa Rentals, which is a vacation rental management startup. I got there through being a web developer. Writing software has been my day job career basically my whole life. I was one of those kids who played with computers. When I was a kid, my dad introduced me to my first one, probably when I was four, which would have been an Apple IIe, maybe. I started writing PHP code when I was in junior high. And when I got to college—well, I had some small-paying gigs before that, got to college and took on a gig with a development shop, and I just worked my way up from there. This is actually the first career job I've had where I've played with hardware at all, and that's been pretty limited to virtual phone systems and that kind of stuff.

Osborn: So then, what got you plugged into the maker culture and the hardware side of thing? What got you excited about making hardware?

Kettenburg: Hardware's always been my hobby in both electronics and computers. And I've always enjoyed that more but never found a career in that and didn't want to be a PC assembler or something. And that goes back to being a kid too.

When I was in high school, I built my first Tesla coil. I was always playing with motors and burning things and taking things apart. So I got involved first with microcontrollers, probably when I was in high school playing with PICs, back when you used a serial programmer for them or made your own for the printer parallel port. So that's always been a strong interest. And then, of course, Arduinos really revived that interest when they came out. I was maybe in late high school or early college when I got my first Arduino, one of the very first ones. And that was awesome because I didn't have all the time I used to have at that point, so having that pre-made for me was great. And then I pretty much just played with Arduinos in my spare time, and tackled projects here and there.

I built an automated chicken incubator, temperature loggers, that kind of stuff. And then I got into designing my own boards. One thing that always bugged me, no matter what my income was—it seemed like a waste of money to stick Arduinos in things. I always had like three Arduinos and twenty projects that needed Arduinos. So I was always ripping something apart.

I came across Kickstarter around about a year and a half ago, and found that there were some Arduino clone projects on there, but they all were very hard to use. Things I could use, no problem, but I didn't necessarily want to. I didn't want to build them or use a separate USB programmer and I didn't want to hand-solder a giant through-hole board and stick it in my project. So out of that, I got the idea of, "How small and simple can you make an Arduino and still have a plug-in that is Arduino compatible?" And so that started the Digispark. I had the idea, "I'll make a couple of these," and then the idea of, "Oh, maybe I'll put this on Kickstarter. Maybe I can make five hundred of them, and that way I can pay for the ones that I make for myself." And that's how the project started. That's why the initial goal was $5,000—because that was to make five hundred of them.

Osborn: So how many of them did you end up making? Are you still shipping them?

Kettenburg: To date we have made forty thousand of them. And we've sold about twenty-seven thousand of them, as of today.

Osborn: I want to backpedal a little bit and talk about some things you mentioned. It sounds like from a very early age you were working on—well, you mentioned a Tesla coil. That's a pretty big early project. Can you remember any things from back then that inspired you? Any projects you remember or people who inspired you to go out and build a Tesla coil or some of these projects that you've built? What was your inspiration when doing these things?

Kettenburg: I think a lot of my electronics interest just kind of evolved on its own, with my dad planting the seeds in that he had a big box of old electronics. The thing that I distinctly—not only distinctly remember but still have with me—is he had two Forrest Mims' Radio Shack books, which were *Getting Started in Electronics*[1] and *Engineers Notebook II*.[2] I don't know if you've ever seen the Forrest Mims' books, but in the seventies, I think probably when he bought them, they were *the* books—sort of an *introduction to electronics,* you know, a consumer book—and they were handwritten on graph paper. The whole book just looked like photocopies of somebody's handwriting on graph paper. I still use those books. They're a little outdated now in that they do everything with 555 timers and transistors, but that's probably the first reference I really read outside of talking to my dad about electronics. He's a high school teacher, by the way.

Osborn: You had this mentor in your dad that could help you get started and plant that seed, but from there you were self-taught?

Kettenburg: Definitely, definitely, yeah. I think he was very interested in electronics at one point, but he didn't keep up with it. It wasn't his hobby at that point. So it was kind of like, "Here's my old stuff. Here's how to do a couple of things." And I kind of took it from there. Of course, I didn't have access to the Internet for the first half of my childhood probably, and so it was pretty much limited to those books and playing with stuff at Radio Shack.

I grew up in Santa Rosa, California, which is about an hour north of San Francisco. We had a Radio Shack about two blocks from our house, so I would just buy things there and hook them up, see what happened. I'd often burn them out and spent all my allowance on that.

When we got the Internet, I was probably in junior high, and at that point, I got on the Tesla coil mailing list, and that's where that interest came from. I don't know why I got on there. I think that I saw my first Tesla coil in one of those catalogs they used to send out that were like called "amazing scientific gadgets" or something. I haven't seen one of those in a while. But that's probably where I first saw a Tesla coil, and I was saving up to buy one of the little $50 ones in the catalog that shot quarter-inch sparks, and I found my way onto the mailing lists.

---

[1] Getting Started in Electronics (Radio Shack, 1983)
[2] Engineer's Notebook II (Radio Shack, 1982)

I actually made some web stores for some of the people who were supplying Tesla coils, homemade Tesla coil parts at the time. And so then stuff started showing up on the doorstep, and my mom started asking why I was buying a four-inch Tesla coil. And I told her, "No, I'm building a 1.5-million volt coil." And there were some trips to Home Depot and some big transformers and stuff. I only ended up running it twice because I could tell it just scared the heck out of my mom, but my parents supported me in it. They even allowed me to drive a twelve-foot grounding rod into their back lawn so that I could run the thing. And that ended up going to Sonoma State University in Santa Rosa, where they were going to use it as a teaching coil.

Osborn: Wow. How old were you around that time?

Kettenburg: Let's see. I was in ninth grade when I built the coil, so what was I? Like fourteen?

Osborn: Nice. I'm pretty sure I just played *Final Fantasy* when I was fourteen.

Kettenburg: About fourteen, yeah. And I think toward the end of high school, when Arduinos came out—I don't know when I switched from PICs to Arduinos, but I got more into microcontrollers or more into small stuff that wouldn't kill me or scare my mom. And the biggest kind of lightbulb moment—starting with PICs and Arduinos—was the ability to interact with the computer, because at that point, I was saving for college by doing web development, doing a lot of contract work in high school on web development. So bridging that gap between hardware and software was really a lightbulb moment for me because I loved the hardware and I knew the software. That's remained my biggest interest, and that's why the Digisparks had to have a USB connector to it. I didn't want just something I could program and stick in a box to do something. I wanted an easy way to interact with computers.

Most of my personal projects with the Digispark have been using its ability to emulate a keyboard to make a random password generator or using it as a USB device to notify me over the network when my laser cutter's done cutting—pretty much simple tasks that would be expensive to do with a full-blown Arduino. And that's even more recently changed my way of thinking. Having thousands and thousands of Digisparks sitting around and knowing what their cost to produce is, it's an easy choice to say, "Oh! I could put a Digispark there." I think that's probably why it's been successful too.

Osborn: Say somebody who's new to the whole maker thing, but they want to get plugged into the culture or movement, or whatever you want to call it. Do you have any advice for the complete novice who wants to start learning things?

Kettenburg: With the Digispark, I see a lot of people who are just starting because I think the price point appeals to people wanting to jump in, but not willing to fork out one hundred bucks in parts.

I think my biggest piece of advice is to find something that you think you'll be passionate about, that resonates with you. I mean, the maker culture is so big now. There's 3D printing. There's electronics. There's all the subparts of electronics. There's the craft side of it, the clothes making, and then of course combining electronics and clothes. I just see so many different aspects of it. I see a lot of people jump into whatever's hot. "I'll get a Digispark because I want to be a maker!" But I think you need to pick an end result that would be cool. Are you after blinking LEDs? Or would you rather make a toy elephant, plastic elephant, or something? So I think that's the first thing. It's so big now that you can really just look around and pick where you want to jump in.

Then once you do jump in, I always jump into things with two feet for better or worse, so I always recommend that. Go for it and get involved in the community. I know we have a lot of beginners who read our forums[3] and don't ever ask questions. And they should be asking questions, because for the most part, the maker community is very friendly. More than any other community, there are so many people who are new to it. I would say that compared to Massimo [Banzi] over at Arduino or Bre [Pettis], you know, those people, I'm pretty new to it even, at least new to having it be a large portion of my life. And I'm still on those message boards asking the stupid questions and getting great answers. So I think the first step is to jump into the community. And there are so many communities to choose from. It's not hard to find one that both has the same interests as you do and is very friendly.

Osborn: So there's kind of the next step, a lot of people have projects or ideas that they're working on that would bring it to the market. Do you have any advice for those people?

Kettenburg: Build a prototype. I get so many e-mails about that. E-mails, Kickstarter messages, and they all start like, "I have this idea. I think it will be a great product. What was your secret? What should I do next?" All those kinds of questions. When the Kickstarter [initiative] was going, I'd get about one of those a day. Now I probably get about one of those a week. Mostly I get people who have an idea and haven't tried to build anything yet. I think often we get held up on, "I have this idea. How do I build that product?" And, really, the thought process needs to be, "I have this idea. How do I build—to use a startup term—how do I build the *minimum viable product?*" But a better question is, "What can I tape together, stick together to do what I want this product to do, even if it doesn't work right, even if it costs five times as much?"

Personally, I always get held up on things like, "I have to design the perfect circuit board." Instead, I should be building it on a breadboard first. So I think the best advice is to do it, build it, test it, and tell people about it. People are always afraid that their ideas are going to be stolen, but you know, you're

---

[3]http://digistump.com/board/

really not that important. Your idea isn't that important. If it's worth stealing, somebody will pay you for it then. And talk about it, be passionate about it, and actually build it.

I think once you actually have a working prototype, the way the economics of starting a hardware company or launching a hardware product, just now with Kickstarter, with all the clones of Kickstarter, is once you have a proto- type, you can test your market really fast, which is amazing, because you don't have to invest the tons of money that I'm sure Arduino invested before they launched their product, and then all the money they invested to get their product out there and get it known, and how many years that took. Now you can do it in thirty days. I think it's important to not spend too much time building that first prototype, to not make it perfect, because the laws of busi- ness still apply: most things will fail.

I actually had a Kickstarter project before the Digispark that failed. It fell flat. Nobody was interested in it. And it was a software project. It was a software as a service dashboarding application, intended to provide real-time metrics. And I thought it was such a great idea. I thought it would be a big hit, and it fell completely flat. With the Digispark, I thought maybe I could sell one hundred of them, and it took off. So I think you've got to build it and test it, and test the waters and not spend too much time on the details until you do that.

Osborn: Great advice. Can you tell me a little bit about—can you give me some examples of hiccups you've had along the way or maybe speed bumps— unexpected challenges that you've had?

Kettenburg: Yeah, definitely. Well, the first unexpected challenge was we set out to raise $5,000—and we raised $330,000 and about another $60,000 in preorders.

Osborn: It's not the worst problem in the world to have.

Kettenburg: Yeah, not the worst problem, but logistically that's a big problem. I went from being a small customer for a surface-mount assembly shop to requiring a significant percentage of the factory, of the whole factory, to produce our product. As a point of reference, to produce thirty thousand of them kept the factory—a good regular-sized production facility—working for three weeks. I'm sure they had other little projects, but that was their main project for three weeks, the first thirty thousand. So that created a lot of scheduling problems, a lot of sourcing problems.

The first thing I found was there weren't thirty thousand ATtiny85 chips, which is the main IC on the Digispark. There weren't thirty thousand of them produced. So we had to go to Atmel, the manufacturer, and say, "You've never heard of us, but how fast can you produce thirty thousand?" This chip generally doesn't sell that well. I think ATtinies—used for hobbies, and another Kickstarter project, the Blink1—was also trying for the same chip and had just been fairly successful. But, generally, the ATtinies were used in things like alarm clocks, where the production was scheduled months and years in advance, and they worked directly with the manufacturer. So we ended up with a ten-week lead time to get those parts. Ten weeks was the longest lead time for several parts.

Almost every part had a lead time. Most had to go back into production to meet our numbers. That took several weeks to get straightened out and get the right manufacturer who could make enough of them.

We knew—at that point, we already had this looming problem of shipping everything. We sold twenty-five thousand Digisparks through Kickstarter and the preorders that followed immediately. At that same time, we sold twelve thousand kits because we offered about twelve different shields,[4] you know, same idea as Arduino shields, but to plug into the Digispark. We did that because people were asking for it, not fully comprehending what we were getting ourselves into. By the time we shipped everything, we had twenty-six different things that could go in any given package, because we offered them both as a kitted version and as just the PCB board.

On Kickstarter, you're always getting pushed to set goals, bonuses when you reach a certain amount—stretch goals, that's the word I'm looking for. If the project reaches certain funding milestones you might offer add-ons or bonuses. So we did free stickers with that. We discounted one of our kits down to $1, which resulted in eight thousand of them being ordered. We had this huge logistics problem. We had to order all those parts. We had to kit them all into little bags, and we had to ship them all.

The biggest issue there was that the Digispark was so cheap that it didn't make sense to pay a fulfillment house to pack them for us. To have a fulfillment house pack them was going to cost about $6 on average per package—not including shipping—and we had put $5 of shipping into our price. So we ended up doing all of that in-house, my wife, Jenni, and I. We pretty much immediately started kitting things and ordering parts. We filled an entire bedroom, probably floor to halfway up to the ceiling, with just boxes of parts and boards. So that was a huge challenge, and it took us just about two months to ship everything, and we ended up shipping sixty-five hundred packages. I had never shipped anything commercially before that.

The other bump in the road—we ran into several bumps in the road with the factory—was that we were programming the chip in a slightly uncommon way, and so their programming hardware wasn't working. So we sent them samples. I hand-assembled some samples and sent them, and then they

---

[4]A shield is an add-on circuit board that attaches to the main microcontroller to provide additional functionality or peripherals.

tried to match that exactly. I sent them five test jigs on which you could hold a Digispark down and it ran through all these self-tests. They couldn't get it to pass the test because it wasn't being programmed quite right at the factory. That threw another month and a half into back and forth—videos, phone calls, e-mails—just trying to get it right.

Eventually, they got the right combination of programming hardware, and it turned out that they had tried to cheap out and bought this slightly cheaper version of the ATtiny85 from Atmel. Luckily, they had only gotten the sample quantities at that point. That version didn't work because it couldn't run fast enough to run the USB end of things. So there were plenty of hurdles there.

Then aside from the hardware side of things, we were trying to do something in software that had only kind of been done. Making an ATtiny chip talk over USB isn't a standard function of that chip, so we were completely bit-banging the USB functions. The version that I showed on my Kickstarter video was the first time I had ever gotten those functions to work. They still had some hiccups in them. I think it would have been no problem, again, if we had had five hundred or so, or one thousand, or even five thousand. But so much time ended up being consumed just by managing everything that it left a whole lot less time for the software end of things.

So in the end, we got help with the bootloader that would actually do the USB functions—do the programming over USB. You know, I had some starting points, I had it mostly working, and then one of our supporters actually stepped in and helped put together the final bootloader that we ran with, and that's an open-source project. In return, we essentially sponsored that project. We kept it, but we don't own it, we don't have any rights to it, so we used it and we sponsored it to keep them going and inspire them to get it done in time for the factory to ship it. I think in the end that was a really great outcome, because in the end that got the community more involved.

The bootloader created this entirely separate project that I know other people are already looking at. Adafruit has a device called Gemma, a device coming out that's based on the ATtiny85, pretty similar to the Digispark. It's made to be sewable. I think it has three input/outputs instead of six, but I saw they're considering using that same bootloader. And people have started contributing to it. It's now on GitHub. There's now like three different versions of the bootloader. When you first power up a Digispark, there's a five-second delay before it runs your code, while it waits for a USB programming signal. Some people didn't want that, so they made the microcontroller check if a pin is tied to ground instead, and if it's not tied to ground, then it boots right into the user code, so already that's evolving. So that ended up being a bump in the road that turned into an even better thing, and a completely new project launched out of it too.

Osborn: That really is a nice result, saved you some time and really got the community involvement going. Building a community behind these projects is a great outcome.

Kettenburg: Yeah, definitely. And I've spent a lot of time on the community end of things like, "This library could use improvements," or "We could use another release of the software that fixes the known bugs so people don't have to download this file or that file depending on which version of Linux they're using." All those things are on my list, but an emphasis has been on the community and it's paying off. We have a fairly active set of forums, fairly active in posts, and extremely active in views. People are helping each other on them a lot already.

I would look at new topics on the forums and anything that hadn't been solved, I would try and help out with. That went from taking me hours a day to now probably fifteen minutes a day because we have some real dedicated community members helping out, and then a lot who just help out here and there when they see something. That's been great to see. I think one of the challenges for Digistump as a company, with the Digispark and with other products I have in the pipeline now, is I'd like to see the Digispark community and the Digistump community tie into the broader Arduino community more. You know, you have people running official Arduino hardware on their Arduino forums. You get people running the Teensy[5] hardware by Paul, who is in—do you know Paul? I can't ever pronounce his last name.

Osborn: Stoffregen, yeah. I've met Paul a couple of times. Seems like a nice guy and his product is super useful.

Kettenburg: He's right outside Portland there, and he's got a very active community. He's great with his community. He offers a lot of really technical help. He's pretty undisputed in his technical expertise on all things microcontroller. And we have all kinds of distinct communities that grew out of the original Arduino community, and they don't tie together very well. Adafruit is going to have their ATtiny-based device and Todd Kurt—the maker of the blink(1), BlinkM series of devices, down in LA—has a community, and the Digispark has a community, and we're all running the same hardware. So I think that's maybe a challenge of the maker community at this point, or I see it as one, that we need to join together a little more and tie that information together a little better. And the same for Arduino libraries. The other day, I was looking at the universal TFT library for driving color LCD displays, and it's like there's this really nice universal library, and then Adafruit has this really nice library too. I can't imagine how much time was spent on both of those libraries, and then in the end, they do the exact same thing. They both do it almost the exact same way. They both have the same issues remaining that no one seems to have time to get to.

Osborn: One thing that I've seen that kind of bugs me is not only that there's duplication, but finding the right library for what you're doing is somewhat difficult. And then for a lot of people, just figuring out where to put those files in the right place in the file system is a challenge. If you're new to it and you find this library, what do you do with it? So I've always thought it would be a great project to see somebody build a package manager.[6]

Kettenburg: I was just about to say that, yeah! With the Digispark, we have to modify the Arduino distribution slightly, and it's such a pain because it's not built for that. The Arduino guys, all the thanks to them, created this whole Arduino ecosystem. They started it all. But they're relatively resistant to compatible hardware being made truly compatible. And I think that's seen most in that there's no plug-in system for the IDE to support other programmers. There's some there. There are board files and you can define other devices, but it still assumes that they're exactly like the Arduino. So you got Paul, who had to make a special version for his Teensy, and we had to make a special version for the Digispark, and it seems like a package manager could solve all that too.

I've put a lot of thought into how to make a good package manager for it, but it's kind of one of those jobs that take a ton of work and very little payoff. If I had, if the Digispark hadn't happened, that's the kind of thing I would pursue but don't have the time now. But it's certainly something that the community needs. I've even thought about making a Kickstarter project for sponsoring a package manager, and then hiring someone to do it, or something like that, because Digispark/Digistump would benefit from it greatly.

Osborn: This is something the community needs.

Kettenburg: The next project I have in the pipeline is probably going to need modifications to the Arduino IDE too.

Osborn: Yeah, I definitely think that's something the community needs. I've looked at the internals too. Even in places where they had made some effort to make things more generic, for instance, the Avrdude uploader. There's an uploader base class and then there's the Avrdude subclass, but the base class has all this very specific code that makes it not generic at all. Even the places where there was some effort or forethought to make it generic, it has been bastardized to the point where it really no longer functions generically.

---

[6]A package manager is tool that manages project code requirements by automating the downloading, discovery, and updating of libraries the project is dependent on.

It's certainly not insurmountable by any means to accomplish this. It's going to take some work cleaning it up, I think, before you could start really building on top of it.

Kettenburg: Yeah, definitely. The biggest incompatibility we had integrating the Digispark into the ID was that you have to use Avrdude, and Avrdude didn't work with our bootloader. We needed a specific specialized upload tool, and we had that in a command-line form, but I ended up having to replace Avrdude with a dummy executable that's called Avrdude, and then rename the real Avrdude, and then pass the flags over to that unless the flags say it's Digispark, and then we pass it to our command-line program instead.

Osborn: Wow.

Kettenburg: It's one of those I could have gotten as an Avrdude source and added support for the Digispark, but you know, then it's like we're getting into branching yet another project, and in the end, it seemed cleaner just to put a proxy in between. And, the—oh, I can't remember the project—one of the robot projects off of Kickstarter, they were taking the same approach, and we exchanged notes to make sure that our proxies wouldn't conflict with each other.

Osborn: That's pretty clever. It would be great to see the community take a bit more forward-reaching approach there, a bit broader approach.

I was wondering what new projects do you see out there that you think are the most interesting? What other things have you just looked at recently and said "Man, that's cool!" A project that someone's building?

Kettenburg: I think that some of the coolest ones to me—and I guess my view, my interests, because of the Digispark and because of trying to build a company off of that, have kind of turned to an interest in do-it-yourself manufacturing, the makers who are manufacturing themselves and building their manufacturing equipment. We're moving that way. Any day now, our first pick-and-place machine will be delivered. It's this little desktop unit that they build in China, and it's pretty much not exported at all. And these Chinese makers are using it to make one hundred boards at a time in their living room.

Osborn: I'd love to see that sometime.

Kettenburg: You know Zach Hoeken, the former cofounder of MakerBot? He lives in Shenzhen now. And has a blog called Hoektronics.[7] And he has a video of the machine that we bought in the form of an interview with the maker in China, who uses it to make boards in his living room. That's where I first saw the machine.

---

[7] www.hoektronics.com

Osborn: I think I might have seen that video. I'll have to take another look.

Kettenburg: Ian over at Dangerous Prototypes—are you aware of Dangerous Prototypes?[8]

Osborn: Yeah, I've got a Bus Pirate.

Kettenburg: So Ian was over in China and saw these too and ended up ordering one for himself. Then he organized a group buy with about seven of us who all bought them direct from the factory and ended up getting a big discount. We ended up paying less than they sell for on the Chinese market actually, so that was great. The manufacturer was so excited to be exporting them to America, because there really hasn't been any market for small pick-and-place machines over here.

So that whole movement of really small-scale manufacturing in the US is something that I get really excited about. And that's not just premade things, like the pick-and-place machines from China, but people who are developing homemade laser cutters. The 3D printer movement is awesome, but I still don't see 3D printers—you know, a homemade 3D printer still isn't practical when I need to make twelve hundred cases for Digisparks that I've sold. So the laser cutter still wins there. I have two laser cutters, and one of them is a big, giant one that we air-freighted from China. It's a beast. It's a great machine, but I've seen a lot of these homemade laser systems—on BuildLog and other sites—coming up, and I think that's really cool.

Osborn: I bought a Full Spectrum 40-watt hobby laser recently. Haven't made anything exciting with it just yet.

Kettenburg: I have that one. Do you have the fifth gen or the fourth gen?

Osborn: I have the fourth gen.

Kettenburg: Okay. I've got the fifth gen, and I liked it. I've kind of soured on Full Spectrum since then, since I've seen how they've treated their customers. I liked the machine. It couldn't keep up with our production. We bought it thinking we're going to make, like, one hundred acrylic cases, and we ended up with orders for twelve hundred, so that's why we flew in this beast of a 60-watt cutter from China. That machine is actually a beautifully made machine, despite what everybody said about buying a laser cutter from China. Of course, we researched the company and everything, and it's built like a tank. It cuts about six to ten times faster than the Hobby one, and so that's amazing to watch.

I need a reflow oven to go with the pick-and-place machine, and I don't like the Chinese options there. They have a lot of safety issues, a lot of fire issues, and generally just don't have the reliability that I need. And we're a little too

---

big for the hot-plate method. I'm going to be doing twenty-inch by fifteen-inch panels with, say, one hundred to two hundred boards on one panel. So I finally settled on it last night. I'm just going to build a reflow oven from scratch. I see other people frustrated with the choices, so I wonder if that's an area that's maybe about to kind of kick off in the maker culture, because people are getting into this lower-quantity production.

I know a lot of people do the toaster ovens, but you just can't get a big enough toaster oven once you're making one hundred boards at a time. So those projects have really excited me.

On the embedded microcontroller side, there's actually a project on Kickstarter right now that's an FPGA.[9] I think that's really cool because I've always wanted to work with FPGAs. And really, there isn't any kind of mainstream, real accessible development board out there for it. The project's called Mojo.

Then there's Parallella—I'm not sure if you've seen that project. It's a parallel computing project. That was probably about four months ago or so. I ended up backing that, and I'm really excited for that kind of stuff. I guess in general, this is like more advanced computing. We have the 16 megahertz Arduinos down. Now it's time for the more advanced but still very accessible options, like an FPGA, like a parallel computing board.

And the next Digistump product that I'm working on is actually a 32-bit platform similar to the Arduino Due, similar in that that's the closest thing out there to it but with embedded Wi-Fi on it. I think that's the next step—making wireless connectivity ubiquitous on these devices. And right now, it's not only really expensive, but there are just so many wireless standards out there. Putting Wi-Fi on your board is resource-intensive and expensive, so then you put an XBee on, but then you need a board to receive the XBee signal. I think the real solution is just to get a Wi-Fi-enabled board down to a price range where every device you make can just have Wi-Fi on it. Or another protocol. It doesn't have to be Wi-Fi, but really bringing those prices down is necessary. My target price for this project, not completely confirmed, but kind of the target price I'm designing around is to have a Wi-Fi-enabled, 32-bit, Arduino-compatible board. Right now we've got about one hundred I/O lines on it, and we're looking at a $35 to $45 price range.

Osborn: Yeah, that would be pretty massive, I think, for the community. People would fall all over that.

Kettenburg: We're hoping so.

Osborn: I would buy a couple. I'm just saying.

---

[9]An FPGA, field-programmable gate array, is a hardware device designed to be configured by the end-user after manufacturing.

Kettenburg: Once you put even a cheap Wi-Fi board on a Due, an Arduino Due, you're at like what—$110?

Osborn: Yeah.

Kettenburg: I'm not going to spend $110 on a project even now.

Osborn: Yeah, with the cheaper $60 WiFly shield and a $30 Arduino, you're still at looking at quite a bit of cash.

Kettenburg: Yeah, you're still at ninety bucks. So I mean, it's not going to be an easy one to pull off, but the Digispark was a lot easier from a hardware standpoint. This one should be more straightforward, or is more straightforward from a software standpoint because we're not trying to do anything with hardware it's not made to do. You know, we're not bit-banging USB or anything. The challenge with this one is purely hitting production numbers to be able to source those parts at those prices. I've been working with some different companies in China that produce Wi-Fi modules to get them in the right price range. We haven't decided exactly how we're going to pursue the funding, but it very likely will be Kickstarter.

And for this one, I'm going to do kind of a prefunding round through our web site with our existing backers and say, "Do you want to be part of this? Do you want to get one of the first prototypes? For one hundred bucks, you get one of the first prototypes and you get one of the final products when it's done." And use that money to essentially go the factory and say, "We want to make one hundred of these, but you can't hand-assemble them. You have to run them like they're a full production run," so that we can work out the kinks and everything before we set a final price. We would like to make sure that we keep the margins tight because we truly believe in making it accessible, but I would like to do this full-time someday, and so it would be nice if we made a little more off it than we made off the Digispark.

Osborn: I just have one more question about Kickstarter. I mean, everybody and their dog is launching Kickstarter projects it seems, and I just want to know about your experiences with it and maybe any hiccups you had or challenges dealing with the Kickstarter model. It sounds like you're thinking about doing it again already, so I'm guessing you had a pretty good experience. Is there anything you can say there or any advice you have for anybody considering using Kickstarter?

Kettenburg: Yes. So we had a couple of bumps in the road with Kickstarter directly, actually. Kickstarter pulled our project when it was around the $200,000 mark. It still worked as a project page, and it was still taking pledges, but you couldn't find it from any of the Kickstarter pages. You could only come in from a direct link. I guess that's what they do when they're pending a resolution because they don't like something you've done. And the communication there was definitely a lacking. We were getting hundreds of messages a day through Kickstarter, and their message came like any other Kickstarter message, and I missed it for a whole twenty-four hours.

So the problem was we had packages that had too many units in them, and we had mentioned that you could ask for them to be in retail packaging if you bought over two hundred of them, and Kickstarter didn't like that. It admittedly wasn't consistent with their guidelines. But I didn't think of it at the time we offered it, because somebody asked, "Can you do this?" And essentially we had to get those people to cancel their pledges, because when you're running a Kickstarter campaign, you can't cancel someone's pledge on your own. "Get them to cancel their pledges, remove that category, or we'll take your project down." And the only way to communicate back with them was through Kickstarter messages, you know, through their ticket system.

With such a huge project and so much at stake, it was a frustrating couple of days. It took four days for them to put our project back on all the pages. So it definitely was difficult to communicate with them. That was a challenge. We felt when a project reaches a certain size, and with the problems it can encounter, there should be more support there. If nothing else, a number we could call and talk to someone at Kickstarter to get things resolved. I've heard that same sentiment echoed by other big projects.

Eric, the guy behind the Pebble watch, is a Digispark backer, and he and I talked actually quite a bit about issues with Kickstarter. He tipped me off to another potential hurdle with Kickstarter. We knew there was this hurdle that you had to wait fourteen days for Amazon to release your money after the project ended, which in our case would have meant waiting fourteen days to authorize production, because I didn't have enough money in my bank account to fork over $150,000 for production. So he tipped me off that you could just ask Amazon to waive the fourteen days. Essentially, I sent them an e-mail and said, "I've been in business. I've had my own consulting business for x number of years. My credit is fine, and all my tax information is entered. Will you waive the fourteen days?" And they said, "Sure, no problem," and they released all the money to us two days after it funded. That certainly was a nice piece of advice. Amazon Payments is actually really easy and good to work with, and supportive of Kickstarter projects. They realize there are some unique challenges there.

The other challenge with the platform is that Kickstarter still isn't built for the volume of business that's taking place on it. You have Kickstarter messages you can send to your backers, and you have Excel reports that you can click a button to generate, wait for them to generate, and then wait for them to download. And there's one report for each reward tier. There's no API. There's no master data dump. There's no way to send automated messages. So then we screen-scraped everything. I wrote screen scrapers, and we were using cURL to fake our sessions and our logins to automatically notify backers of different things to download the reports and update our databases. So not only did we have to build an entire system on our own to handle the sales and backing, keeping track of pledges and all that, but there was no way to directly interact with their system. We had to do all this in roundabout ways, which certainly led to some pretty major hiccups, and if nothing else seemed like a waste of time. But in the end, we couldn't have done it without it. I get a lot of e-mails from new Kickstarter-type sites saying, "Launch your project with us. We have fewer fees. We have this, we have that," but the visibility of Kickstarter—you can't beat that.

Overall, I'd never be one to complain about anything that enables me to start a business with essentially zero capital. And I actually have a degree in economics. I studied business. I've worked with lots of startups. I've seen how much capital people can burn through, and I understand investing money to make money and all that, but I never dreamed I could start a business with essentially none of my money at risk. So overall, I would say it's a great experience.

There are certainly some big challenges there. I guess I'd add that another challenge at Kickstarter is that there's no limit to the funding. You can limit your rewards, but no one is going to limit their rewards. So I think a lot of the projects I see having a lot of issues result from ideas that aren't fully fleshed out and then run a while. And a lot of times, the amount of money those ideas were asking for in the first place—if they had only got their $500, it probably would have come out fine. They probably would have made their backers happy. But then when they have $50,000 and still don't have a fully fleshed idea—and I don't know what the solution is there, because that's certainly part of Kickstarter's success too, but that can be a challenge. You can go to sleep and wake up and have a much bigger problem on your hands.

Osborn: There's definitely some nuance on Kickstarter's part to balance people's expectations with the project's risk. I mean, there's only so much that Kickstarter can do to make sure the project is going to be successful, but if it is not, people tend to be upset that they invested their money in it. Personally, I feel like I want to back some projects where there is some risk involved because those are the projects that are doing new things. The projects where there's no risk involved are just basically established companies that are releasing the new version of their product, and that's not really moving the needle forward, right? I mean, there's definitely a lot of balancing of priorities and risk, I think for everyone there.

Kettenburg: I think a big threat to Kickstarter from within is the number of commercial products. And when they changed their rules[10] within the hardware category—that you could only sell one unit—it would have killed the Digispark! Well, it wouldn't have killed it. We would have made our five

---

[10]www.kickstarter.com/blog/kickstarter-is-not-a-store

hundred. I would have been happy, but it wouldn't have been the success it was, because something like seventy percent of the backers were buying three or more, maybe even more like eighty-five percent. About half of all backers bought three of them, which I figured, if I had seen the project, that's probably what I would have bought, because it made the most sense to ship them at that price. So I cringed when they did that. And a couple of people interviewed me about that, and I talked about how I felt that that was a bad move. I still don't think it was a good move, but I do understand the problem they have there of wanting to support projects and not just the sale of finished products.

The other thing they did is they made the hardware category not just open source. I think that was the worst move because I think that has encouraged commercial products and I think it's also encouraged people who have more of the mindset of looking to make profit than looking to launch their projects. That's kind of how I think of things: there are products and there are projects. The projects can have a product, but when you look through Kickstarter, you can often clearly see who's trying to sell you a product and who's trying to launch their project, and that's kind of what influences my backing of things. I want to make sure that even though we have this little company now, that the next Digistump project that goes on Kickstarter is truly a project. It's doing new things, it's opening new doors, and it's providing something for the community.

An example of one I've felt a little torn about right now is the Hydra bench-top power supply. It's a cool idea—a lot of people in the electronics community have been really getting into these homemade bench power supplies that run over USB, and you can set them and log from the computer. And that was a realization of it, but I just can't get over the fact that it's not open source because I can look at their board and see that they've pulled from everything out there, all these projects from the EEV Blog,[11] from Ian's blog at Dangerous Prototypes,[12] you know, all this work people have been doing. And it's on Kickstarter and it's really killing it. I look at the comments, and I notice that no one's even asked them, "Why aren't you open sourcing this?" So, you know, coming from the Digispark, which wouldn't have been possible without all the open-source projects before it, I have trouble with that.

I see the commercial versus open-source issue that MakerBot is very publicly dealing with right now, and I don't necessarily agree with the route they've taken, but I certainly am carefully considering that for our next product. I've heard that DF Robot, one of the Chinese companies, is already working on a Digispark clone, so, you know, that issue is alive and well. But I do truly believe that if your product is successful, good, and unique, and you support the community, the community will support you.

---

[11] www.eevblog.com
[12] http://dangerousprototypes.com

I think that really shows in Arduino. There are so many clones in Arduino, and there are even mainstream clones and American-made clones of it, and still, most people buy an authentic Arduino. I own Arduino clones, from Seeed Studio and the like, but I still buy the Arduinos. I do see a place for licenses, like creative commons, noncommercial, and that's what I'm considering for some of our future products. Just to say, "This is for everyone. But if you want to make a product off it, you'd better make it a new product." And that's why we actually chose to make the Digispark completely open source. But the name is not open source. It's kind of like Arduino did the same thing. You can't make our product and call it a Digispark. And I get a lot of inquiries about, "Can you send me the files? I live in this country and I'm planning to produce the Digispark because you're selling it for too much." And I usually respond, "We really prefer that you license it from us," or "We'll give you wholesale pricing. We can work with you, but the files are public." And some have even gone so far to send follow-ups to tell them all the details of how it's produced and what they should tell the factory and everything.

Osborn: Oh man. Yeah, you don't get everything for free. You have to do some work if you're going to steal the whole item.

Kettenburg: Yeah, I tend to emphasize to those people that there's test jigs involved. There's all this stuff you're going to have to do if you want to produce it. We didn't release the plans for our test jigs. If some maker e-mailed me and said, "I'm trying to make a test jig for my product. I'd really like to see how you made yours," you know, I'd send it to him in a second, but I think there is something to be said for finding that balance as an open-source company. And you do have to protect it somewhat, but I'm afraid that people are starting to take that too far. And I think the public manifestation of that is MakerBot.

Osborn: It's interesting to see this evolving in the hardware space, because I've seen this kind of thing in software for a long time. I think WordPress is a great example of an open-source community. Wordpress.com powers a large chunk of the Internet, but they also enable all their competitors to go out and just roll their own WordPress and self-host it. There are pretty successful companies whose business model is hosting WordPress and they enable that.

Kettenburg: Yeah, definitely. Being a PHP developer, I've never been a WordPress user, but I've seen people make a lot more than me just installing WordPress. People seem to be making a very big deal about the hardware world facing these challenges, but it's only a big deal because the hardware world has been so locked down historically. Even if the MakerBots go and come up with some quasi-open-source business plan, there's still going to be the Adafruits and the SparkFuns who—well, SparkFun is kind of in between, because they use a noncommercial license too. And in the end, we're still miles ahead of where we were ten years ago in the hardware world.

Osborn: Yeah, and there's the open sourcing of the firmware and the software that's running on the device, but then there's the actual physical open source. Open-source schematics, open-source silicone, and stuff like that, which is— even on the projects that are very open, like Raspberry Pi, Broadcom has no interest in showing you how they make their processor.

Kettenburg: I have a lot of reservations about Raspberry Pi calling themselves open source, not just because of Broadcom, because they have kind of taken this attitude of, "Our hardware is open source, but you don't really want to see it because you'll never be able to make it anyway."

And then on top of that, they represent themselves as a nonprofit, but make far more units for sale than for nonprofit use. They're a really unique case of it because in the end, they released their schematic. I looked at it and saw a lot of ways they saved money and thought, "Well, this is a great guide." Someday, if I can do this as a full-time gig, I would love to make a true open-source Raspberry Pi, as many have already. So that's certainly some useful information to the community. And there's no denying what the Raspberry Pi's done for the ubiquitous and embedded computing community. But, yeah, they're a very interesting case. Very mixed feelings there.

Osborn: Well, all right. That's some great insight. Especially into the sort of challenges that come with Kickstarting a physical product and getting it through manufacturing. I'm looking forward to seeing what Digistump has in store for the future.

David Merrill

Cofounder
Sifteo

David Merrill holds a Ph.D. from the Massachusetts Institute of Technology (MIT), where he was part of the highly regarded Media Lab program. He has devoted his studies and career to exploring alternate user interfaces and interactions between humans and physical computing objects. He now runs a company called Sifteo (sifteo.com), which has commercialized the work he began at MIT.

The first time I saw a Sifteo Cube, I recognized that it was something totally unique. They are simple to use and understand, yet challenge our assumptions and conventions around how a computing device can be used.

Steven Osborn: Tell me a little bit about the projects and the people who inspired you to make things.

David Merrill: I think the reason that I started making things came from my dad. He should have been an architect or a mechanical engineer, but he didn't wind up studying either of those disciplines, so he wasn't. But he was a really mechanically inclined guy and was really good at sketching and building. I have this one picture that he sketched for me after he had disassembled my bike to ship it to me on the East Coast. He had drawn an exploded-parts diagram, basically of the whole handlebar assembly with arrows and labels, so that I could put it back together once I got it. He was a natural maker.

When he was younger, he built things like musical instruments. He built a couple of mandolins. When he became a homeowner, all that energy was directed at improving the house. I saw him re-roof the house and build additions, and he once built me a lofted bed in the bedroom I shared with my brother. He would pour new concrete paths until they went all the way around the house.

So I grew up with this role model in my family and a feeling of being empowered. If you had an idea for something you wanted to build, you figured out how and did it. I think in addition to that more abstract feeling of empowerment, just watching him build and solve problems gave me an intuition about problem solving. That was where it all started for me.

When I was a kid, I used to build things too. I built a coaster car, a wooden car that you pushed up a hill and then rolled back down with gravity. It had a steering wheel and brakes that were basically a piece of wood on a pivot that you could pull up, and the other end would scrape the ground to slow the car down. What else? I built a minibike with a lawnmower engine, my own little DIY motorcycle from a kit, basically. I had to go find the engine and put that together.

Osborn: Did you scare your mother to death with that one?

Merrill: Yeah, yeah. I think the reason that she let me do it was that my dad was very supportive because he had actually built something just like it when he was thirteen years old. I think he loved the idea that I was following in his footsteps and wanted to build this little minibike.

I tried to build a miniature steam engine once out of wood and it turned out it wasn't airtight enough—none of the seals were sealed enough to actually make it work. But I loved physics class in high school because we had to build little pneumatic cars with a two-liter bottle and pump it up with air to see how far you could make your car go. We built a little roller coaster for marbles with weed-whacker cord as the tracks. So that was just the childhood I had, loving to make things. I had a lot of physical toys like blocks and Lincoln Logs. My earliest blocks were a set that my dad had made out of two by fours that he had cut down to a couple different lengths and standard sizes. He gave me a whole set. I grew up really thinking that one of the fun things you could do in life, or if you're bored or whatever, was to make things, or think up good ideas for making things. So that's kind of the background of my personality and why I love making things even today.

There are a couple of other key moments I would point to. When I was probably seven or eight, my dad got a computer for our house. That was when I started having access to a computer. I mostly just played games on it. I didn't start programming at home at a very early age. But when I was about nine years old, I got exposed to the Logo programming language when I went to a summer day camp. I didn't think about it that much after that summer, but I think it planted a seed for programming. I had Logo access in school, too, when I was in fourth grade, which continued that interest. I built up some pretty elaborate animated scenes, almost like I was directing a movie using Logo, by creating very simple graphics and moving them around programmatically. Then, I started playing videogames, although my parents never let me have a game system like a Nintendo or PlayStation, or anything like that. So I had to play shareware games on the computer.

I kept playing whatever videogames I could find, and then when I was in high school, my next programming experience came when I was taking calculus as a senior. It turned out that I could write programs in BASIC on my graphing calculator to make some tiny programs that were useful to the other students in the class. So I really got into that.

I think the thing that was so satisfying about that was that I got to make something that was useful for other people. Since then, I've recognized that that's one of my primary motivators in life, and in my pursuit of technology, and in entrepreneurship. I just love making things that are useful for other people, and then putting those things in their hands and getting the feedback that yes, indeed, it is actually a useful, life-improving thing. So that was, I think, a transformative moment in high school.

Osborn: What was the nature of the program?

Merrill: I think it was a successive approximation under the curve to do a discrete simulation of an integral. I wrote this program that would iterate and you could put in the bounds and what you wanted the step to be each time, and it would calculate the area under the curve with a bunch of rectangles. That was a satisfying thing because I made this program and it worked. I debugged it and made sure it worked for me, and then I handed it off. Everybody else in the class started using it on their calculators. So that was—before anyone was doing much with the Internet—my first experience with sharing software and experiencing that exponential, multiplicative growth of utility that comes from software being able to replicate. That was really cool and fun.

When I got to college, I thought I would be a physics and Spanish major. I loved both of those topics in high school. I think what I loved about physics was that it got me playing with things that were really more like mechanical engineering concepts. I learned pretty quickly in my freshman year that physics wasn't for me, after I got an A, then a B, and then a C—one quarter after another.

But what I discovered at the very end of my freshman year was programming. I took the introductory programming class—this was at Stanford, Computer Science 106A. It was a programming class that massive numbers of students on campus take. I think it's the most popular class on campus. Especially at that time, when the Internet was getting going. This was 1996 or '97. A lot of people wanted to know how to program. So I took this intro class and totally loved it. It brought back this experience from senior year, where I had made this program and shared it. The exciting thing about it for me was that there's a certain level of behavior and utility that you can make with physical stuff, but you can breathe a totally different kind of life into something when you can program it with code. And that was just so exciting.

I wanted to make videogames. That was my motivation at the time. I grew up not having a Nintendo but loving games like *Super Mario Bros*. And my primary motivation at the time was, "I need to get good enough at programming so that I can make a game like that." And so I got into computer science and started taking more and more classes.

Osborn: So you ended up majoring in computer science?

Merrill: I did not end up majoring in it, but majored in an adjacent field called Symbolic Systems. At other schools, they would call it "cognitive science." It's computer science, psychology, linguistics, and philosophy all rolled into one. So I got a broad base of experience in computer science and really loved learning about perceptual psychology too. I had a couple of classes that really shaped my way of thinking about technology, because they were really about us humans - about the human perceptual system and body and how that related to technology.

One was about the human vision system, like how do our eyes work? The first half of the class was about that, and the second half of the class was, "Okay, so now we know how people's eyes work. What does that mean for how we should design imaging technologies like printers, and displays, and projectors, and things like that?" I thought that was super cool because it was a way to ground our design of technology in the truth of how our bodies and brains work. That's something that changes much more slowly than technology. We're not evolving anymore, but we can change the way the technology works to match us.

So, anyway, to wrap up this part of the story, I took a bunch of computer science classes. And that was great and fun, and I kind of expected that I would leave school and go into doing something related to software. But then I started to take computer music classes at the Center for Computer Research in Music and Acoustics (CCRMA) at Stanford, and really got into that combination of music and technology because I'm also a guitar player. And one of the key things that happened was I took a class taught by Bill Verplank that was about designing and building new music controllers—new musical instruments out of technology.

The key thing that happened in that class is I realized what I could build with hardware, too, because the class taught some very basic electronic circuits and simple microcontroller programming. At the time, we were doing BASIC Stamp programming. We put together our own custom controllers with buttons, and sliders, and force sensors. I used cameras. It was this amazing revelation for me! My palate of tools expanded and I could build interactive circuits that could explode beyond what was inside the screen, and keyboard, and mouse of the computer. I didn't have to make things that just lived on the screen in the software of my laptop computer anymore. I think the reason that was so exciting and so transformative for me was that I grew up playing and building with very physical things, like blocks, and building things with wood and metal. All of a sudden, my two worlds of building stuff, one from childhood, one from college, had found a way to meet each other. And at the time, building musical instruments and interactive music installations was an amazing fun thing.

Osborn: And then you moved on to MIT, right?

Merrill: So I went to MIT, to the Media Lab. At the Media Lab, you're basically an artist in residence as an engineer, which is a great life. You have a lab to work in. You've got a bunch of smart people around. You've got a budget to buy materials. You have a lot of freedom in terms of what you want to build, almost whatever you're interested in. That was a great opportunity to just keep it going and keep honing my craft, to keep learning, getting better at building systems, and to learn how to work with analog electronics and microcontrollers and other peripherals and do wireless stuff. It was amazing.

I built a bunch of interactive art installations. I built more music controllers. I built wearable technology, like a wearable system that would let you forage for information in a physical space. And then the focus near the end became the topic of my Ph.D., which was this prototype that we called Siftables at the time. Jeevan Kalanithi and I have been friends ever since undergrad, and he wound up at the Media Lab at the same time and we started talking about ideas, and eventually collaborating together as cofounders of Sifteo. There was this moment at the Media Lab where I think we had just finished a class on sensor networks and were inspired by the possibilities of systems of little interactive pieces. And we were thinking about interactions with computers and how they still could be a lot better. We were thinking about how you use your hands and body when you're playing with physical stuff like LEGOs. Imagine if you had a pile of LEGOs on the table in front of you. Think about the way that you could just jam your hand into it and move it around, even use your arm to push some of the pile one way, some of the pile the other way. And we were so fascinated by this idea that maybe there's a way to interact with computers in a manner that's a lot more physical than what we have now. This was 2006. Multitouch was just becoming known. Jeff Han from NYU had just shown his great multitouch demo at TED[1] at that time.

Osborn: I remember watching that TED talk. I was blown away by it.

Merrill: Yeah, it was amazing. The iPhone wasn't even out yet. He did a great job demonstrating this new core interaction paradigm, which was so exciting to me, because I have this interest in making things that are useful—making tools for people is one of the things that I really love. I think that there's a need for what I call "new hand tools for the digital age," which work in a way that is more analogous to the tools we use with physical materials. A traditional hand tool is very specifically crafted to shape the material to work within a certain way. Whereas woodworking tools shape wood, I think we need a lot

---

[1] www.ted.com/talks/jeff_han_demos_his_breakthrough_touchscreen.html

more tools for shaping digital media in ways that are expressive and direct and an expressive extension of thought.

Osborn: I'd never thought of it that way. Computing has the mouse, which we use as a hammer to shape things in the electronic world, but until recently, that has been the only way to interact with the digital things.

Merrill: My personal history of the greatest moments in computing is mostly about the interface, not about the underlying depths of the computer itself. I'm a huge fan of Doug Engelbart and the invention of the mouse, and all the stuff that his team at SRI[2] did in the sixties. And then Ivan Sutherland and the sketchpad work—that's basically the precursor of tablets and stylus-based computing, which he did in the sixties at MIT. Watching Jeff Han was another moment like that. I was like, "Wow. This is really important because this is a new way that we can get a little bit closer to having a way to directly translate our thoughts into the computer doing something." That's really what the interface is. You want the most efficient, the most natural way to translate an idea in your head into something you can get the computer to do.

So Jeevan and I were thinking about this, and we thought, "Well, we've got all these collections of little things on computers, like files, and e-mails, and icons on our desktops." At the time, we had this single cursor way of interacting with them, which is like having one fingertip to play with a pile of LEGOs. Imagine if you had a pile of LEGOs in front of you and I told you, "Build something cool, but you can only use one fingertip." That would be so frustrating because you are capable of a lot more. Eventually, you would figure out how to cheat that constraint: "Maybe I can use a fingertip plus my elbow on the other hand. Or maybe I can use fingertip plus my nose. Or use my fingertip plus other objects." And that's exactly what the desktop interface with a mouse wound up doing, which was basically to cope with this fundamental limitation that you've only got one touch point. That's why we have Shift-click, and Shift-Option-click, and right-click, and all these coping mechanisms, where the real problem is that you just need more direct access to what's inside the machine.

So, anyway, that's the long way to say that we were really inspired by the ways that we could make people's interactions with information more direct and immediate. The original idea was about building an interface made up of a bunch of little autonomous pieces that could all represent items of digital media, and that you could manipulate them with your hands by just moving them around—gestures like shaking them or bumping them into each other, or pushing them into a pile. We got so fascinated that we just started sketching, and writing, and prototyping, and trying to figure out what this idea could become.

---

[2]Stanford Research Institute.

Osborn: It sounds like you're leading up to the birth of Sifteo Cubes, and what they are and how you came up with the idea.

Merrill: Yeah, like I said, our hands are really good at that kind of interaction, like picking up and moving little objects. It's something that we humans do all the way back to when we're kids, playing with blocks and little trucks, and trains, and rocks, and sticks. It's such a core human ability. Why isn't interacting with our computers more like that? We got the vision—this one afternoon while we were sitting in the kitchen at the Media Lab—for a new interface that would be more like a collection of little physical objects, but those objects could represent digital items, digital pieces, and you'd interact with them by hand, more like a pile of LEGOs than a mouse and a keyboard, or even a multi-touch display.

We had the vision pretty much identified from the beginning. But the key questions were: Number one: What kind of specific capabilities does a system like this need to have? And number two: What are you going to actually do with it? What is the right application for this new interface? New interfaces tend to enable certain things really well and really specifically. In the Jeff Han multi-touch demo—most of what he showed had to do with photographs, which is all really common and well understood today, like resizing photos by pinching and zooming, and panning photos by swiping across. With our interface, we started to think of a ton of different things we could do with it, anything from tools for creative professionals, like make a video editor where each little clip would show up on one of the screens, and you'd make your video by arranging the tiles in the right order. And as soon as you had made an arrangement, then a full version of your clip would play on the bigger screen of your computer—not for manipulation, but for review. Or managing your digital photos—say, you come back from outside with a camera-full of photos. A thumbnail of each one would show up on each cube, and then you'd manipulate the cubes as a way to organize the photos. You'd push them into piles to get the originals into folders, or make linear arrangements of them to put in a slideshow, things like that.

Osborn: Were you just thinking about games or media uses?

Merrill: We also thought briefly about tools for business professionals. Maybe you could make Gantt charts with cubes, and then rearrange them quickly to see what would happen if you had different arrangements. I made a "physical Photoshop" where you could add filters to a photo by arranging cubes—each cube represented a filter, and one of the cubes would show the photo. You'd make a sequence of filters that you could apply just by neighboring the filter cubes against that photo cube in a chain. You'd have the photo on the far left, and then just to the right of it, you could put the cube that showed "blur" on its screen. And just the right of that, you'd put a cube that said "threshold." And you'd get the original photo blurred and thresholded, and you'd see the result on your computer screen.

There were a ton of different application ideas that we thought of for this interface. We started prototyping and playing with a lot of them. At the Media Lab, we probably went through four iterations of the platform, along the way figuring out that the cubes should be wireless, that they should have color screens on top, that they should be able to sense motion, and that they should be able to sense each other when they got next to each other. We determined those capabilities were a basic set of really useful functionality that we could do a lot with. That became the canonical form of the platform.

The implementation of the platform has completely changed since those early days at MIT, but the cool thing about those days was that we had what seemed like all the time in the world to explore different application ideas and show them to people and get feedback. We hadn't focused it yet on a particular domain, a particular application. I think that's exactly right for research, to just play around with different ideas—and see what works and find out what doesn't. We got to incubate this idea for a couple years at the Media Lab.

Osborn: And some time in there you did the TED talk, right?

Merrill: In the fall of 2008, I'd just defended my PhD based around this project, and I'd been trying to finish up the writing. My advisor Pattie Maes came to me and said, "Hey, I got invited to give a talk at the TED conference and Chris Anderson, the curator of TED, wants to know what my talk is going to be about. I told him about a lot of the work that our research group was doing. When he heard about Siftables,"—we called it Siftables when it was a research project—"he got really excited and he wants that to be a big part of the talk. I think what I'll do is talk about Siftables as a case study of what our group does, and then I'll add more detail about some of the other projects we're doing. So Siftables will be maybe half the talk, and then I'll split the other half with a bunch of our other work."

I heard this and I thought, "Hmm, well, that would be okay. That would be nice to get Siftables on stage." But I was thinking back to Jeff Han's talk, where he had the spotlight for an entire talk to show this one spectacular user interface invention. And so I thought, "Well, maybe I can do what Jeff did!" And so I asked, "Why don't we see if Chris will let *me* give a talk about Siftables, and that will free you up to talk about everything else the group is doing."

At first, she didn't go for it. She said, "Well, I don't think that's going to work because they're *very* selective about who gets to give a TED talk. Just the fact that I've been offered one talk is already pretty special, and so I doubt that we're going to get two."

I kept pushing. I'm an optimist. "It doesn't hurt to ask." I said, "When you talk to him later this week, why don't you pitch that and see what he says?"

So after the phone call later in the week, Pattie came back and said, "Okay. Chris is open to this idea, why don't you get in touch with him and work out the details?"

I sent Chris a note, and I said, "Hey, this is great. I'm really looking forward to giving a talk about Siftables."

He said, "All right, well, first you have to convince me. Tell me what the talk's going to be like. What are you going to do? Give me a script."

Jeevan and I spent the next twenty-four hours writing a script of the talk and we sent it back to Chris, and he said, "Okay. That sounds great. It's going to be fabulous. Go for it."

Osborn: When you say "twenty-four hours," you mean consecutive hours?

Merrill: Yeah, pretty much. I think we slept a little bit, but we took it very seriously. We knew that we had to pitch a pretty complete, compelling talk. So we went over different scenarios, what demos should be in, what demos should be out, what would be most exciting to the audience, what was the strongest thing we could show. We came back, and I think it was about twenty-four hours later, and sent him the proposal, and he green-lit it.

At that point, I was supposed to be finishing the writing of my thesis so I could turn it in and graduate, but instead, I started working on the talk and the demos. We had this dilemma, which was: How much live demo we should try to show onstage at TED. The key thing was it had to work. It had to be smooth. At the time, we actually had a good working demo. All the stuff that was in the talk was working the way it looked like it was working, but there were two things. First, it was kind of awkward to switch from one application to another, so I was worried about the time that I would lose switching between apps, and then, even more scary, I was worried about the wireless control of these cubes failing in a room with fifteen hundred people with cell phones in their pockets. I figured, "If there's ever a time when wireless is going to fail, it's when I have fifteen hundred people in front of me in an auditorium."

So we decided, "Here's what we can do that we think will work. Let's only do demos that don't require the wireless. Then let's show videos to demonstrate the other stuff because it will allow me to get through them faster, and I won't be worried about whether they're going to work or not." So that was what we did. We spent a couple months building these demo applications, and then I spent a week in the sound studio in the Media Lab filming them, trying to get a lot of footage of these nice applications working. Then I put together the talk. I gave it to my group, and I gave it to other people. I iterated it, honing and honing it, until it was really tight and exactly seven minutes long, because that's how much time I had been allocated.

The week of TED came along, and my talk was mid-week, I think. I was having fun, and going to the talks, and meeting a ton of people, and having the time of my life. But every evening, I would go back to my hotel room and rehearse the talk, pacing back and forth in the room to make sure I was memorizing every word of it so I could really nail it, because I knew the stakes were high. TED—even at that time—had caught the world's attention.

Osborn: Sounds like you were completely prepared.

Merrill: The day of the talk came. My session came, and I was backstage. I was talking to Ev Williams, the founder of Twitter. He went onstage right before me. We were making small talk, and everything seemed ready to go. Ev went out and did his talk, and then he was done. Then I went onstage and was introduced, started giving my talk. It was going great. I was hitting all my points. I felt good because I had internalized it so well that I wasn't worried about missing any parts of it. I could just focus on the delivery and walk around and make eye contact with the crowd—I love delivering a talk in a way that feels natural.

Then all of a sudden, I realized that the video segments I had recorded had no sound coming out when they were playing. It was okay for some of the clips because I could talk over them and explain what was happening. But at the end of the talk, the grand finale was a music sequencer demo that would make no sense at all without audio. So I alerted the IT guys by just saying into the microphone, "Hey, by the way, backstage, I'm missing audio on my videos, and I'm really going to need that by the end of my talk."

I just kept going, went through video after video. I didn't know if they had fixed it by the time I got to that very last clip. I got to that music sequence, introduced that video, turned around and looked at the screen with everybody else in the auditorium, and clicked the clicker. It started rolling and there was no sound! There was still no sound. I had to tell them, "All right, stop. We've got to back it up. We've got to figure this out, because this isn't going to work." I had the clicker, so I backed it up and started the video again. No sound. Did it again. No sound.

The guys backstage started doing the same thing. We were having this tug of war over the slides. After 30 seconds, I just decided, "Okay, I've got to let them figure it out and entertain the crowd." It felt like when you're onstage playing music and someone in the band breaks a guitar string and you've got to tell jokes or stories until that person puts a new string on. So I just started talking to the crowd.

After a minute, Chris Anderson came up and said, "Look, I don't know what's going on, but here's what we'll do: We're going to have you sit back down in the audience. We'll run another couple talks, and then you can come back up and finish your talk once we figure out the audio." So I went back down and sat down. It was kind of surreal. It was like one of those dreams where things happen out of order. You're in a place that's not where you should be. Being back in the audience but not having finished my talk yet was just bizarre. But that's exactly what we did.

After a couple of other talks went by, I got back onstage. They had figured it out. I got to crack a joke about getting to do *two* TED talks rather than one, and then I finished it up. In post they just stitched the pieces together to make the video. I kind of knew they would do that, so I just gave them enough overlap that they could make a clean edit.

The result of that whole thing was that they put my talk online the week after TED and it just blew up. It got more than a million views very quickly. That talk was—in a way, like our Kickstarter before there was such a thing because it was a public validation of this idea, and it gave us the momentum we needed to decide to turn it into a company, and push it forward and build a product that we could get out into the world.

Osborn: Wow—a million views. That must have led to some interesting developments.

Merrill: You know, I knew that TED was going to be important, but I couldn't have told you that it was going to be that important before it happened. After the talk went online, my e-mail inbox was never the same. I started getting e-mails from people that were interested to buy the system, developers that wanted to make stuff for it, angel investors that wanted to see if we were starting a company, VCs[3] that had the same question, and educators and teachers that wanted to use it in their classrooms. I basically finished up my thesis as quickly as I could, and then we came out and started the company in California. Sifteo has been building commercial products around this idea ever since then.

Osborn: Besides the issues at TED, can you tell me a bit about some challenges you had along the way building the product, either through physical manufacturing or software engineering challenges? Any technical speed bumps that you've hit along the way?

Merrill: Both of those are really hard. Let's see. In our physical manufacturing, sometimes things that you don't think should take very long will take a long time. In our first-generation product, we got delayed for about four months after we changed one small piece, which was the hard cover on top of the screen that protects it from getting scratched. We changed it out for a more scratch-resistant version of the same little piece of polycarbonate, because we heard from some early users that their screens were getting scratched. It wound up costing us like four months to work through all the implications of that—getting this new piece in enough quantity and re-jiggering the mechanicals to make sure that it would still fit. It wound up being much more difficult than we thought to get that all the way through.

Then on the software side, one of the challenges that the team faced was when we were moving from our generation-one to our generation-two

---

[3]Venture Capitalists

system. The first-gen system used a computer as the control center. Games ran on the computer, which via a little USB radio, would control the cubes wirelessly. We realized right as we were launching the first-gen system that we could make it more convenient for people and a much better product if we could make the whole thing self-contained and portable. So we started working on that, and we gave the team this challenge: "It's got to be portable, lower-cost, and have better performance." The first-gen system sold for $150, and people wanted it cheaper. The graphics should feel snappier and there should be less latency.

Osborn: Those requirements aren't necessarily compatible.

Merrill: Yeah, it's like better, faster, cheaper. Usually, an engineering team responds to a request like that with, "Okay, pick one." Or maybe, "Pick two, and we can do that." But the Sifteo team is comprised of people who are so talented and so enthusiastic about what we're doing that they picked up the challenge and ran with it, and over the course of a year, created the second-generation system, which has much better graphics and animation capabilities. It's totally portable, because of the base that runs the game and stores them ships with it. And it's cheaper—the system is now $129.

There are tons of details about what had to go into the system to make it all work, but a couple of the most interesting ones were that the cube itself got changed such that there's a little microcontroller inside the radio chip on the cube. That little microcontroller does way more than even its designers would have thought possible. It gathers data from the sensors and sends it back over the radio, which is probably what they designed it for—to be like a wireless joystick, or gamepad, or keyboard. But it also drives this entire little 2D graphics engine, pulling bitmapped sprites and tiled background images out of a little bit of local flash storage on the cube, and assembling them to the screen at frame rates up to thirty frames a second. It is so tightly wound that there's not even a byte left over for extra code on that microcontroller. So I think of that firmware as more of a nervous system than a firmware image for the cubes behavior.

Then on the base, the team developed what we call the Sifteo Virtual Machine, which is a very lightweight virtual machine that accomplishes a lot on a pretty low-power processor. It basically runs apps on a processor that doesn't have the kind of hardware peripherals normally required to run apps. What I mean is that it doesn't even have hardware support for memory management or file system access. We're running applications in a way that it's both sandboxed so the applications can't harm the device—even if there's malicious code—and very performance-oriented. It pretty much lets the apps run right on the bare metal, as they say, of the microcontroller. Great performance and also low power—we get good battery life out of the system. There's a ton of really excellent engineering that went into the creation of our second-gen system.

The other thing I would say, if you're interested in challenges, was there's a creative challenge that the game studio at Sifteo tackles all the time, which is: How do we design games for this new system. It's a new platform. Before Sifteo, there were no platforms to design games for that worked like this. So we are continually challenging our studio to figure out how to design a really fun, engaging game on this platform. There's not a long history of designing for this system, so it takes a lot of creativity. This is really just as difficult and interesting as the technical challenge.

Osborn: It sounds like you guys have been working on this concept since 2006, so there's a lot of history there. You've put a lot of effort and a lot of tears into bringing this physical product to market. I wonder if you have any advice for people who are building things in their garage, or are at a university right now creating things. Just advice for them to transform these projects from something in their garage into a real product.

Merrill: I guess the number one thing I can say is to talk to other people who have done it before. People who have brought products to the market that have something in common with what you want to do. If it's a hardware product, talk to other entrepreneurs who have brought hardware to market. Software, same thing: talk to software people, especially if you can find someone who's done something related.

We became friends with the guys that made Guitar Hero. We picked their brains. We got to know the founders of Fitbit. We actually share investors with them, too, which made it easier. We got to know founders of other kinds of hardware companies, like Jawbone and Ouya. There aren't that many people who have taken hardware products all the way to market. Everyone's busy, but most are willing to share some experience and sit down for coffee with an entrepreneur who is just getting started to give some advice. That's one thing I find that's been really cool about making a hardware product for a platform. I can usually get a meeting with people that have done this kind of thing before and pick their brains, and they're happy to help. I think part of that, especially in hardware, is that the community of people doing it commercially is actually still small enough that there's an intimacy there. People know each other and they're still going to meetups. That's one of the cool things about hardware these days.

Osborn: What are some new projects that other people are working on that you find interesting?

Merrill: I think that there's a ton of interesting things. Let me name three in particular that I think are really cool that are just getting off the ground. One is some guys making a motorized skateboard, Boosted Boards.[4] They're a group of grad students from Stanford that showed this project at the TechCrunch

---

[4]boostedboards.com

Disrupt conference last year. They have this super cool motorized skateboard that you can control—it looks really fun. You can basically make the skateboard your commuting vehicle because it will even go up hills.

I'm also really interested in this new surge of quadcopter and RC helicopter flying machines that are appearing. There's one project called the Crazyflie[5] that's made by some Swedish guys. It's the tiniest little quadcopter you've ever seen. The whole thing is not much bigger than your iPhone. It looks like it has insane maneuverability, and it's just miniscule. It's like the mosquito of quadcopters, where everything else is like an albatross. I think it's pretty exciting, the better and better ways we have to control those things. The possibilities for entertainment and photography are really exciting. Personal drones may sound pretty threatening to some people, from a surveillance Big Brother point of view. I know that's another side of the coin—most technologies have this kind of good side and dark side. But I'm pretty excited about the consumer applications for these things.

Osborn: And it's getting easier to prototype product ideas.

Merrill: Yes there has been this succession of better and better hardware prototyping tools, going all the way back to BASIC Stamp, which was the standard for a long time. Then the Arduino became the standard. And the Arduino is continuing to evolve, but there are also these other new platforms that offer really exciting stuff, like fully integrated development environments with debugging capabilities. I've been watching one called the Galago[6] that's particularly interesting to me because it has the same kind of microcontroller in it as the Sifteo Gen2 Base, but with the Galago, you fire up the development environment in a browser window on your computer. It talks to the hardware and lets you debug it the same way you'd expect to debug a software application. I think that's pretty exciting. It's basically reducing the barriers to entry for people that want to work with hardware. I think that is going to be just as empowering as what happened in software, especially as the Internet took off.

We're starting to see it now with the wave of hardware startup companies—like Sifteo, like Fitbit, MakerBot—that are popping up and growing big, and showing that there's a world of startups that can actually make physical goods because the development of the Internet makes it possible to market them to the entire world and get it out there fast, in a way that you just couldn't before.

Most of the companies that are making hardware also have a software aspect to them. They're not just selling a thing. They tend to be, like Sifteo, a platform. Or they may have a subscription or some sort of digital revenue stream that

---

[5]wiki.bitcraze.se/projects:crazyflie:index
[6]logiblock.com

makes it a more comprehensive product. It's both a product *and* a service. So I guess that third category is partly the new development tools, but the point is that there's this movement happening that's getting bigger and bigger, and is fundamentally about lowering the barriers to entry for people that want to build new things with hardware. I'm really excited about that because I think the kinds of devices that we're going to see come out of this are going to be really different—it's going to be like the personal computer era again, but a much more wildly varying set of systems and devices. I think that's going to be exciting.

Osborn: When you mention all the new development platforms. The key to me is not that there are so many more of them, but that it doesn't cost $2000 anymore to go get a development kit to start. Your barrier to entry is as low as a $20 bill. You can get an Arduino-compatible board and start programming microcontrollers in a couple of hours.

Merrill: Yeah, it's amazing. That's totally the thing. It used to be really expensive. It's getting cheaper, but it's also getting easier. The kinds of tools that people are making available are just getting better and better, so you don't have to be a domain expert in embedded systems anymore to get an Arduino and plug it in and make an LED blink, and then you can start to iterate from there. For some of these new development boards, the ambition of the people making them is they'll actually be low-cost enough that you will consider designing it right into your product. You don't actually have to do this two-step process, which is usually the way it's done, where you build a prototype on the developer board and then you build your actual product by totally redoing it for lower cost. I don't know if they're quite there yet in making it really cheap enough, but it's heading in that direction.

Osborn: David, thank you for your time and insight. There seems to be a ton of people coming out of the MIT Media Lab doing extremely interesting things for computing and electronics, and you are certainly no exception. Keep challenging the way we interact with the world and the way we approach devices.

Merrill: You're welcome. It's a great time to be making physical things that have intelligence and personality.

Nathan Seidle

CEO
SparkFun Electronics

*Founded in 2003 by **Nathan Seidle**, SparkFun Electronics (sparkfun.com) is well-known and loved by hardware hackers everywhere. Nathan started SparkFun while attending college at the University of Colorado. Since then, SparkFun has been recognized as one of the fastest growing companies in Boulder and has served as a learning tool and source of discovery for many people exploring the world of electronics. One of my favorite weekly traditions is opening my browser on Friday mornings to see the SparkFun new products video.*

Steven Osborn: Nathan, I'm wondering what inspired you to become a hardware hacker. Can you think back to some projects or even a person who inspired you or got you interested in electronics?

Nathan Seidle: It started back in, I think, middle school. My friends and I were trying to program calculator games on the TI83 series, or maybe TI85 series calculators. That was about the same time that I started playing with bulletin board systems [BBS], calling them up and transferring files. I came across a schematic to build a link from a computer to a TI calculator. I also came across a repository of TI calculator games. So I thought, "Oh wow! I've got to get these on my calculator, but I don't have this link." So I tried to figure out how to build one from the schematic, buying parts from Radio Shack, and managed to get one assembled and plugged into a parallel port. I guess it was an open-source schematic of sorts. At the same time, I managed to cut my thumb pretty good. I still have the scar from building those things. I built one for myself and, because I had all the games, my friends started hooking their calculators up to my calculators to get games.

They said, "How'd you get these games?"

I said, "Well, I built a download cable."

"Great. Can you build me one?" So I started building and selling TI calculator connectors.

Osborn: I've talked to a couple people whose first experience with programming was on a TI calculator. To switch gears here slightly, a lot of people seem to have this person in their life—in a lot of cases their dad—who was a role model or mentor. Did you have someone that helped you learn electronics? Or did you just see this problem to solve with the calculator, and then went out and read about it, and figured it out yourself?

Seidle: My parents were pretty understanding. They would always find broken devices, be it a blender or a CP/M 80, a really old computer, and allow me to tear into those and dig them apart. I didn't really have a mentor. It was just sort of tearing stuff apart as a kid. I guess we were all curious people. It wasn't until college that I discovered that I could build microcontrollers and blink LEDs but I've been playing with stuff all my life.

Osborn: Tell me a little bit more about yourself and your background, your education and early projects that you worked on.

Seidle: Let's see. How it all started was I got into college and I was pretty good at math and science. I said, "Okay, let's go into engineering." And then I took some circuit classes, and at the same time I was doing my engineering degree.

I was also on the crew team.[1] The crew team had these weird electronic devices that they used for voice amplification and they were very old, very troublesome; they broke a lot. So I started to look at what it would take to build a better device. We wanted to make something to do voice amplification as well as a handful of other metrics like boat speed—via GPS, stroke rate—via accelerometers, and whole host of features—data logging and stuff. On top of all that, it had to be waterproof and rugged.

I thought to myself, "I need to read the switch. I need to have a display." I concluded, "Well, you need a computer." But it's impossible to put a computer into these very small crew boats, so that's when I started to read about the Parallax BASIC Stamp, and started to teach myself electronics. I got a Parallax Board of Education, and wrote some code, and maxed that out in about a day and a half. That's when I started to really look into and learn about microcontrollers, because the BASIC Stamp was great to get me started, but within a couple of days, I needed something a little cheaper and a little beefier.

Osborn: Did those efforts eventually turn into SparkFun? You just celebrated your ten-year anniversary, right?

---

[1] A sport in which competitors race boats propelled by oars.

Seidle: In 2002, I was in Salt Lake City as an employee of the Winter Olympics. I was basically an underpaid security guard. I just stood out in the middle of the night guarding some gates. In my free time, I was learning about how to hook up microcontrollers and control LEDs to do different things.

When I moved back to Boulder, I started looking for parts to build the projects that I wanted make, like a GPS logger. I got on the Internet. I looked at all these web sites and I said, "Oh cool. They've got a GPS module, but they don't have a connector for it, and they don't have a breakout board, and they don't have a data sheet, and oh my goodness, there's just a phone number to call. I don't want to talk to a human. I just want to order these parts." So I realized, at that moment in 2002, that the state of electronics stores, electronic parts—it was really hard to get anything online. So I thought, "Well, maybe I can start my own little store." The goal was just to feed my own addiction. The goal was to make enough money so that I could continue to build my own side projects.

Osborn: So your goal was to have it all online, even in 2002? From really early on?

Seidle: Yeah. In 2002, I assumed that there were other people like me that didn't want to make a phone call, didn't really have a fax or want to fax in an order with a credit card number. In 2002, I said, "This should be easy. I should be able to add stuff to my cart and check out with a credit card, just like all these other web sites that sell stuff." But at that time, the electronics-parts world was nowhere near that. So I decided I could start a web site and sell weird electronic parts online. On January 3rd, 2003 SparkFun opened for business and we've been trying to catch up ever since.

Osborn: You guys sell a lot of different things, a broad spectrum of things. Can you tell me about some of the cool projects that your customers have built or are working on that you think are interesting?

Seidle: There's dozens, if not hundreds, and my memory is pretty poor. The one that often comes to mind is a young man who came into the office. I think he was twelve or thirteen at the time. He wanted to get a tour of SparkFun and he wanted to show off a project he had built. He had taken a series of our flex sensors and had attached them to a glove, kind of like the Nintendo Power Glove. He used an accelerometer to detect the level of his hand, and then based on which fingers were flexed and the tilt of his hand, he could decode sign language characters.

Osborn: Oh, incredible.

Seidle: Yeah, and so he piped that into an LCD display, so he could actually sign characters and have it print out. Eventually, he sent that to what's called a speech jet, which is a voice synthesizer. So he could sign stuff, and then after a couple of seconds, his device would start talking. It was at that moment that we realized this kid was going to take over the world someday. It is just amazing to see what twelve and thirteen-year-olds can build with the tools these days.

Osborn: Do you have an example of a more unusual or a more oddball project that you've seen?

Seidle: Let's see. We had a customer, maybe five or six years ago, who sent us an e-mail, with an image attached, that said, "Hey, thanks for selling this distance sensor to me. Check out what I built with it." So I clicked on the image, and it was this gentleman jumping on a trampoline with a gigantic flame behind him. What he did was place the distance sensor underneath the trampoline. The distance sensor went to a microcontroller. The microcontroller went to a valve on a propane tank, so the harder you jumped, the bigger the flame was in the background.

Osborn: Now that's fun, a little crazy maybe, but fun. In recent years, at least from my perspective, there has been an uptick in interest in electronics. I don't know if it's just because of the ease of entry or what, but it seems like a lot more people are buying Arduinos. The Kickstarter hardware projects tend to get a lot of attention. Can you describe what you've noticed there? What do you think might be feeding that? Do you think it's going to continue to grow?

Seidle: When we started SparkFun in the very beginning of 2003, it was obvious that we were selling to electrical engineers, and hobbyists, and people that were exactly like me—who wanted to build projects that were just a ton of fun. Then I think *Make* magazine came along in like—'05, '06—and showed folks that it was kind of fun to use your hands. So they had all these really great tactile, sort of getting-back-to-building stuff, making things. Then Maker Faire came along and people started discovering each other, and they had similar passions and some new passions, and it was really fun. The first couple of Maker Faires were *amazing*.

Shortly after that—'07, '08—Arduino really started blowing up. I remember when Tom Igoe first came to me and said, "Hey, Nate. I think SparkFun should carry this Arduino." I have to admit, I didn't get Arduino. As an engineer it looked like just another AVR developer board, but I was very wrong. But Tom was a trusted friend so we started carrying it, and it started to sell really, really well. We noticed that it wasn't shipping to universities. It wasn't shipping to engineering schools. It was shipping to these really creative art schools, these really creative digital media programs. I think it was the combination of a series of storms that made SparkFun at the right time and the right place in the middle of that, and it worked out really well. Arduino has brought an entirely new category of people into electronics. It's not just electrical engineers. It's not just hobbyists. It's *amazing* artists, and *amazingly* creative people doing things engineers never would have dreamed of.

Osborn: Can you talk a little bit about open-source hardware? What it means to have open-source hardware, and what it means to you?

Seidle: Way back in the day, when we had some of the first products that we released, they were little breakout boards. Actually, it was an accelerometer on one side and a PIC microcontroller on the other, and all this little device did was convert the accelerometer values to a serial signal, so that you had a serial accelerometer. This was the easiest protocol, so people liked it. The problem was that SparkFun was just me at that time and I couldn't really handle the tech support. I was really worried that folks would want to change certain aspects of the product and I wouldn't be able to do that. I wouldn't be able to help them.

So I decided in that moment to open up that product, in whatever year it was—'04, '05—and say, "Okay, here's the schematic. Here's the firmware. If you want to make changes, go for it." At that point in time, there was no concept of open or closed. It was just like, "Here's this thing. We want to share. Do whatever you want with it." As time went on, it became more and more obvious that folks were learning from our designs, so that the more we shared, the faster our customers learned and the more stuff they needed from us. It was beneficial to us to share everything that we developed.

In the last couple of years, the open-source hardware movement has turned into a significant thing, and I'm really pleased with it from two aspects. One of them is making humanity better. By sharing these things, you fulfill the human need to learn from each other. If I learn a hard lesson here, let me share this hard lesson with you so that you don't have to go through that same pain. That works really nicely with hardware. There's a lot of "gotchas" that can be avoided if you can learn from somebody else.

On the opposite side of OSHW,[2] there's the business benefits. What we found at SparkFun is if we open-source our design, there is a good likelihood that our business competitors will also learn from the design. But what that does is force us to pay attention. It forces us to innovate. It forces us to always be thinking about the next product. Over the past two or three years, that has caused this great effect within SparkFun to streamline, to get really fast and good at coming out with new versions, and new features, and new products. So I find open-source hardware to be really beneficial from both a humanity stance and a business stance.

Osborn: What license do you use? Can you give me an overview of what the spirit of the license provides, and what that means for people and why did you guys go that route?

---

[2]OSHW – Open Source Hardware

Seidle: The products that we've released as open-source hardware have a variety of licenses, whether it's GPL or MIT. A lot of our firmware is actually released under "beerware," where we just say, "You know what? If you ever use this and you happen to be in the same conference or the same place, you buy the beer." And it's worked out really well on the innovation front.

Osborn: Is there an official text for beerware?

Seidle: Yeah, if you Google beerware,[3] there's a gentleman who actually came up with it a number of years ago.

Osborn: I love it.

Seidle: We just sort of started using it without really thinking about it. I've actually gotten two beers from it so far, so it does work from time to time. We released these things out into the wild effectively—you know, public domain. Then the side effect of that is we don't have the luxury of sitting on our laurels and trying to enforce patent lawsuits against folks. At the speed at which technology changes in our world, you can try to get a patent. It will take three to five years. And you can try to enforce it and you can spend all your time fighting people. Or you can just innovate, and release stuff, and get creative. I think it's actually a lot healthier and can be a lot more lucrative going the nonpatent route to open up.

Osborn: So you haven't standardized on something like Creative Commons?[4] It's just sort of whatever makes the most sense for that project?

Seidle: Correct. There is some really technical stuff about compliance to works of art with Creative Commons. Like the schematic could be considered a work of art, the gerbers[5] could be considered a work of art, but the PCB layout is actually a technical document. So that could be potentially patented. Actually, there are some very smart people—smarter than me—that have looked at all this and have said that Creative Commons, even though it is very simple to understand, doesn't apply very well to hardware. So we're still trying to figure out what license works.

Osborn: So, no general advice for a good hardware open-source license?

Seidle: I don't have a good recommendation right now.

Osborn: Even if you did, it would have to come with the "I'm not a lawyer" caveat, I suppose.

Seidle: Exactly, and it's probably going to change in six months anyways. Right now, I believe in the spirit of open-source: "Hey, here's this thing. I don't know what license to put on it, but if you want to use it, you totally can. Go for it."

---

[3]http://people.freebsd.org/~phk
[4]http://creativecommons.org
[5]A *gerber* is a common file format for describing layers of a PCB (printed circuit board).

Osborn: So if I'm just a complete beginner, maybe I'm a designer, maybe I'm only interested in the software side of things, what would you recommend? Or what would be the best way for someone to get plugged into the maker culture?

Seidle: It depends. If you're a complete beginner, it's always best to learn a new hobby with a friend, right? If there's a way, go to a meetup or something, where you can meet folks in the maker crowd, the people that build electronics, or even just build stuff at all. That's a great way to learn. If you don't have that, then I would say go buy an Arduino. Our community is really moving in that direction. When you buy an Arduino, you go through the first few tutorials, and it tells you how to build a circuit to blink an LED. That first moment, when you realize that you have control over this thing—this blinking LED, and it's independent of a computer—is great. It's really, really exciting to see folks' brains explode when they first experience that. So once you realize you can control hardware, that's really the gateway into a lot of fun products.

Osborn: You said something about, "Go find a meetup group." I think Dorkbot[6] is one example. I'm sure there are other meetup groups. I know you guys host a number of events throughout the year. Can you talk to me a little bit about the events you host in Boulder?

Seidle: We have between one and two classes per month. They range anywhere from a "learn to solder" kit, where we'll help you put it together. We'll help you solder your first joint. Then you solder all the other connections on the board. Then we offer classes on programming and e-textiles and all sorts of machine shop classes. We don't think that we're a replacement for a hacker space, by any means. I love hacker spaces.

Really, we're just sort of helping folks learn the specialty that is SparkFun. On top of that, there are a couple of events here. In 2012, we had our first soldering competition. We had, I think, sixty or seventy competitors come out. It was a fun, crazy time with a bunch of different folks who were very good at soldering come show off their skills. We had a good time doing that. Coming up in June [2013], we have our autonomous vehicle competition, which is our version of the DARPA Grand Challenge, but on the student level, where it's much, much cheaper. You can build an autonomous vehicle for two or three hundred bucks, and then come compete against other little autonomous vehicles. This is our fifth year of having that competition. Every year, the autonomous planes show up, and the quadcopters show up, and some really exciting wheeled vehicles show up.

Osborn: I just saw a blog post about AVC[7] today. It looks like there's going to be a new course and some interesting things there. Maybe that's my next project.

---

[6]http://dorkbot.org
[7]AVC – Autonomous Vehicle Competition, avc.sparkfun.com

Seidle: It's a tremendous amount of work and a tremendous amount of fun.

Osborn: There is a lot of buzz these days around personal manufacturing, or on-demand manufacturing, or insourcing, which are not necessarily all the same thing, but all kind of fall into this bucket of things that people are interested in. How do you see the current maker movement and culture playing into that? And do you have any examples of this sort of thing happening now?

Seidle: That's a really good question. The gentleman who started Tindie—his name escapes me. I could find it in my e-mail. What's his name?

Osborn: Emile Petrone.

Seidle: Emile has done some really amazing stuff with Tindie, showing what this kind of microdemand can do. Instead of designing a product that needs mass-market appeal, SparkFun came in and said, "Okay, cool. We can build products even when only five or six hundred people want the product." Tindie came in and said, "Well, what does it look like if only five or six people want a product?" So I'm really excited by that.

At the same time, the sellers behind those five or six sort of the Etsys of the world,[8] seem like they're still doing it by hand. They're manufacturing the electronics by hand. In the past six months, I have been in contact with five or six people that are trying to crack the nut of short-run manufacturing. So I wouldn't be surprised if in the next twelve months, there are options, very low-cost options, which allow you to do some pretty interesting electronics manufacturing.

Osborn: Dangerous Prototypes[9] has a blog post where the guy was using a pick-and-place[10] he purchased from China for maybe $3,500. That's something that people are starting to roll in their garage, which is pretty interesting.

Seidle: I haven't seen the Dangerous Prototypes post on the pick-and-place machines. The one that I saw was Zach Hoeken, one of the founders of MakerBot. He did a really great post about his $4,000 pick-and-place.

Osborn: I believe it's the same pick-and-place. They ended up doing some group buy or something. If you talked to Ian Lesnet, he would introduce you to his guy in China and you could get some ridiculous discount—but only if you wired the money to China. It's kind of like, "I know this guy who knows this guy in China, and if you wire him thousands of dollars, he'll hook you up." It sounds completely shady, but apparently has worked for a number of people. I'm not sure that's exactly how it works, but that's my understanding.

Seidle: Awesome, I'll see if I can't get on that list!

---

[8]www.etsy.com
[9]http://dangerousprototypes.com/
[10]A machine that picks up small components and places them on printed circuit boards.

Osborn: A lot of people seem to be getting into 3D printing. I have a 3D printer and a CNC laser, for instance, and I've even seen pick-and-place machines in people's garages. Have you seen 100kGarages[11]?

Seidle: No I haven't.

Osborn: It's basically Airbnb for like CNC or 3D printer rentals. So if you go on there, you can just search for an eight-foot-by-four-foot CNC router and find one in someone's garage who is willing to rent it out. I searched for just that and there was one twenty minutes from my house. So it is pretty cool to just think about the possibilities there.

Seidle: Very cool! Yeah, I haven't heard of that site, but I'm definitely seeing more tool sharing services. One for CNCs and pick and place machines makes a lot of sense.

Osborn: Let's see. So another theme getting some attention is the "Internet of Things," which some people see as being the next big evolution of the Internet—monitoring and controlling everyday things remotely over the Internet. In your words, can you describe what that is and the impact you see it having?

Seidle: The Internet of Things? I'm an electrical engineer, and so everything looks like an electrical engineering problem. We've been building a lot of stuff for a large number of years. As the processors get cheaper, and the development boards get cheaper, it's easier and easier to hook up Ethernet and push some data around. So to me, the Internet of Things is not as revolutionary as some folks are excited about. It's good to be passionate, it's good to be excited about stuff, but to me, it's a natural progression of—you know, it's just easier. It's easier to move data around if my thing is on the Internet, so, yeah, let's hook it up. It's going to be great. Everything is going to be wired up. I still think you don't need microwaves on the Internet, but there's always going to be really creative ways of using the Internet.

I've got some good friends who did Botanicalls.[12] It was a project, five or six years ago, where they used a plant moisture-monitoring system to kind of Twitter out different things about the status of the plants. But instead of just, "This is my relative humidity. This is my temperature," it was more snarky than that. It was, "Why don't you love me? Why don't you spend time with me? Nobody loves me enough to water me." Those sorts of things are, I think, the creative spin that I'm really interested in.

Osborn: So there's the short-run manufacturing, 3D printing, the Internet of Things, these common themes throughout the maker community. Do you see

---

[11]www.100kGarages.com
[12]www.botanicalls.com

any other interest groups or topics, maybe wearable computing or something else that's taking off?

Seidle: We just got back from South by Southwest and we've been to every Maker Faire since the beginning of Maker Faire. It was amazing to see the night-and-day difference. Where Maker Faire is a collection of tinkers, and inventors, and people obviously making things, South by Southwest is this collection of really creative types—the designers, the visionaries of the world—getting together and kind of revolting. They have been promised this great interactive experience for a number of years, and it's just been on an LCD screen. So when we showed up for this first time this year, we didn't know what to expect. We had so many people at our booth. It was nonstop for a week. People were coming by and discovering the missing link to their world. We had a booth set up that did e-textiles. So we showed folks how to use connective thread to wire LEDs. It was like this thing they had been searching for all of their lives, and they had just found it. It was so exciting and rewarding for us to be able to show folks some new stuff in the world.

I think you asked, "Is there an upcoming theme?" I really think we still have this untapped resource of really creative, very visual designers of the world discovering what it means to have physical stuff again. When they can learn to use e-textiles, when they can learn to use electronics, we're going to see some really amazing projects.

Osborn: Awesome. So one other thing I want to talk a little about is the SparkFun national tour you guys have coming up in 2013. What do you have planned, and what's your purpose?

Seidle: Kind of like South by Southwest, we really enjoy teaching and sharing all our passion with other folks, and we think it's not at all limited to adults. We really want to show middle school and high school kids what it's like to use something other than a touchscreen. With the national tour, we really want to visit schools that have an interest in changing the way that they teach various curriculums using electronics. So there are currently about seventy cities and school districts that signed up for the national tour to have us stop by for a day. We show up, we bring hardware for forty students, and we teach an all-day class on e-textiles and how to use microcontrollers to control the world around you. The goal is really to not necessarily teach students—we really enjoy teaching students—but we also want to teach educators, show them sort of the new tools that have come out in the past two or three years.

Osborn: Right, you can teach forty students, or you can teach an educator, who can teach forty students each semester. You started this business in 2002, right? I don't think you've taken venture capital, so you bootstrapped the business in 2002. How long was it before you were able to quit your job and do this full-time?

Seidle: In 2002, I was a junior at the University of Colorado. When I started SparkFun, it was with a credit card. I started SparkFun with $2,500 worth of debt, an inventory shelf in my bedroom, and a tape gun. As the orders very slowly started coming in, I started shipping out orders, and I then found myself having to run to the FedEx depot and the post office every day, having to ship out three, or four, or five orders. At the same time, I was taking a full load at the university and working part-time as a motorcycle mechanic. So when I graduated from college, everybody asked me, "Where are you applying? Where are you going to work?"

And I said, "Are you kidding? All I have to do now is work? I'm not applying anywhere. This is great. I don't have to do school. I don't have to do the motorcycle mechanic thing. I can just run SparkFun." It was sort of a shaky job. It wasn't a guaranteed thing. But SparkFun was big enough when I graduated that I could just run that full-time.

Osborn: That's great.

Seidle: To answer your question about venture capital, I am still the ninety-six percent shareholder in SparkFun. So we've never taken outside investment. We've bootstrapped the whole thing, and it's been very tricky. Every month that went by, we were thinking, "Oh my goodness. We have to pay the credit card bill off this week. We have to make payroll next week. And then we have to sort all the inventory back onto the credit card the following day and ask them to raise the limit." It is just this constant sort of cycle. But it worked out, and now we have the fortune of being in control of our own destiny. We enjoy being in the pilot seat.

Osborn: What are some of the challenges you've had as part of the business? I'm sure it hasn't always been just up and to the right? I'm sure you guys have had some bumps along the way.

Seidle: Oh my goodness. That's an hour-long question right there. If you ever get the chance, come out to Boulder and come take a tour. I'd love to show you all the crazy. Some of the bumps along the way—one of them, we still refer to as the "cash death" of 2010. SparkFun had been growing for whatever it was—five, six, seven years at that point. We're in an inventory business. We're into physical things. We have to build these widgets and we have to ship them to our customers. So as you grow, you're managing everything on dry-erase boards, and then you're managing it on spreadsheets, and then you get to a certain time where you're thinking, "This is crazy. How does the real world do it?" And they start talking about these massive pieces of software to manage their entire inventory. So we were sort of learning as we went. I like to joke, "I never took this class in college," so we're just figuring it out as we go.

In March of 2010, I got together with our purchasers, who are one or two people responsible for buying the inventory. I get together with our director of finance. She was running the inventory as well at the time. We looked at the money we had in the bank. We're like, "Okay, cool. We're out of stock on all these parts right now. We've got a couple hundred thousand dollars. Let's go buy extra inventory. Let's go buy enough so that we can have almost nothing out of stock." So I told the purchasers to go buy more. I told the finance person, "We've got the money." We've also got this line of credit with the bank, so that's all good.

So we started. We went out and we bought stuff, and it was between four and five weeks later, we started noticing that there was no cash in the bank, that we had way too much inventory, and we couldn't touch our line of credit because of some fine print in the agreement with the bank. So there was this really bad couple of weeks where we nearly didn't have enough money to make payroll because we had purchased the wrong inventory items and we hadn't worked with the bank long enough to secure the line of credit in the way that we should have. It was one of those weeks where I realized that I don't have a lot of business experience. We learned a lot of lessons. We made payroll. We were lucky that we made payroll, but we also learned a lot of lessons about how to handle inventory correctly and work with your bank. It was pretty close. It was pretty scary.

Osborn: I've worked for companies who've been in that situation before. It's not a fun place to be.

Seidle: There are tons and tons of other examples. In 2009, we got a cease-and-desist letter from SPARC International, which is a really big conglomeration of Oracle and Fujitsu. That was the day that I got to learn about what a cease-and-desist means, and about trademark law. Luckily, the Internet came to our rescue and SPARC International backed off. We've also been on the other side of it, where we're starting to get a few companies that are copying our logo and copying our font and colors to make electronics. Just sort of dealing with the challenges of having a business. It's not that exciting unless you're in the thick of it. It's crazy. Every day it's something different.

Osborn: I would love to take a tour when I'm there sometime. Do you guys do tours regularly? Do you just show up? Or do you have to schedule something?

Seidle: We give tours every Friday afternoon at three to the general public, whoever wants to show up. It's a lot of fun. It's the end of the week. Folks are kind of more laid back. And then whenever we have friends in town—like this Saturday, I'm giving a tour to some friends of mine and their sons, just to show them what a warehouse looks like. It should be pretty interesting. So, yeah, if you're ever in town, drop me a line. I'd love to show you around.

Osborn: How many heads do you guys have now?

Seidle: Currently, it's somewhere between one hundred thirty-five and one hundred forty, and then we've got—last check it was forty-one dogs, so that puts us as the second-largest kennel in Boulder, if we were out to put up a kennel.

Osborn: Forty-one dogs on premises at any one time?

Seidle: So they don't show up every day of the week. It's sort of whenever the owners want to bring them in. But we have ten to twenty-five over here on any given day.

Osborn: Wow. That's pretty incredible. I thought that it was a Portland thing to have a dog or two in the office, but that puts away what I've seen. It's one or two, not twenty.

Seidle: Yeah, this is a little different.

Osborn: In Portland, the thing is you have to have extremely large room to park bikes in. When we were at eighty people, we had maybe thirty people that commuted to work by bike. Once a quarter or so, we would bring in a bike mechanic who would maintenance your bike. Fix a flat, realign the cassette, and tighten up your brakes, whatever needed to be done. That just served a perk that we offered the people because there were so many people who rode bikes in. We didn't want them to have to take time off to take their bike to the shop, and we didn't want people getting injured because they were riding something, you know.

Seidle: That's a great idea. That's awesome. We've got a handful of folks, not as many as forty, probably twenty or thirty, that ride to commute, and it's that time of year when folks are starting to break their bikes back out because it does get pretty cold and icy in the winter here. So that's a cool idea. I'll see if we can basically just get everybody together that knows about bikes and just get it ready for the spring.

Osborn: Well, I'm looking forward to a tour soon. I'll definitely be around for AVC if I don't make it before then. Keep making great stuff! I look forward to the new product videos every Friday.

Laen

Founder
OSH Park

In order to help out his friends and fellow geeks, James "Laen" Neal organized and collected orders for printed circuit boards (PCBs) for them. This service grew to be Laen's full-time job (OSHPark.com), and the unique purple circuit boards he offers can be seen all over the Web inside thousands of projects across the globe.

Laen is heavily involved in his local maker community, specifically the local Dorkbot group (dorkbotpdx.org), where he helps out in numerous ways. I learned to design circuit boards using Eagle CAD at a local workshop that Laen taught.

Steven Osborn: So, first, I want to know—is it James or Laen?

James "Laen" Neal: Yeah, my name is James Neal. I go by Laen exclusively in this circle of my life.

Osborn: I'm always confused how to address you in e-mails because—anyway, you go by Laen.

Laen: Everyone in the makers' sphere knows me as Laen. James Neal is a pretty common name and there are a lot of us out there. In fact, there's one who I worked with who's in the same line of work as me, and about the same age as me, and was hired into a job when I left it at one point.

Osborn: That was confusing for HR.

Laen: And for him! That must have been awful. The first three times he signed up for an account, one of the other admins deleted it, thinking it was me fooling around.

Osborn: Ha! So tell me a little bit about how you got into this maker community. What got you started?

Laen: Well, back when I was a kid, I was interested in electronics. But back then, electronics education was pretty much just, "Let's light up an LED," or "Let's have a 555 timer do something," and microcontrollers weren't really a part of it. At the time, I was more interested in computers and that sort of thing, so I kind of fell out of it. In 2008, I saw one of the makers' blog videos, *Introduction to Arduino.* It was a Halloween-themed project. It showed how easy it is to make interactive electronics through microcontrollers using Arduino. It was just a blinking LED, but how easy it was shocked me.

Osborn: What early projects inspired you?

Laen: That's a hard question. At that point, I started browsing through the SparkFun[1] library of all the different tools you could use to make other things, and I saw how inexpensive it was to put GPS into things and all that. One of the first things I wanted to make was just a little GPS logger to stick on my mom, who goes for just the longest hikes during the summer, so that she could record her trips, and chart where she was along the trail and elevation, and all that.

Osborn: You were just browsing SparkFun, geeking out on the possibilities?

Laen: The possibilities, yeah.

Osborn: Was there a certain person you remember who was influential for you?

Laen: Definitely Limor Fried at Adafruit.[2] That was really the kind of thing where I was like, "Wow." The documentation that she did with all her projects and releasing it for free was all really cool. Coming from a UNIX system in the past, seeing how open-source software would work with open-source hardware was really inspiring.

Osborn: Tell me a little bit about how you got involved in making this PCB service.

Laen: At the time I started it, I think it was late 2009, early 2010. Now it's called the OSH Park PCB Order. It grew out of the DorkbotPDX PCB Order. DorkbotPDX is our local electronics group, which started about the time I started getting interested in electronics, in 2008. Many of us in the group were just learning how to design our own circuits, our own circuit boards, and getting them manufactured. We were all ordering them from China. It would take more than a month to get those boards turned around and back to us. So I priced it out and saw that we could order a panel from Advanced Circuits[3] with a three-day turn around, and get them back in a week. So that's how that started.

---

[1]www.sparkfun.com
[2]www.adafruit.com
[3]www.4pcb.com

Osborn: It was really a need to scratch your own itch, or solve a problem for your buddies and makers in this Dorkbot group. So the next question is: Why purple?

Laen: That was just sort of a lucky accident. I had just switched providers. This one had a lot more options than green. Then someone brought to Dorkbot a development board from Nuvoton,[4] a little arm board. It was this gorgeous purple color, and I was like, "I want that." So the purple came about and I was like, "This is great because I can go through Flickr and I can see which boards people made that were made through my service." And I really like to see what other people have made with it, because I don't make many boards myself anymore, but I really like helping other people make. That was the reason to make it even more distinctive: so I could find it easily when browsing the social networks.

Osborn: Regardless of whether or not you like the purple color, one thing you can't argue with is that it's distinctive. I see your circuit boards all over the place, and there's no question that it's an OSH Park board because it's purple and gold. I like to go on Tindie, and every day I see a new cool project, and I'm like, "I know where that PCB came from," which is cool. So I think the purple certainly worked out for you.

Laen: Yeah, I really love it. It's a nice color for me. I like it with the gold. And I really like being able to see these projects as they explode across the Internet—and know I had some small part in making it happen.

Osborn: I don't know if other PCB services have the level of Web interface that you provide. I have personally uploaded PCBs before and ended up using your service to error-check my design. I just upload it, and then I notice something out of place. Before, I would have found out two weeks later, and that's a big reason why I like using your service, because without that feature, I would be losing a lot of money and time.

Laen: Not when this was the OSH Park PCB Order, but the Dorkbot PCB Order, people would just e-mail me their files and put it on the panel, and it would come back a couple of weeks later, and they'd go, "Oh, man. Why is this all messed up?" I'd go, "Well, that's what the file said." Gerber files can be a little confusing because they're all laid out as though you're looking through the board. You have the top layer, and then when you look at the bottom layer, it's mirrored. So I really wanted to show people how the board would look when they got it, because it really cuts down on the number of e-mails saying, "Hey, this isn't how I wanted it." And those were always sad e-mails for me, when someone was expecting it one way and it didn't come out that way. It really cuts down on [disappointment] a lot, which makes me very happy.

---

[4]www.nuvoton.com

Osborn: I think it's really a killer feature. Can you give me a rough estimate of how many boards you've produced, maybe lifetime or even on a regular basis?

Laen: So it's really grown a lot. It used to be about a panel a month. And one panel is usually about eighty to one hundred ten board designs on a panel. So I was doing about one hundred designs a month, then one hundred designs a week, and now it's about up to that about every day.

Osborn: So it's grown up to one hundred designs a day?

Laen: Yeah.

Osborn: That's very interesting. A lot is kind of an understatement.

Laen: It's really a big pile.

Osborn: Incredible. I've seen a lot of people use these boards in production. They print your boards and sell their products on them, not just for prototyping, but are selling real products built on purple PCBs.

Laen: That was another requirement when I was finding my fabs. I wanted to make sure that they're very high quality. The profit margin is vanishingly small, so I really can't afford a lot of returns. The fab we use—they're more used to working with Motorola than hobbyists. Their design specs are such that I get about one bad board in every thirty thousand, which is I think very important—being able to rely on the boards that you're getting back as being good and being production quality.

Osborn: Tell me about some interesting projects that makers have made on purple PCBs.

Laen: There's a lot. I really like the projects where it's geared toward education. Wayne and Layne is a group of makers, or a couple of makers in Minnesota and Pennsylvania,[5] who design kits to teach people how to solder, both surface-mount and through a hole, and how to program. The boards have very focused reasons for them, and I really like those. Every now and then I see weird things on the silk screen and want to know more. There was one that was a time-travel controller. I would have liked to hear the story behind that. I don't know what it is.

Osborn: Did it have a flux capacitor?[6]

Laen: A big flux capacitor.

Osborn: Was it surface-mount or through a hole?

---

[5] www.wayneandlayne.com
[6] http://en.wikipedia.org/wiki/DeLorean_time_machine#Flux_capacitor

Laen: It was 1980s tech, so it was through a hole.

Osborn: Oh, that's good. At least they kept it real.

Laen: I see a lot of people make different effects pedals, like guitar effects pedals. I think that's very cool. There's a DJ in Ontario who made this custom all-in-one MIDI effects project. It was the biggest board I've had in the order so far. It was, I think, about a foot by a foot square. He sent me a disc of an album he made with it and a video of it in action and stuff, and I thought that was awesome.

Osborn: People talk about the "maker movement" and what that is, and if you ask five people what it is, you would probably get five different answers. How would you describe it?

Laen: I think it's simply a desire to scratch an itch that's now been made possible due to these personal prototyping abilities that we have. Like 3D printers are now commonplace in the maker community and laser cutters and C&C mills. Things that were very difficult to do yourself twenty years ago are now becoming easy, and I think that's opening up a lot of possibilities in a lot of people's minds. Where you at one point would have to say, "Well, the dishwasher broke. Bummer. We're going to have to spend a bunch for a repairman." Now you can say, "Hmmm. I can do some measurements and 3D print my own part, and replace it and make it better." You can redo all the design mistakes that other people have made in your life and make an improved thing that you can share with others.

Osborn: There seems to be this huge insurgence of crowd-funded projects. There's talk all day about the Teensy 3, the Digistump, and then the consumer products, like the Ouya game console. A lot of which are a line of things that wouldn't have ever made it to market before. A couple years ago, if you were to say you were making an open gaming console on an ARM chip to sell and compete with Nintendo, it would be laughable. This is something people would snicker at—like, "Sure you will." And then they raise $9 million on Kickstarter. Now they have this capital to go out and do it. Money that they've raised because they have the backgrounds and expertise, and people believed in it.

I'm wondering: Where this goes from there? Do we see more of those types of projects, or do you see consumers buying more and more products that are produced in people's garages, and grassroots manufacturing via crowd funding?

Laen: I hope so. I think that a lot of things become easy when you spread out the work. I think that there are just a lot of products that have a much smaller audience and that you would never get a manufacturer to agree to twenty years ago. Now you can say, "You know what? I'm going to make it, and I'm going to see if people like it. If they do, I can grow organically and expand to do new things." And that just wasn't as possible back when you had to convince an investor. Now you can either convince a lot of "backers," who want nothing more than the cool project you're making, or you can just do little onesies, twosies, and sell them on Tindie[7] and see if there's an interest—and show that there's an interest—to make larger runs. I think that's really exciting.

Osborn: There are a lot of new technologies. There are like one hundred 3D printer companies now.

Laen: The Maker Faire last year was replete with them.

Osborn: I was at TechShop yesterday and saw a company called Type A Machines[8] that builds things like the size of a Volkswagen. I'm exaggerating—but it's like the size of a small…

Laen: Table?

Osborn: It's about the size of a small coffee table with a massive, massive build platform. It's a beast, but again, it's one of dozens.

Laen: Hundreds. And the stuff like Shapeways, with the really high-end 3D powder printers, where they throw down the layer of powder and "Zut-zut-zut-zut-zut-zut," melt down the layer very quickly, with a really decent resolution.

Osborn: The cool thing about that technology is that as they are printing it, they can lay down color pigment, and so you have a full-color object. One cool thing I saw at TechShop[9] was this massive water jet capable of cutting eight-inch-thick steel. Not new technology by any means, but now it's available to me for a few bucks a month. I have no use for that, but the fact that that's available to me is amazing.

Laen: Yeah, knowing that it's there opens up a lot of possibilities in your mind.

Osborn: Right, you're no longer limited by the tools in your garage.

Laen: Right now I don't have a laser cutter, but I can send something off to Ponoko and have it back in a week and make whatever I want. I made a little scanner table that you put your iPhone on top of to get better images of documents. I think it cost me $50. It's cut out of nice wood that's joined together. You put the phone on top, and it's an instant document scanner that folds away.

---

[7]www.tindie.com
[8]www.typeamachines.com
[9]http://techshop.ws

Osborn: I think there's a Kickstarter project for that, and it was like $50 and it was made out of cardboard. I'm like, "I'm not going to pay $50 for a cardboard box."

Laen: "Give me the PDF and I'll order it myself," in a polymer or an acrylic or something.

Osborn: Plus, you would get it on time since it's not a Kickstarter project.[10] Something in that realm that I find really interesting is Thingiverse.[11] This repository for printable objects, which to me is an amazing thing, but creates a bit of controversy. A lot of people are worried about the IP around a 3D object, like, "What happens if I go and scan a 3D object and print it?" Something people haven't really had to deal with before because of the cost.

Laen: The cost of actually replicating something. Yeah, now there's software for using your smartphone for scanning and—ta-da!—you have a pixel map that you can then print yourself. There was something on the news just a few days ago about that.

Osborn: For people who are new to this maker culture, what would you say is the best way for someone to get plugged into the maker thing and start learning things? What would be the recommended thing for people to do?

Laen: I really love the new Adafruit learning system.[12] I think that's a really awesome curriculum. They've gone to some pains to address people who are interested in making stuff with really fun and relevant projects. They're very well documented, so you're not going to fail your first time. It will give you some of that early confidence that you need when starting something new. Then it will give you lots of stuff to build on. You work up to more advanced projects.

Osborn: I've seen some "beginner tutorials" that were only a little more high-level than a data sheet. It was like, "Here's some code that doesn't even compile. Good luck."

Laen: For beginners, you need to have those early confidence builders. There's a lot to learn from failure, but in order to learn that, you're going to need some confidence early on. It's tough.

We have people in Dorkbot who come in and say, "Hey! I've got this idea for this cool thing I want to do. I want to hook this *Dance, Dance Revolution* pad up to the computer." And the other Dorkbotters are like, "All right, well,

---

[10]Kickstarter projects are notorious for shipping late because many teams underestimate the time it will take to deliver a product.
[11]www.thingiverse.com
[12]http://learn.adafruit.com

here's an Arduino." What they really need is someone to walk them through hooking it up and writing those first few lines of code. They have their first project and could really use the hand of somebody to get this first one going, more hands-on learning, because this is their first electronics project. It's not a doozie, but it's a good one. This is how I felt in elementary school electronics class, "Okay, so I got the 555 timer blinking a light. Now what?" Then not being able to build past that.

Osborn: The new Adafruit learning system is pretty great, but it is hasn't been around for a long time.

Laen: Yeah, for me it was the MAKE videos—I'm not even sure they still make them, but was it Thursday maker videos, or something like that. I forget what the name was exactly.

Osborn: So it sounds like good advice to find help locally.

Laen: Yeah, find other people in your neighborhood.

Osborn: Find other people who will help you. Find a mentor or somebody who can get you through that first project.

Laen: Absolutely. And there are groups all over the country. If you're in a college town, then going to the electrical engineering department and seeing what's posted on the bulletin board [will help you discover them]. Dorkbot is awesome, but I think that Dorkbot Portland is unique among them in that we have huge meetings every other Monday.

Osborn: You mentioned Dorkbot[13] several times. Can you talk about what it is and how you got involved in that?

Laen: Dorkbot is people doing strange things with electricity. The idea is to join people doing art with electronics—artists and engineers—to make cool electronic art. In most places, you go to a meeting and people will be presenting the cool things that they did. In Portland, it's really a social hour. And it probably has a bit more of an electronics focus than an art focus, to the chagrin of some in the group.

Osborn: It seems that across the spectrum, this maker thing is making an impact in any city you're in, but the projects that come out of it are unique to that city's strengths. For instance, there are a lot of silicon companies in and around Portland. That shows up in the group. There's a lot of low-level hackers building microcontroller projects or Arduino-compatible boards from scratch.

---

[13]http://dorkbot.org

Laen: Yeah, that's something that I really like about the group, that there's as much low-level as high-level. With makers in general, a lot of people will just say, "Hey, I've got this cool idea. This is something that can sense you're coming at it and turn on a light." There's not a good use for this, right? It's not like a finished product, but it makes a great art project and you can explore these different ways of interacting with electronics through the umbrella of, "It's an art project." Some people think it's cool and some people don't. It's just an art project, nothing that needs to be any more than what it is.

Osborn: You'll see Ward Cunningham hacking on his distributed wiki for Raspberry Pi or something like that. It's really casual. It's just people having beers and talking about stuff that they are building in their garage and they're passionate about.

Laen: And there are all sorts of neat interactions. That's what I like. There's a guy who, a year ago, had a bunch of plaster masks hooked up to a wall and a little camera watching, so that as you walked by, the masks would all point to you and just follow you around. That's awesome. That's a really neat way of interacting with it. A neat use of the technology.

Osborn: Freak people out a little bit maybe.

Laen: Totally. I think all the best projects do. "Well-behaved projects rarely make history." Is that how the saying goes?

Osborn: That's a good one. Do you have any advice for people who have a project that they want to make into a product and bring to market?

Laen: Do it. Just try it out. Start at a small scale, and build it out. Share it as widely as you can. And then listen to the feedback to see how you could make it interesting to not just yourself, but to other people. Because a lot of people say, "Hey, I have this itch, and this is a great way to solve it," but maybe not everyone has this itch, or maybe it's close to what other people want, and it's great to be able to adapt your project so that it's useful to other people. It may just be that I'm a support guy. My day job is IT, and that's always been my passion. I want to help other people do their thing, so it really makes me happy to be able to tweak something so that other people find it interesting.

Osborn: I think a big thing about making something into a product is building a community behind it, to get interest. That's how you market it, to build this community behind it, which is really what I think all of the Kickstarter projects are about.

Laen: Yes, seeing who else is interested in drawing them together. I agree.

Osborn: So what are your next steps for OSH Park? Do you have anything interesting in the pipeline?

Laen: Well, I just recently quit my job to work on it full-time. At the same time, I took over BatchPCB, which is a similar service that SparkFun offered its customers.

Osborn: Wow, that's great. You should be able to continue growing your service.

Laen: Yeah, I'm really excited about it. Doing this full-time wasn't really a goal of mine when I started it, but I'm excited to have this opportunity.

Osborn: Well, I will certainly continue to use it. Thanks, Laen.

Zach Kaplan

Founder and CEO
Inventables

Zach Kaplan found his passion over a decade ago somewhere at the intersection of design and engineering. In 2002, he founded Inventables (Inventables.com) to meet the need of the industrial design world. With the arrival of crowdfunding platforms and the growing interest in the maker community for physical products, Zach has transformed Inventables into an amazing resource for makers to discover new materials and tools.

Steven Osborn: Zach, what got you interested in making?

Zach Kaplan: When I was little, my parents used to buy me construction toys and things like LEGOs and Erector sets. When I was in fifth grade, my grandpa taught me how to solder. Then I got to high school, where we had a full machine shop with CNC equipment, including lathes and mills. I got the chance to build a scale-model roller coaster all out of steel, steel rails, and a CNC car. That really ignited my interest and passion in building things by learning how to combine design, engineering, and making.

I studied mechanical engineering at the University of Illinois. Each summer, I had a different internship. I was a mechanic at Six Flags. I was an engineering intern at General Motors Locomotive Division, in the Turbocharger Group. Then the next year I worked at Yaskawa. They are a motion control company. They make devices that control manufacturing equipment, automation equipment. They were working at the intersection of mechanical and electrical systems— they called it mechatronics. They make a lot of robots for assembly lines and packaging equipment, which companies like Procter & Gamble use to package consumer products.

I was really interested in starting my own company. My junior year in college, I met up with someone at a business plan competition, and we ended up starting a custom software company called Lever Works. Upon graduation, instead of getting a job, we just kept going with the start-up. It was a consulting business. We hired a bunch of interns to help over the summer, and they got credit at the university. It turned out that in December of 2001, after graduating, Leo Media bought out the company. Shortly after that, I started Inventables.

Osborn: How long have you been doing the Inventables thing?

Kaplan: Since 2002.

Osborn: Wow, over ten years already. Was it just you in the beginning?

Kaplan: It was Keith Schacht and myself. We're the two cofounders. He also worked at the first company with me. So we sold the first company, we had a little cash, we went through a process of brainstorming and prototyping what kind of business or what kind of product we wanted to be part of.

At that point, we knew—based on our first experience—that we didn't want to do consulting because we were selling our time. The other part of consulting that we didn't like was the fact that you were working on somebody else's project. Whether we were building a shopping cart or building a content management system, it was the client's ideas and the client's requirements that drove the coding. We wanted to work on something that we were interested in as opposed to the customer. And so we thought if we had a product that we could pour our passion into, we could sell that and we would make our money that way. We prototyped a lot of different things. What it came down to is that we were most passionate about product design and product development at sort of the intersection of design and engineering. Most of the start-ups in that space, at that time, were consulting companies, and we really did not want to do a product design consultancy.

We ended up doing what we called "interviews." We interviewed about forty different industrial designers and engineers—at big companies, at start-ups, at consulting companies, places like IDEO and Black & Decker—to try to understand that if we were going to sell a product to those kinds of folks, where were the opportunities? What were they working on? We were just trying to get "a day in the life of" [the people we interviewed], because we had just graduated and had never worked at a full-time job before outside of internships.

Osborn: What ended up coming out of those interviews?

Kaplan: The theme that kept coming back, where people were struggling, was around materials. So we did a pilot program where we launched a small material library. It was called the Innovation Center. It was similar to a rolling tool chest, which we had filled with about fifty different materials. We gave it to two companies locally here in Chicago and one in St. Louis. It was a prototyping success but a commercial failure. They all said that they loved it, but they were not willing to pay any money. That was sort of crushing, because how could they love it so much but not want to pay?

While we were picking up the last prototype at Insight Product Development, up in Ravenswood a neighborhood in Chicago, I remember the owner, who must have felt that he had taken the wind out of our sails a little bit. I think he felt bad, after they had just pumped us up and told us how awesome it was. He says, "Hold on one second. I have somebody for you to meet." He leaves the room and comes back, and there's this guy. His name is Dave. He's says, "Hey, Dave. I want you to meet Zach and Keith. Just tell them what you just told me." So we go through the whole thing, and Dave says, "I'll take one." And we're thinking, "Who's this guy?" It turned out that Insight was a consulting company, and Dave was his client. So it turned out that the clients had the money, not the consulting companies. So Dave took one.

If you look at it in terms of Geoffrey Moore's technology adoption curve,[1] it turned out that Dave was, in every sense, an early adopter or an innovator. He didn't know what the product was, like how much it cost or anything. He knew that he needed something like that and we were going to figure it out. So what we ended up selling him was a subscription to the library, because we didn't have a full library yet. We told him it would come in quarterly installments. And so for the next set of years, we published a little kit we called Design Aid, which had twenty innovative materials and technologies. The idea was that it had things that you probably hadn't considered but you probably should, or that had some unexpected property around them [to help you think of new ideas] as you're going through your design and engineering work.

Osborn: So about what timeframe are we talking here when you were doing this?

Kaplan: That was February 2002. We shipped the first kits in November.

Osborn: So this was well before you guys had a web site and stuff?

Kaplan: We had a web site. It was more like a brochure, but still a web site.

Osborn: You've always sold materials to inventors?

Kaplan: No. We didn't launch the hardware store until early 2011.

Osborn: Before that you were selling things through door-to-door sales?

Kaplan: It was subscriptions. The original subscription was seven grand a year. Actually, I think that first subscription was $3600 a year. And then we

---

[1] Geoffrey A. Moore. *Crossing the Chasm: Marketing and Selling Disruptive Products to Mainstream Customers* (HarperCollins, 2002).

increased it to seven grand a year. And then, in 2006, we upped the price. There were three packages—at $70,000, $120,000, and $360,000 a year. Then we added more service. So we would go out and install it in a physical display and everything. But, yeah, in the beginning it was more of a research subscription, where advanced materials research groups and industrial design groups at companies like Coca-Cola, Black & Decker, Milwaukee Tools, Nike, and Procter & Gamble would subscribe for a year. It was a physical display library. If you type "Inventables Innovation Center" into Google, there's a How Stuff Works article that features it.[2]

Osborn: Cool. So what was the growth like over this period? It's a pretty long period of time. In these days, where the life of a company is often measured in months, you've been at this for quite some time. Has growth been pretty consistent? Or have you seen a pretty large uptake recently with the whole maker movement?

Kaplan: Yeah, what happened was there was an inflection point. We consistently grew—we were growing linearly every year, getting more customers, getting more subscribers, because with the subscription business, some percent renew every year, and then you keep adding more people. Then a bunch of things happened all at the same time. Kickstarter launched, transaction volume on Etsy broke $100M I sellers using Fulfillment by Amazon stowed more than one million unique items in their fulfillment centers. Then we started getting inquiries from start-ups and actual people who were doing their Kickstarters and needed the materials. At the time, we didn't sell the materials. We just connected you directly with the vendor if you were one of our subscribers.

What we saw happening was the interest, energy and excitement for all this stuff was coming from start-ups and small companies that didn't have $120,000 to spend. The folks who were paying us all that money, while they had product development processes, the passion wasn't there in the same way. When you do a Kickstarter, you are sort of obsessed with your project, but when you're working at a big company like Microsoft, it's different. They're not coming to work with the same intensity. The other thing that happened was the cost of the tools that these places were using—when we started in 2002, I think the cost of the average 3D printer was about $450,000. Then the MakerBot launched. I actually bought the first one, the Cupcake. I paid $1,000 for that machine. I got into this originally because I was passionate about design and engineering.

So all these things happened at the same time and I realized we could really direct the business toward the part I was most excited about. I believed that all this stuff happening with the maker movement was going to be the future.

We had just worked on a project with Palm, with their docking station that took two years to go from "I have this idea" to "it's in the market," where they used

---

[2]http://home.howstuffworks.com/technology-library1.htm

the suction cup tape on the bottom. The guy that we were working with, the main point of contact was Peter Skillman. Peter is one of my heroes because he had worked at IDEO. Do you remember the IDEO shopping cart video?

Osborn: I don't think I've seen that.

Kaplan: They were on *Nightline* with Ted Koppel. It was when I was in college, and my parents actually sent me the tape. Peter was the main character in that episode of *Nightline*, where they had redesigned a shopping cart.

So all these years later, I got to work with Peter. I just thought that was the coolest thing. But the project ended up taking two years because Palm, at that time, was a pretty large company, I think close to $1 billion or just over $1 billion in revenue. Roughly six months after the two-year-long Palm project, we got an inquiry from these two guys. They had just graduated college, did a Kickstarter, and they used that same suction cup tape material in their product. The whole thing took six months. It was just the two of them, they made all the decisions, they found a factory, and they went.

They actually placed the same order that Palm had placed for that material. So going from like two years to six months for the same thing, I was like, "Wow." All these things are making the maker movement—start-up hardware, open-source hardware—build faster and get products to market faster than in 2002.

So we launched the hardware store for designers. We now have about ten thousand products on the site, and it's all merchandised around selling the equipment and materials to help you design beautiful products.

The core mission of the company didn't really change. What changed is the delivery mechanism for how we were going to market. The new model is that of a hardware store that inspires and empowers designers to disrupt the establishment. We're empowering this generation of smaller start-ups and individuals who can use these low-cost manufacturing tools to make whatever they want, especially products they can sell.

Osborn: The shift in product coming to market is pretty interesting. Ouya recently raised $9 million on Kickstarter. You know, it's an open-source gaming console, and two or three years ago, if somebody told you they were going to do that, it would be…

Kaplan: Laughable. Nine *million* dollars.

So I just did a blog post on the third industrial revolution.[3] I really believe that that's happening right now, where there is this idea that people are excited about things like 3D printing. People are excited about personal manufacturing. People are excited about Kickstarter. I used to feel like I worked on stuff that I was interested in. You sort of had to be an engineer to understand.

---

[3]http://inventables.blogspot.com/2013/02/the-third-industrial-revolution.html

Now, my mom is sending me articles about 3D printing. It's not just that it's happening to industry. The world is taking notice. What I wrote in the blog post is that the first industrial revolution happened in Great Britain in the late eighteenth century. The revolution was about the mechanization of the textile industry. Textiles were first made by humans, by hand. Then, it changed, and machines started to play a role in the textile industry, instead of people doing all the work. The famous example of this is Eli Whitney and his cotton gin.

The second industrial revolution was in the early twentieth century, with Henry Ford, when industry moved from making things one at a time to mastering the assembly line, which ushered in the age of mass production that we know today and we sort of expect. This movement was driven by lowering costs through economies of scale. Henry Ford's famous quote "Any customer can have a car painted any color that he wants so long as it is black" epitomized the idea of making large quantities of standardized products as cheaply as possible.

Then, the third industrial revolution is what I believe is really happening today and that's manufacturing and production going digital. It's just being accelerated in the same way as what happened with desktop publishing, because the cost of these tools is so cheap and the Internet and computing are ubiquitous.

As you've seen, you can buy a CNC laser for $2,300, and we're selling a $900 3D printer and a $600 CNC mill. If you can afford an Xbox, you can afford a mill. Most people interested in these kinds of things already have a computer, so the barriers to entry are extremely low just to get started. There are free versions of all the software you need. It really comes down to, "Are you passionate? Are you interested? Do you have ideas of what you want to make?" Then, when you start seeing people going on Kickstarter and raising all this money, like $9 million for an open-source gaming console, you know, people start to take notice. Like Scott Wilson, whose office is a couple of blocks from ours, he did a Kickstarter. He raised something like a million dollars for a watch band called the Luna-Tik.[4] It wasn't even a watch. It was just a watch-band that plugged into your iPod Nano. So people start to take notice. That's compelling. It's interesting. I describe it as manufacturing that's going from the factory onto the desktop. There has been a transfer or risk and a reduction in startup capital required to launch a product. This makes it possible for smaller teams to bring products to smaller markets than multibillion dollar companies can afford to focus on. That's why we launched the store.

Osborn: Yes, it's exciting to be able to bear witness to that type of thing. I mean, really for you to be able to be part of that and to help make that happen.

---

[4]www.lunatik.com

Kaplan: It's like a lifelong dream—the world just sort of caught up to what I was hoping for. It's not even that. The world started being interested in what I was interested in. That's what it really boiled down to.

Osborn: What would you say are some of the biggest challenges you've had in building this business?

Kaplan: Well, in the beginning, nobody cared. So it was convincing everybody that all this stuff was necessary. It was definitely very niche. Now you don't have to—I mean, *The Economist* is doing an article every day on the third industrial revolution, the *New York Times*—and everybody's on board. It's hot right now. But in the beginning, you know, I guess they thought it was just too technical.

Osborn: It's just a lot of patience or a lot of waiting—I guess for the world to catch up to your vision of how things should be made?

Kaplan: I wouldn't say that I had a vision in 2002 that you could make stuff on your desktop. I think that I was aware of the fact—like I think one of the ideas I had talked about was making a 3D printer. I remember doing a little prototype of a 3D printer with a hot glue gun and an arrow that we bought at a hobby store, like forcing the hot glue through the arrow, through a very small hole in the tip of the arrow. I wonder if I still have that thing?

Osborn: That would be awesome to see.

Kaplan: I messed around with it for a little bit and eventually gave up on it. But I think that at some level, we knew that it was going to happen eventually, but we started pursuing things that were more near-term because it was just really early. My core idea was that we were going to help companies innovate and help companies with the product development process. And just by staying true to what I was really interested in. Eventually, when all the technology caught up to my interest, I was there to be able to continue to participate in a more meaningful way.

Osborn: Do you have tips for makers who are building these things in their garages, who might want to move into manufacturing to scale up their hobby?

Kaplan: Actually, what I would say is that a lot of makers have it backward. We're seeing this over and over. It's something that happened with our experience with Shapeoko, the $600 CNC mill, and it really solidified my thoughts around this. A lot of makers order machines from us, and they make stuff, and they think that because they can make stuff, it means that they have a commercial success. There is a big difference between having a hobby project and having a commercial success. What we're seeing is that the people who are having commercial successes, they're starting with the community first. They're first building a community, and the community is helping them contribute and play a part in the development of the project. And then they go out and do Kickstarter.

Kickstarter serves as a way to unleash all this energy and excitement toward the prototype, or toward the idea, like, "Okay, I could make this, guys." And then, you know, after the Kickstarter, it's like, "What's next?"

With Shapeoko,[5] we launched it on Inventables in more of a commercial way, and there was a second unleashing of all this energy and excitement. [People really] wanted to buy the machine. Now we're doing upgrades. It's like the community just keeps getting bigger and bigger, and building the community is first, and then delivering the product back to the community is second. And what we see happening is that a lot of makers, or at least first-time makers, their thinking is the opposite way, "Okay, I need to make this thing and then bring it to the market," as opposed to "build my community and then give them what I made."

Osborn: It sounds like Shapeoko has been pretty popular. What type of material items are people really interested in? What are some of your top sellers?

Kaplan: Shapeoko is the fastest-selling digital fabrication machine in the history of the world. In the Shapeoko, people are milling plastic, wood, and soft metals like aluminum.

Osborn: So the Shapeoko is driving a lot of your sales for materials too?

Kaplan: Yeah, lots of people are buying acrylics and anodized aluminum. A lot of soft metals like aluminum. Also, people are really interested in wood and the filaments for the 3D printers. It's all the materials that you can use to do fabrication, like sort of short-run custom fabrication. The cool part about the mills, as compared to the 3D printers right now, is the materials you can use, and the fact that the products that come out of them are store quality. We have customers that have a wrist watch businesses. We have customers that make skateboards with the mill.

Osborn: Can you give me a couple of examples of good products that people are building using your materials in the Shapeoko?

Kaplan: There is the Mistura[6] watch. The clasp and the face where the time-piece is set into is milled. There's also a skateboard company. There are a lot of companies with an Epilog laser or something similar. They buy the acrylics. They're doing things like jewelry or wedding cake toppers or signs. Lots of sign shops where they're doing a custom sign. We actually made our sign at Inventables using a laser.

[5]www.shapeoko.com
[6]www.mistura.com

Osborn: So that's an upside of being a company of makers—you just produce the things you need.

Kaplan: Yeah, it's fun too. We just actually built a fab lab in our office, so employees have a budget and they can go make stuff.

Osborn: Awesome. You guys are in Chicago. I was wondering what the maker culture is like there and how it's evolved. I'm guessing there has been a bit of an explosion, like most places.

Kaplan: It's exploding in Chicago. Everyone's interested, from the mayor's office to the library—we just sold the Chicago Public Library the gear and materials to build a Maker Lab that is free for the community to use.

There are a couple of fab labs, there's a maker space called Pumping Station: One, there's a whole start-up ecosystem where people are making hardware-based start-ups. The Midwest has historically been a center for manufacturing in the country. A lot of the big industrial supply companies are in Chicago, so it turns out that it's a good spot for Inventables because lots of our suppliers are in the Midwest, and so we can get next-day delivery for our inventory. We can meet with the suppliers in person, and stuff like that.

Osborn: I think what you described in your city you see anywhere. You go to Portland or Seattle, Boulder, New York—all these places have this great uptake in hacker spaces, but each city has their own vibe. I think that in Seattle, it's a lot more of design or art-type projects, and in Portland, there's a lot of semiconductor companies like Intel and Maxim, so there's a lot more low-level hardware hacking, RF projects. So it's definitely interesting how large the scope is, and to look at each city and see a theme evolving. But it's all tied into this fact that it's extremely cheap to build and prototype and manufacture things today.

Kaplan: Yeah, it's awesome. I call it "digital fabrication."

One of the things we launched with the Shapeoko is `MakerCAM.com`, where we took an open-source CAD and CAM package that's in the browser and it's free, and it lets you go from an idea to the machine cutting in under five minutes. Historically, that has been impossible. You needed a really expensive CAD and CAM package, and even the free ones are cumbersome and hard to use. So now, with $600 and a free web-based tool, you can go from idea to finished product pretty quickly and very inexpensively.

We recently hired Edward Ford, who is the inventor of the Shapeoko. He came on full-time. We started selling the machine with him in April, but he came on full-time as an employee in October.

He independently had the same vision for what we were doing, and he's got this concept that he calls "crawl, walk, run." He's been working on the Shapeoko for like eight years. Actually, four years ago gave up, and then scrapped it and forgot about it, and then came back. It was sitting on a shelf in his basement. So crawl, walk, run. The idea is that making stuff is hard when compared to some other things, because you're dealing with the physical.

It's not as easy as just writing software, where you click Enter and then push it out,. You have to make the thing. So the idea with this is, at first, people can come to the Inventables website, download and make something that somebody else has already made. Then they can fork it, or modify or copy it, and adjust it and customize it in the way that they want to make that same thing. Then they can go and be sort of a Rembrandt and design their own.

We're partnering with places like the library, and the fab lab, and the university to get kids going into this process of crawl, walk, run. First, just making something that somebody has already made, because all of the tools are open-source, and it's just another way to access the components in our warehouse, to make it easier for people. Maybe they're interested in making, but they haven't really dug in or some of the tools are sort of complicated. This way, they can go from, "Hey, I can make that," and then fill in the blank. Some of the things on there are simple, and then the idea is that they'll get more sophisticated. But for people who are just getting interested and started, it's a pretty powerful tool.

Osborn: I think a lot of what is driving interest in making things is the openness in the community. Starting with companies like yours—that don't try to have a secret sauce. When they make something, the whole recipe is out in the open. That level of sharing and education is important—and to me, it's what is making the "maker thing" happen.

Kaplan: Exactly right.

Emile Petrone

Founder
Tindie

Emile Petrone is an entrepreneur who has been part of many web start-ups, and most recently is the founder and CEO of Tindie (tindie.com), a marketplace for hobbyist electronics and open-source hardware. Before Tindie, he founded both Housefed and Knowble. He also worked for companies like Yelp and Urban Airship building consumer and B2B web applications.

Steven Osborn: So Emile, tell me a little bit about yourself and what inspired you to start Tindie.

Emile Petrone: Prior to Tindie, I was a self-taught web engineer. I learned Python I about a year and a half, almost two years, before founding Tindie. But I guess my background starts off more on the sales side, working in sales for various start-ups, like Yelp and Red Beacon.

Then I decided to take a gap year and teach myself how to code. It was just something that I've always wanted to do. I had the interest pretty early on. In middle school, two friends and I taught ourselves HTML, and it was something that I wished I had followed through on, but, once we got to JavaScript, there wasn't anybody to point us in any direction, so it kind of withered away. But that nagging desire to learn was still there, and so once I took the gap year, that's when my professional career changed toward engineering—at SimpleGeo as a developer advocate, and then with Urban Airship.

Osborn: So what was your education background? Did you go to college for business?

Petrone: My education background was actually a political science major at the University of North Carolina at Chapel Hill. I completed that in a year and a half, the degree, but I had to fill hours, so I did take some entrepreneurship classes. In one of those classes, I launched a site that allowed researchers at the University of North Carolina and other universities around the world to connect across disciplines, and that was called Knowble. The university helped fund that project—I think about $30,000—back then. We ultimately didn't get the grant that it was associated with, so funding dried up and that help spur the move out to Silicon Valley.

Osborn: So you got into this engineering role at a couple start-ups. At what point did you start Tindie, and what inspired you to do that?

Petrone: Looking back, there were a bunch of key points that I think led up to Tindie and led up to tinkering with software and getting interested in hardware.

Growing up, my grandfather made RC planes. He had a room in his house and that's what he did. My brothers and I would go out with him to the flying field and he would fly those planes. So I was always around building and making things from a pretty early age.

Early 2012 was when Arduino and Raspberry Pi started to pick up a lot of steam, and people were getting really interested in a really small computer that was very cheap. I was following the articles in the press that were coming out about that, and I could see that it was something that a lot of people were getting excited about. It had a lot of potential. I already had that interest in the RC side of things, but it seemed to me that what would happen with cheap computers all over the place had the potential to be mind-blowing. People couldn't predict exactly what the impact would be. It would just be massive. At that point is when I really began to dig into it in earnest. Since I had already learned how to code, it was a bit more tangible at that point. That's when I could dive in and start playing around with Arduino.

From there, it really just became a question of what projects could I build and where could I find them? What I was seeing was a lot of interesting projects pop up on web sites like Reddit, Hacker News, Hackaday. Basically, it would be a one-off project, where the maker would say, "Here's the design. Here are the instructions. I'm done with this project. I'm moving on to whatever else I'm interested in." The problem for a beginner was if I was to start off by building some little project, you're probably going to have a tough time figuring out how to source parts, what parts you need, and all of that. You'd rather just buy a kit, and I couldn't find kits that allowed me to build a widget I wanted, whether it was a headphone amplifier, a robot, or small drone. I couldn't really find those for cheap and that were at a skill level that was comparable to where I was. That led me down the path to what ultimately inspired me to build Tindie.

Osborn: Now that you've got this idea for Tindie, tell me about how you got it off the ground and about the launch.

Petrone: With the idea that I couldn't find kits or projects that I could personally build as a beginner, I tossed the idea up on the Arduino Subreddit.[1] For people unfamiliar with Reddit, it is basically the site for people to find lots of smaller communities that they can join with. The Arduino and Raspberry Pi sites are just two of the Subreddits that I was interested in. On the Arduino Subreddit is a bunch of Arduino enthusiasts, and I just asked the question, "Would you be interested in a marketplace for people to buy and sell their projects, or am I just totally off-base and I've just got my head in the clouds?" Fortunately, the feedback was positive, overwhelmingly so. I didn't expect it to (a) get a response, but (b) get a response of "Yeah, that sounds great. Build it. I'd love to see it. I'd love to do it. I've got projects to sell."

Osborn: So it started just by you putting the question out to this community to see if anyone thought it was a good idea or a bad idea?

Petrone: That was the start of everything. I threw the question out there. There's clearly an audience that's interested. I don't know how big that audience is. I didn't know how big the Arduino world was at the time, but Raspberry Pi at that point was only two months old. So as the weeks followed, as the days came and went, I would post updates. I remember posting things like, "I found the name. What do you guys think of 'Tindie'?" And that came basically from wordplay with "indie" and "tech" and then flipping it, so you get "Tindie." People liked that.

Then I had one that was something like, "Here's a logo idea. What do you guys think of it?" and more people would throw in their feedback and say, "That looks great." So it was very much a community-driven process, where as I came up with new ideas, I'd throw it out there and people would give a yes or no. I had immediate feedback on every aspect of the business creation. That led through the entire development process, starting from when I first got a landing page up. The first page originally said, "Reserve your username," and people would actually register. That's how we got our first few hundred—maybe few thousand people—signed up. People were just coming to the page. They were interested in reserving their username before the site was even out. The next step was that I threw a post up that said, "We're now stocking the shelves."

So once I got the backbone code that was just handling products and connecting a seller and the notion of a product together, people could upload products, prices, photos, descriptions, titles, that sort of thing. This is all still

[1] www.reddit.com/r/arduino/

while the site isn't open. People began submitting products. We were getting things like a robot that plays Angry Birds, a mini electronic xylophone kit, different Arduino projects—I think there were a few Arduino cases—different light projects, LEDs. It was very clear from the beginning that there was a much bigger world out there than I even recognized or knew about. It was just starting to find me.

The day I flipped the switch and turned the site on was Wednesday, June 27, 2012. And I can still distinctly remember the day before, going back and forth in my mind whether this was actually a good project—whether anybody was going to show up. What if I turn it on and nobody shows up? I still didn't know right up until the end. Basically I said "Why not? Just do it. If no one shows up, it's no harm, no foul. Just wasted a few weeks of development time," and that was that. Fortunately, when I launched the site, I put it up on Reddit and I put it up on Hacker News. I think it went to number one on Hacker News. From basically that first day, there were ten thousand to twenty thousand people on the site. At that point, we had roughly twenty projects on Tindie and had our first orders that day. I guess that kind of set the wheels in motion.

Osborn: So you just had your one-year anniversary. How many employees do you have now? You started with just you, right?

Petrone: Right. So right now, we've got a total of five, including myself. In September of 2012, I raised $500,000 from two investors and that allowed me to start hiring engineers from California and Canada. We're very much believers in a virtual company and a virtual system. Everything is actually online. I still haven't met three of our employees in person, but we get along great. It's something that works for us, that's where we are at.

Osborn: Tell me about the fundraiser feature on Tindie.

Petrone: We launched the fundraiser a few months ago as a way for makers to basically test their concepts and get preorders. We're really focused on straight-up preorders. We weren't trying to do a Kickstarter model where people are having various tiers and try to raise money for a venture. The businesses on Tindie are more focused on, "I've got a product. It's developed. Here's the finished prototype. Is this something people want? And can I get enough preorders where it's financially viable for me to get a run at these made?"

We had that going for a few months, and it did well. At a certain point, half of our revenue came from fundraisers and half came from store sales. In the process, we actually got in contact with Texas Instruments and Element 14, who are interested in using fundraisers as a way to promote the Launchpad community into building what they call booster packs, basically accessories for their Launchpad series. So right now, fundraisers are on vacation while we upgrade them and do some work to get that ready for our launch next month with Texas Instruments and Element 14. They are still on the site, but they are down for the time being while we work on it and get it ready for bigger projects.

Osborn: Do you have any tips for makers who are building projects and want to make some money on Tindie? What kind of projects to build or how to approach it?

Petrone: Right now, a year later, we've got two hundred fifty-six or so businesses on Tindie and we're approaching one thousand products. With that scale, we have access to a lot of the trends and lessons that makers learn as they get started and as their business evolves on site. As they launch new products they learn different tricks of the trade.

I think that the main thing is for people to start small. There's a misconception out there that launching a massive project on Kickstarter is going to be the way to succeed. I think that we've seen with many of the projects that have gone through Kickstarter or IndieGoGo is that if they become too successful too soon, it can swamp the project and ultimately lead to the project not being fulfilled because of lack of planning, lack of funding, and inexperienced makers keep jumping in a little too deep.

So the first thing is start with a small project and start with a small run. If you've never made something before, then you really need to start out with ten, twenty, thirty units and understand the manufacturing process, understand that you're going to have to test whatever your product is. You're going to have to really understand the manufacturing process from a business side which most people haven't even thought of before, because most of them are just electrical engineers. The majority of our sellers are electrical engineers that have a day job, and this is their first step into building their dream business and working for themselves.

So start small, understand manufacturing, understand shipping, customs, ship times, and packaging. If you decide to ship internationally, packages getting stuck in customs are a reality and uncertainty that you have to face. You don't know when your packages are going to get stuck and you don't know why. Then the next thing you know you've got customers e-mailing you asking, "Why hasn't it gotten there?"

The other bit is pricing and understanding the financials of running a maker business. There are some good articles out there on how to price your product, but basically, most people don't take into account their labor, their overhead, and they price it at the cost of goods. When you do that, you're shooting yourself in the foot and you're saying, "I will pay other people for the privilege of giving them products." Your time is very valuable, and you're not actually working that into the equation. So really understand the economics of what you're doing and how much time it's going to take. You need to factor that into the price that you sell, whatever your product is.

If you start out small enough, you can figure this out as you go along and as your business grows. That's a much smarter approach than, "I've got this great idea for the best widget the world's ever seen. We're trying to raise $150,000." If you do succeed, there are a lot of ramifications that come with that that I think most people don't foresee. My advice is to start small.

Osborn: When people see someone raise a half-million dollars on Kickstarter they say, "Wow, they made a half-million dollars." But in reality, if they were working a job at a large company making salary, they would often have made more money at the end of the day, once all the expenses and materials and shipping and their time are accounted for, as a couple of engineers. I don't think people really think about it. They see this big number and think, "Wow, they made a lot of money." In reality, maybe they came out with $40,000 apiece to split over six months or a year, which is a poor engineer's salary.

Petrone: Maybe they don't make anything at the end of the day because once you have your first run you realize that it's faulty. That there's a fault built into your project and you have to scrap that first run. That costs you a third of your funds right there. That's not a one-time story. That story's been told many times. The reality is that bigger projects that end up making, let's say, $500,000, a million, multiple millions—they end up going and seeking outside VC and outside investment because of the costs that they accrue which they didn't see upfront and they have to seek outside investment just to fulfill the original orders. That's a part of the story that people don't see. That's not actually the amount of money that they walked away with. You're dead on right. Maybe they come out with a few thousand. Maybe they come out with nothing. So there's a lot more to it than people recognize other than a bunch of zeros.

Osborn: So I guess to paraphrase your advice would be to keep it simple, to expect the unexpected, and don't underprice yourself or undersell your product.

Petrone: Yes, exactly.

Osborn: So you guys have a lot of products on Tindie now. Can you give me an example of a product that's doing well and heeding that advice?

Petrone: The most recent example is the Femtoduino. This is a story that's been going on for a while—has been in development for a few years I think. The maker who is selling those, Alex, started out with a small run. He sold out of those quickly. Then it was at least a few weeks, maybe a month or two, before we got another run in. In that time, the word of mouth had spread that (a) this was a great product, and (b) it was everything it said it was. It is a derivative of Arduino, and a lot of people understand the Arduino platform and there's already a sizable community that's interested in using it, so the waiting list grew pretty quickly. When that second round came in, we sold out in less than four hours and the waiting list started back over. He just sold out of his fifth run maybe, but basically, what's happened is every single time we get more in, they sell out and he grows that run more each time.

The community continues to support him, and his business has basically grown with the interest in the project. I think that that has helped him understand what goes into it and inadvertently has also helped market the product as well because of the limited supply has caused I guess some word of mouth and artificial demand of some sort—that people say, "Okay, it's back in stock. I've got to get it now or it's going to sell out in a few hours," so you see people buy ten or more just because they don't know when it will come back into stock because we're basically now beholden to factories to getting production runs just as fast as possible.

Osborn: It sounds like he built a community up as he was building the product along the way. That was a good example of a guy making something in his garage. I think that's how a lot of people would describe the maker business, or maker movement. Where do you see that going? Is it always going to be people building things in their garages? Will it evolve into something beyond that? Will all the interesting projects get bought out by TI to where there are only a handful of key players the way the software world has done?

Petrone: That's a large question that I'll break it down to different parts in the answer. The first is that you will always have the big manufacturers, the big monoliths who will be making things in bulk supply. You'll also have the niche little maker businesses. The majority of what's on Tindie right now is businesses that are one-man shop in your garage like you were saying. I think that is only going to continue to grow as people come up with new ideas and continue to access manufacturing techniques.

The other part is the maker business that takes advantage of larger manufacturing processes and streamlines their business with technology. One example of that is Tautic Electronics. He's one of our sellers. He has many products for sale. He just invested in his own pick-and-place machine, which is sitting in his garage right now.

Osborn: Is this the one from China that Ian Lesnet blogged[2] about?

Petrone: No. I don't know what model it is, but it's a big boy that's $10,000 plus. He is manufacturing at a larger scale than your average maker, and I think that that's only going to continue. He's invested in that future and that's the direction he's going to go. So you're going to have a wide range of the sizes of these businesses. That wide range of businesses is the first part.

---

[2]http://dangerousprototypes.com/tag/pick-and-place/

The second is that businesses of all sizes are actually starting to buy, consume, and use open hardware. They recognize that projects developed by individual makers can have the exact same quality as a project by a larger Fortune 500 company. And that's what we're starting to see, that it's not just hobbyists that are buying these projects. We've got Fortune 500 companies that are buying parts. We've got government agencies. We've got the biggest tech companies in the world, and universities labs. It runs the gamut in terms of who is buying products through Tindie right now. I think that says everything about what is happening with this revolution in hardware.

It's growing very quickly, and it's going from zero to very high quality and scaling as quickly as demand needs it. I think that's exciting. It's ultimately because of two things. The first is the dropping price in manufacturing, the low cost of components and access to inexpensive manufacturing. Manufacturing hardware has been a very expensive process, to come up with an idea, prototype it, refine it. That process took years and a lot of capital. Nowadays, it takes weeks.

The final thing that is driving this innovation is the open hardware itself. What I mean is open schematics, open designs, open-source code. The notion of open-source hardware is something that is really starting to come of age right now. It is something whose impact I don't think we will really truly know for years to come. We can see a lot of changes, and we see people integrating things, whether it's an Arduino into a commercial 3D printer or adding a Raspberry Pi into a rocket—whatever a project is.

We're seeing a lot of different interesting applications, but what does that actually mean for business, for electronics, for hardware in general? I think we're just starting to see that, and that's really where we're pushing Tindie, to promote the idea behind opening the schematics and be a place where people can find open designs and the blueprints to get an open-source product whether you want to build it yourself or buy it through the site. We really want to help define a directory of finished open designs. So if you're looking for an open design for anything, you can come to Tindie and you'll be able to find it.

We're going to roll out a feature with Arduino that will start to integrate the whole ecosystem together and really connect the makers with the content creators, because that whole ecosystem is very fragmented and we think that a much tighter integrated system between the manufacturing side and the people that are designing and creating the open-source schematics and code—that's ultimately what this ecosystem is lacking. We're going to be developing a feedback loop for those two groups to come together. That's where we see the future of this ecosystem going.

Osborn: When I think about the impact open-source hardware is going to have, I think about the analog and the software world. Even if you think about simple cases, like your web browser, like in 2003, the browser wars were won. Internet Explorer won. Netscape fell away because at the time Internet Explorer was just a better browser. And then out of that, Netscape's open-source became Firefox, then WebKit[3] came about. Now if you look at the most popular browsers, Internet Explorer is pretty far down on the list. All these open-source browsers have not only replaced it, but the competition has really changed the pace at which the web is evolving.

HTML5, JavaScript, CSS3, all this stuff has happened in the last few years, whereas HTML4 was standard and everything was stagnant for a good, solid ten years. I think really it's the people making the browsers that are moving that forward rather than the standards body. That wouldn't have happened without competition and the open-source community coming together to build these browsers.

You guys are doing well and growing, but surely you've had some challenges along the way. Can you talk about some things that maybe didn't go as expected?

Petrone: I think that every web site has their hiccups along the way.. Our big outage was after we raised that $500,000 in funding, I decided to throw an AMA on Reddit,[4] which is an "ask me anything" to the Reddit community, who were the ones who initially supported it, started it, and fueled it. I thought some people might find it interesting to understand the story behind the business. What are some of the lessons learned?

In that process, I was on the East Coast at the time. Our team is prominently on the West Coast. I launched it in the early morning, and it put the site down for a good four or five hours because of the demand for people just visiting the site. I was still answering questions, but the team hadn't woken up yet, and I couldn't bring the site up and answer questions. I was basically juggling balls in the air. It's a good problem to have when people are so interested in what you're doing, but when it takes the site down for a few hours, that's a different beast entirely.

At the end of the day, the ecosystem is much bigger, much more diverse, and much more interesting than I ever dreamed it would be. I'm sure that most of the community on the site would agree as well, because up until now, there really hasn't been a Tindie, a marketplace for this community. We're the first real success story that's been able to organize the community in one place and recognize the peoples' achievements and the creations that they are building.

---

[3]WebKit is the rendering engine that Safari and Google Chrome use.
[4]www.reddit.com/r/IAmA/comments/1562wk/iama_founder_of_tindiecom_etsy_for_tech_that/

Osborn: Do you see Tindie growing beyond hobbyist electronics projects to projects for everyday consumers? Can you talk about Tindie's vision for the future?

Petrone: There are really two camps that I see emerging out of what people are considering a new hardware revolution, in terms of the products that are coming out. The first is what most people consider "maker" products. Which is just parts and kits—basically components. The second is more the—what do they call it? The Internet of Things? Basically, what happens when you have a bunch of consumer products that are smarter than they are right now and much better designed, and how does that improve people's lives? So there are two different camps.

Right now we're really not focused on the consumer side, and we don't have any plans to focus on the consumer side anytime soon. Our goal is to provide a platform that can just facilitate open-hardware as a community and connect the content creators and the manufacturers. So we're going to be rolling out a platform for people to start uploading their projects and say, "Here's a project that I made. It's under this open license." We'll then allow manufacturers to see the different open designs that are out there and then manufacture and sell them on the site while sending a percentage of their sales to the content creator.

Osborn: So it gets the content creator past the point of solving the scaling and production problems?

Petrone: Exactly. It allows people to specialize. Some people want to sell products and deal with shipping. Some people don't. And at the end of the day, we want to be a clear and transparent marketplace where you can do that. For example, with Arduino, many people built on top of Arduino, but there isn't a way that connects those projects back to the original Arduino project. So we'll have Arduino on the site and people can say, "My product is built on top of Arduino, and I'm kicking back fifteen percent of the sales back to Arduino." We'll facilitate those transactions and allow those projects to be recognized as projects that are supporting the ecosystem.

At the same time, Arduino can now say, "Here are a bunch of projects that are actually bringing value back into the ecosystem. They're supporting us so that we can continue to build on the platform and keep doing what we're good at," let other people develop on top of it and build different shields and components and parts, but bring it full circle so that you can start to see what this ecosystem looks like.

If you've got one person who's built an open shield on top of Arduino, what does the next person down the line do on top of that shield? What is the next evolution? We really see that kind of thing a lot with code, but not a lot with hardware. Right now you can't see these actual connections that are already there because there isn't an ecosystem that enables that community continues to evolve. That's what we're working on now, how can we expose that ecosystem? How can we connect the creators, like Arduino, with manufacturers and businesses that may be building on top of their platform and allow them to have a symbiotic relationship where they benefit from each other and help each other to grow at the same time?

Osborn: Awesome. If you guys get it right I think it will add a lot of value to the community.

Do you have sellers selling 3D-printed things? Is there some concern if they 3D-print a Yoda head, which seems to be a typical test print, and then sell it?

Petrone: That's a very loaded question, but to break it down: patent law hasn't caught up with where technology is. You've got issues of marketplaces trying to regulate 3D printing and different marketplaces having different ideas and different rules, because no one has any idea of exactly what the standard should be. I don't think using a solution from the last decade or the last century is ultimately going to be the right solution. I think trying to protect 3D designs with lawsuits is going to be a lost cause. You're never going to be able to squash everyone.

Right now, there are multiple 3D printer web sites that are saying, "Let's put DRM on 3D design," and people will pay for it. It's just absolutely insane. It's crazy. If you look at it, iTunes has been around now for I don't know how long, and it hasn't squashed piracy. The only things that have made a dent in piracy are services like Spotify, which is a modern solution to this problem, because it's better than having to hunt down individual files. That is what we need with the hardware revolution. We need a modern approach to this modern problem.

Osborn: An analogous example I guess is all the Arduino clones. There are a ton of them, but people still go out and buy the blue Arduino because that's the brand. Really, they have the brand and the community behind it more than anything, and I think that is key.

Petrone: That brings up the other part, is that we're now at a point where you're not competing with a business in the next city over, the next state over. It's truly a global marketplace now. On Tindie, we've got sellers in forty countries the world around. We've got them in China, Japan, UK, US, Germany, Brazil, Egypt, all over. If you want to get a patent or protection here in the States, that does not give you protection worldwide. Even if you try to protect your design, you're never going to succeed. You're going to have competitors in countries around the world that are not going to respect it, and there's no way that you're going to be able to litigate your way through it globally.

Osborn: There are Apple-product clones all over that you can buy on eBay. I don't think they threaten Apple's business, but even a company that has more money than many small countries can't really keep a cap on clones. It's almost silly to even attempt it. It seems like a waste of time and effort when you could be focusing on your product or your business.

Petrone: Exactly. You can worry about protectionist policies and trying to keep a lock and key on your IP or you can worry about innovating and moving even faster. Speed to market and quality are ultimately going to be the things that differentiate your product from a competitor. For businesses trying to worry about it, it's not worth the time, energy, and money. You've got other problems, other things to worry about.

Osborn: There do seem to be a lot of people in this community that are feverishly passionate about open-source hardware, and I personally really hope to see it proliferate.

Petrone: Well, I hope Tindie can play a small part in making that happen. It's an exciting time to be part of it.

CHAPTER

7

bunnie Huang

Founder

bunnie studios

---

*Well known for several of his projects, **Andrew "bunnie" Huang** is one of the people who define maker culture. Driven solely by natural curiosity, he reverse-engineered a key portion of the original Xbox security. He was also the hardware lead for a consumer electronics project called chumby, which Wired Magazine touted as one of the top gadgets in 2008.[1] More recently, bunnie helped design a Geiger counter for people in Japan after the nuclear power plant disaster in 2011.*

He now lives in Singapore, where he runs his own hardware consultancy connecting US companies with the hardware ecosystem in China. If you are interested in learning more about bunnie and reverse engineering, I recommend picking up a copy of Hacking the Xbox: An Introduction to Reverse Engineering.[2]

Steven Osborn: I want to know what inspired you to become a hardware hacker. Can you think back to any projects or people who inspired you to get interested in electronics?

bunnie Huang: When I was very young, probably eight years old or something like that, my dad took a trip to Taiwan and came back with an Apple clone, which didn't come back as a fully assembled device. It was a motherboard with a bunch of chips, and he had to put it together himself. It didn't have a case, so it was just sitting out there, to be seen on the desk. So, you

---

[1] www.wired.com/gadgets/miscellaneous/multimedia/2008/12/YE8_gadgets?slide=7&slideView=2
[2] Andrew Huang (No Starch Press, 2003).

know, I found it really fascinating because it was a cool piece of technology. It was aesthetically very nice to look at. It had all these shiny chips and the green circuit board, and these cool-looking inductors and stuff. Of course, I wanted to touch it, and I saw my dad put it together, so I knew the chips came on sockets and stuff like that.

When he saw me start to poke at it and try to pry out the chips, he got really freaked out. He said, "Hey, you can't touch it. It's verboten. You can't do these kinds of things." Of course, that was one way to tell a young boy, "You absolutely have to find a way to play with it." So it became an object of fascination, partially because you could play games on it, and program it, and do interesting things, and it was there, but partially also because it was a fascination with things that you're not supposed to do but you think you should be able to do.

Then it just turns out that the Apple II came with a full set of assembly code for the bios and a full schematic as well. It took me a while to figure out that the manuals had the schematics and stuff on the inside. It's all written in Chinese. These are clones, right? It came from Taiwan. But I eventually figured out that this huge sheet corresponded roughly to what was on the motherboard. These chips had some meaning, and they all had some correlation. And it opened me up to the idea that there's a lot going on underneath here that could be understood. From that point, I kept playing with stuff.

My dad had also got some Heathkits—the old Heathkit experimenter series. Like the Apple clone, we had to build them ourselves. They had these tutorials and manuals. So when he wasn't around and whatever, and the manuals are sitting out, I would just start reading them and learning about this stuff. I had an uncle who also worked at Bell Labs, and he gave me all kinds of books that were discards from his laboratory. They had all kinds of great stuff on the inside about programming and design, and so forth.

Osborn: It seems to be a common theme that people got started in electronics because their dad played with electronics, ham radio, or built PCs as a hobby. Tell me a bit about your education and some early projects you worked on.

Huang: I started doing hardware and hardware hacking before I went to college. So I started learning from the Forrest Mims' books[3] from Radio Shack and *The Art of Electronics,*[4] and all those kinds of books, just reading them on my own. I had *Byte* magazine, and so I would build some of the projects in there.

Before I went to college, I had built a speech synthesizer with a voltmeter so you could measure your battery, and it would tell you something like,

---

[3]www.forrestmims.com
[4]Paul Horowitz and Winfield Hill (Cambridge University Press, 1989).

"1.4 volts," in a computer voice. For my high school project, I did some electronic-type stuff. But for sure I didn't really understand what was going on. It was mostly a lot of just hacking around. I got into MIT, and there I learned a lot more of the formalism behind what was going on on the inside, which was really helpful to get some strong fundamentals behind the electronics.

Then I got my master's degree there. Went out, tried to go in the workforce for a little while. It didn't work out too well, for a lot of reasons. Then I went back and got my PhD at MIT.

Osborn: At MIT, were you part of the Media Lab?

Huang: I worked at the Media Lab as an undergraduate for two or three years, but my actual thesis, my dissertation, is at the AI[5] Lab, which is now defunct. It's now part of what is now called CSAIL, the computer science and AI Lab. They merged together. So I did some work at the Media Lab back then, but just as an undergrad.

Osborn: Were there some interesting projects that you worked on? You said you went back and got your PhD at MIT.

Huang: I just like building stuff on the side, so back in the day, when the Internet was starting, the Web didn't exist yet and e-mail was just a curiosity, I built a temperature sensor. I had this x86 machine running NeXTStep, and it ran a service to tell you the temperature outside and the graph of the temperature over time, which was neat and a lot of fun.

I lived in a frat, so we wired a discarded traffic light to a circuit that would switch the lights to music. Then as I started going through my thesis program, I had to come up with some actual research topics. So for my master's thesis, I built a reconfigurable hardware image-processing solution. Then for my PhD, I did some work on supercomputers and architectures for them and how to deal with a lot of the contemporary challenges that they're facing in terms of latency, access, and parallelism, and a lot of the issues that they are going to face down the road. So I built some network simulators using FPGAs[6] back then and wrote a simulator for that in software, which is what my dissertation was based on.

It's funny—that piece of hardware, the network simulator, formed the basis for one of the projects I'm better known for, which is when I extracted the security keys from the Microsoft Xbox – which was procrastination [instead of working on] my thesis at the time. But, you know, even before I did the Xbox stuff, I had habitually taken apart all of my videogame consoles and pulled the ROMs out of them, because back then it was easy. You just sucked out the

---

[5]Artificial intelligence
[6]Field-programmable gate array

bits and you disassembled them and started doing stuff with it before they had really hard security on them. So throughout college, it was always these little wacky random projects I would do on the side, primarily as procrastination, sometimes to learn something new, sometimes to play around.

Osborn: Can you talk just a little bit more about the Xbox hack you did? I think that was pretty interesting. It got a lot of people's attention.

Huang: It's funny that it got that much attention. I didn't expect that it would. At the time, I was doing my dissertation on computer architecture, and my advisor said, "Hey, let's look at videogame consoles, because they're the highest-performance-to-dollar machines you can buy." They're a bit like super-computers in a box, right?

So we got a bunch of them, and I started taking them apart. And as par for the course, I started pulling out the ROMs and stuff like that. Xbox had an encrypted ROM. So that was new and interesting back then. People spent some time trying to find out what the encryption key was and so on, and so I got involved. Eventually, because I had this FPGA board lying around and I had a fair bit of knowhow about how to do high-speed buses. I looked at one of the buses on the inside, where I thought maybe the security bus is going across, and I thought, "Hey, let's just have a look to see if the secrets are being passed along there." So I built a little board to adapt from the Microsoft Xbox to my other board, and glued the board in the system and wrote up some code, did some calibrations, and so forth.

I got really lucky that the security keys are just sitting there in plain text on the bus going across in the bus. Then a whole bunch of stuff came out after that, like the DMCA[7] and the fear of being sued, and then MIT pushing me away and saying, "We have nothing to do with you." And then professors in the lab getting really mad about that and saying, "You should publish anyway." Then MIT had some conversations with Microsoft, and the EFF and other lawyers. A lot of pretty life-changing events happened as a result of that. I got a practical lesson in IP law, a hands-on lesson in IP law in the ugliest way. But it's actually been really beneficial. I think having been through that process, I feel like I have a little more of a gut feel of what the issues are there. I'm not a lawyer, but having been on the other sides of some pretty nasty lawsuits and threats and stuff, I think I feel a lot more comfortable with the boundaries, and I know where to push and when not to push.

Osborn: I see. That's a really quick way to learn things, maybe not the most recommended way, but it certainly got you there. It sounds like you have a pretty upbeat outlook on the whole situation.

---

[7]Digital Millennium Copyright Act

You mentioned that you entered the workforce and then realized maybe that wasn't for you. Or you wanted to do your own thing. Did the Xbox experience have any bearing on that, or was this just your personality? Can you tell me a little bit about that?

Huang: That's an interesting question. The whole workforce thing—when I was working up to my master's degree, I had this very conventional idea of what I would do after college. You get a job, you join a big company, and you do the big company things, right? I always wanted to work for Silicon Graphics doing high-end computers and visualization, so I thought it was really life changing to do computer graphics and see things in three dimensions. I was like, "All right, I'm going to work really hard, study really hard, and then maybe I'll get a job at this place, and I can make a big impact and make people's lives better."

So, you know, I work hard all throughout college, get the interview, get the job, and join the organization. It seems awesome. Just as I'm enjoying my new job at Silicon Graphics, these startup companies no one ever heard of—nVIDIA and ATI—just gutted Silicon Graphics. They hired every person out of that building in the six months I was there. When I started, the whole area of the building I was in was full of really bright, smart engineers who were pretty fun, and one by one, they all packed their cubicles and left. By the time I decided I would leave, I had to walk around every half-hour just to keep the lights from turning off because it was just like you'd hear the winds whistling in the hallway.

There were just a few guys left in my group, we were doing our kinds of things, and we were basically the people who weren't picked for the draft of the nVIDIA or ATI start-up crews. At the time, I had no idea what was going on. I was like, "Man, this sucks. You came out here, and you worked hard, and you joined the premier company, and everyone just leaves and they go do this start-up thing."

So I was thinking, "Obviously, the world doesn't quite work like I thought it did." I thought the best way to learn more is to go back and get my education, which is wrong, but I did that anyway because that was the only thing I knew how to do. The previous twenty-some-odd years of my life were spent being in school. I might as well go back to school and try and figure it out again. But my PhD experience was extremely different from my undergraduate experience. It was really formative.

Osborn: Awesome. So now you do your own thing and work for yourself and do your own projects? You started chumby. Is that correct?

Huang: Between when I finished my PhD and now, I had been through three start-ups: a start-up called Mobilian, a start-up called Luxtera, and a start-up called chumby. At Mobilian, I was doing mixed-signal ASIC[8] design. With the wireless start-up I was doing Bluetooth/802.11 combo solutions, back when it was the hot thing. They folded, and then I joined a company called Luxtera, doing nanophotonic integrated circuits. And that was just a super-awesome experience because we were doing just completely cockamamie things with process technologies and really bending all the rules and really hacking silicon at a very low level, which gave me a background in silicon hacking, It is really good to know how to design chips from a fundamental level and that's what the Luxtera experience gave me. You understand a lot more what's going on when you go deep like that. But in the end I decided chip design really wasn't for me.

Then I was invited by Steve Tomlin to start chumby and decided to join the team. At chumby, I did a lot of open hardware stuff and tried to build this "little Internet appliance that could." It turned out that it couldn't, but start-ups come and they go. In the process of doing chumby, I got the opportunity to do a lot of manufacturing and mass-producing. I really couldn't say before I started chumby that I actually knew how to actually make something. I mean, I could make a single prototype.

I have a saying, "You can do anything once." I could pull out the Xbox keys exactly once. I couldn't mass-manufacture the solution. So it felt like a fluke, right? You can coax a lot of hardware systems to do amazing things exactly once, like the overclockers[9] and stuff like that. But producing something that a million people can buy and it performs, and people are happy with it, and it's reliable—that's an art in itself. It's actually extremely difficult to do that. One of the things I wanted to do at chumby was to learn what it really means to go and build these things.

chumby was a great opportunity for me to get into China, learn the ecosystem, get my hands dirty out there, learn how to do tooling and mechanical design, industrial design, how to do cost reduction, testing, manufacturing flow, the whole thing, from supply to logistics, everything you need after you've built prototype one. How do you get from prototype to one million units on time? That was again a hugely eye-opening experience.

In that process, I realized, "My God. The hardware ecosystem is in China. It's not in the United States anymore." I was just spending so much time in China that it didn't make sense to live in the US. So we moved the chumby hardware office overseas to Singapore. That existed for about a year before chumby went under.

When the chumby hardware office went under, I decided to stay in Singapore and just go independent and see what I could do. It's funny. It sounds a little bit

---

[8]ASIC – Application Specific Integrated Circuit
[9]Someone who modifies a computer system to run faster than the manufacturers specifications.

different maybe, to not have a job and do your own thing. But actually, when you look at a lot of the Chinese makers and entrepreneurs, that's what they do. A lot of them are loosely employed guys with very vague organizations around them. And they will start up with a handful of capital, like $10,000, $50,000, something like that, and build businesses that go to $50 million in two years because the ecosystem out there is capable of doing that. It's amazing what they can do. So I'm trying to decode that ecosystem and try to figure out what does it mean, how can we do it? What can we learn? How can we mix it with things I know from the Western ecosystem? See what we can learn.

Osborn: Of all the people I've interviewed, you have the most experience and ideas about the difference between manufacturing in China compared to the US. One thing that concerns me is that places like Portland, where I live, are considered a center for silicon companies in the United States. We have Intel, Maxim, and Tektronix, but if I want to have a PCB made and build a prototype, besides etching some board in my garage, my only option takes two weeks through the mail. Two weeks to get my prototype on a PCB. Then even simple resistors, capacitors, and other basic components are all going to be shipped via DigiKey. There's nowhere to go to just walk in and buy those things. Even tips for my soldering iron, like my Hakko. There's not a store in town I can go and get tips for it. Those get shipped to me via Amazon Prime.

Huang: It seems like everything is unduly hard in the US. Even in Silicon Valley, it's unduly hard to get a lot of things done. Now that I'm out here in Asia, I try to live one month a year, in Shenzhen, just for the experience. It's so convenient: it will be like two a.m. and my soldering iron will stop working for whatever reason, and I'm like, "Oh shit. I really, really want to get this project done. I just can't wait until tomorrow," for whatever reason. "Let's go and see if I can find a soldering iron." I walk around the street, and like one block over, there's a hardware shop that's open at two a.m. that has a freaking soldering iron. It's like five bucks, you got it, you walk back, half an hour later, and you're online again putting down your stuff. That is great. That is freaking awesome.

Osborn: I might be able to get a Radio Shack firestarter if it was between nine and six. Do you have any insider ideas as to how do we fix that? What can we do in the US to try to build that culture around and foster hardware engineering here? This is obviously not something you solve overnight. Maybe it's a decades-long effort to make that change. Or maybe it just doesn't happen or it doesn't make sense. What is your opinion? How do we enable makers to build more, faster here in the US?

Huang: I think companies don't have this problem so much because they have so much money to do prototypes, they don't care. It's really the individuals and the makers who really suffer because they can't afford the FedEx charges, and the big purchasing, and ops, and the logistics guys to get disparate vendors in fifty different states to try to come together and do the thing for you.

I think it's a little bit of an attitude shift. Between the late eighties and today, hardware just wasn't sexy anymore. No one really wanted to do it. It went through this phase of massive outsourcing, and then software just became the new thing—like the whole dotcom boom and everything. Everyone wanted to make money by writing software, and it was cool. And hardware just didn't make any money. I think because of thirty years of this cultural bias in the US against hardware, it's really hard to get the right mindset to approach hardware.

I mean, at the moment, there's almost this mysticism of what's inside the box, right? Like you're just hanging out, and you go and start pulling out screws from the box, and they're like, "Holy cow! You can pull the screws out of that! You're going to electrocute yourself!" When the net goes down, you go and reboot the router, and it works. Everyone is like, "Wow!" But it's like, come on, guys, this is not that crazy, right?

Then you go to China, and you walk into the markets and the stores, and it's a family affair. They have babies and kids running around in electronic markets, inside these stalls where Dad is like soldering the cables and Mom's hawking chips and stuff like that. The kid comes home from school and does his homework on top of a glass case full of SMT[10] ICs.

These kids just live surrounded by components and electronics. They don't think it's weird. It's so normal to them. It's what they do. Then when they become teenagers, they are like, "Hardware? Whatever. I don't want to do that. My dad does that. I want to go into fashion," or something like that. You get a lot of that in China. That's typical. But the thing is, you go ask these kids who want to go into fashion, "Can you solder this?" They go, "Sure, whatever." They're like, "Of course. Everyone can solder. What are you talking about? People can't solder?" You know what I'm talking about? It's just this completely different mindset that they have out there that is just lost in the US.

It's a cultural thing. You just have to get over this mysticism that hardware's hard, like it's immutable and that it's expensive and all these kinds of problems. If you can get around all that, it's actually not that bad, but I think maybe part of the problem is the ecosystem just doesn't exist in the US.

There's Thief River Falls [Minnesota] and DigiKey. I'm like, "If I move back to the US, I'm getting a house near Thief River Falls." I'm just doing will-call to DigiKey all the time and walking in and getting my stuff, because that would be awesome, right? But there's only one place in the United States that has that. I mean, maybe there's another one. There's Jameco in Silicon Valley and a couple of other spots. There are not a lot of places that have that feel. Another thing is that those places are all distributors. You still order on the Web and

---

[10]Surface-mount technology

you can't really browse the inventory. The great thing about China is that you walk in these stores, and they have all this inventory. They're like, "Yeah, come on in." You walk in like, "Oh, you have those? That's awesome."

Osborn: And you can pick it up and touch it.

Huang: You can pick it up and look at it. You say, "I want two of these." And they're like, "You can just have it, whatever. It's just two of them. I don't want to deal with invoicing you for it." It's a really different world. That ecosystem and mentality doesn't exist in the US. If we could bring that back somehow, that would be great, but it's just not there.

Osborn: I wonder if the whole hobby hardware hacker movement will help soften that. I've met a lot of people in recent years who are career web developers or career software engineers who have been introduced to hardware through Arduino or something, and start out blinking some LEDs and it snowballs from there. I don't know how much that's really going to help or not.

Huang: I think it will create a new generation that won't be recognizable from today's generation. I think it will have an impact in the long term. Hardware has moved beyond circuit design and chips and stuff. It's more about what you want to do. The question is, "What do you want?" Do you want just some wireless widget that can have GPS and all these other things and take wind measurements and stick it on your roof, whatever it is? Do you want a dog collar that can tell your dog where it's not supposed to be? Do you want something that can control your thermometer on your house from Twitter or something? All these things are bits that require hardware to enable them.

Hardware currently becomes this barrier between a lot of applications that people want because they just don't have the coupling to get it. So I think the innovation ecosystem right now is creating a lot of building blocks, which is what Arduino's great for.

We already have awesome terminals for almost anything. They're called smartphones. They have great touchscreens. They have interfaces that can talk to almost anything. The really hard barrier of "I've got to build this computer with UI and a touchscreen and speakers," isn't there anymore. Pick up a smartphone. You just figure out how to co-op those and have them control the bits of hardware that you actually need to do to get your job done. That seems to be a winning strategy. I think they'll continue to advance.

Osborn: At this point, there are so many good building blocks. There are so many LEGOs out there where if you want to build a GPS dog collar, you don't really need a good deep understanding of electronics. You just need to buy a couple things from SparkFun, and they go together like LEGOs. You can just download some code, and modify it to do what you need it to do. I think that's exciting. I've seen a lot of products at the prototype stages that get people excited about the possibilities that way.

Huang: That's exactly right. The big difference between China and the US around that is that in the US, you go buy a GPS, you need an Arduino and all this stuff together to build the collar. You've spent like $150 or $200 in the day, right?

Osborn: Yeah.

Huang: In China that would cost you like $10 or something like that. If in the US, you wanted to go and mass-produce these things—like your friend says, "Hey, that's awesome. I want one of those," well, you can open-source your plan up on the Net and that guy can spend $200 and buy it with SparkFun. That's great for SparkFun, but it just doesn't scale because there are not a lot of guys who are going to buy this and put them together. In China, if somebody says, "Hey, that's pretty awesome. I want to market it." They say, "Oh, oh, oh, cool. I'll just place an order with the factory, and then how soon do you want it? Like six weeks? Ten bucks?"

"Okay, fine. Here's a thousand."

Then you say go. Everything you need from prototype one to mass manufacturing exists there, whereas in the US, everything to go from prototype one onward is missing. That's the big contrast.

Osborn: I'm going to jump a little bit to a different topic. I don't know how much you were involved with Safecast.[11] I saw that you had built one of the early prototypes.

Huang: Safecast is a big organization. There are a lot of different aspects to it. I built a device—a Geiger counter, actually. And there are two or three lineages of sensors they've built at Safecast. A team in Japan built the one that they're using to do a lot of the geographic logging in Japan. They are building huge data sets. I have some involvement, but I'm mostly on the manufacturing ops end for that. That's basically a GPS unit with a Geiger counter also. Then the other thing I built was a consumer Geiger counter. I wanted to take the Geiger counter you can buy today, which is this very lab instrument–looking thing that is very expensive, and merge it with modern design principles of today—which is simplicity, ease of use, good user interface—and build something that I could see a concerned father using to determine if the playground's safe for the kids to play in. And it wouldn't require a degree in nuclear physics to operate. It wouldn't have to be scary and bright yellow and scare you when they bring it out, like you're about to do an analysis, you know what I mean?

Taking radiation measurements should feel very normal, right? It shouldn't be something you should be exceptionally worried about because, in fact,

---

[11]Safecast is a global sensor network for radiation sensors.

there are many sources of radiation in the world. Granite is radioactive. There's radon in the tiles. If you just want to know what's out there, it shouldn't be this taboo to measure it, right?

So I designed a Geiger counter, which I open-sourced and released to the world. One of Safecast's commercial affiliates, Medcom, picked it up and decided to build. They had a Kickstarter around it, and it's currently shipping out like any day now.

Osborn: That's great.

Huang: I'm pretty stoked about that.

Osborn: What projects are you working on nowadays? Are you building the next version of chumby or are you doing a freelance job for other people?

Huang: It's a little bit of everything these days. I'm not working on chumby anymore per se. I am still building Linux computers like I did at chumby. I'm working on an open-source laptop that's based on a quad-core ARM CPU. I'm working on a couple of research projects. I'm looking at the insides of full-size SD cards and what the firmware is on the inside. I do a little consulting on the side. So I'm helping a group in Oklahoma build a robot controller for an educational program.

Osborn: I'm originally from Tulsa, Oklahoma.

Huang: Cool. You might know them, the KISS Institute for Practical Robotics, KIPR. I think they're with the University of Oklahoma. So I helped them build the next generation of robot controllers for that.

Most recently, I've been collaborating with this lady. Her name is Jie Qi. She's at the MIT Media Lab and she does a lot of papercraft and electronics. She does a lot of blending of unconventional materials with electronics. So we're trying to build a toolkit of electronic parts that are suitable for being put into books and flexible situations like—flexible as in physically flexible. Things that have to curve, bend, be wearable, that kind of stuff.

We're building things that are almost like electronic stickers. You stick them on things. You run copper tape or aluminum foil to them, and then they flash and do their stuff. So that's fun. Then, you know, some consulting. The odd consulting job. I work with MAKE, Maker Shed, on helping them get stuff done in China, that kind of thing. I also do some start-up advising. So I have a few start-ups that e-mail me every now and then for advice. Some of them I have a formal arrangement with. I may represent the investors, or I may represent an independent advising source. Other ones are just whatever. I just think it's cool, and I want to help them.

Osborn: What new projects are out there that other people are working on or building that you find really interesting?

Huang: Interesting? There's a lot of that stuff I have my eyes on at the moment. I've been looking upstream at what's coming down the chip pipeline. I'm looking forward to the 64-bit ARM CPUs, because I think those will really give ARM a strong bid to compete with the Intel CPUs in the desktop and server space, and not just mobile. I'm watching what those guys are building and really closely following when those are being released.

The other thing I'm actually really interested in is the mobile phone ecosystem in China. I recently bought this feature phone for $12. I mean, it's like $12 full stop. It's not like $12 on sale or $12 used. It was a brand-new phone and I bought it for $12. It has Bluetooth and quad-band GSM and an OLED display and keyboard, and can play MP3s and all this stuff. I'm just like, "Wow, this thing—it's a phone, right? And it's twelve bucks." So that got me interested in trying to figure out how this is cheaper than an Arduino and it has *all* of this on the inside. You know what I mean?

Osborn: Yeah, definitely.

Huang: I'm like, "You know what? We need to figure out what's going on inside of this thing. How do we build more of them? How do we get them into the US?" Because why are we where we are in the US? Why do I feel like we're backward almost?

I mean, not to knock Arduino, but you pay like $25, $30 for an AVR microcontroller with a few kilobytes of memory. In China, you pay $12 and you get a whole freaking phone, full retail, over the counter. What's wrong with this picture here, guys? I'm not willing to accept "Oh, it's China. Ha-ha. That weird ecosystem of stuff." Let's laugh them off as this curiosity. I'm like, "No, no. Something's going on out there that we don't understand, and we're going to be hurting in a while if we don't figure out how to take advantage of what's happening, right?" Or if we don't at least understand what the barriers are to innovation, to get this disruptive cost model, top-performance feature thing into other ecosystems, right?

Osborn: One thing that really bugs me is connecting things to the Internet is way harder than it should be. "Let's put a Wi-Fi module on this microcontroller project." So you go look for this shield or this unit, you're looking at $60 and up—$60, $100 to add Wi-Fi. Why? I can get a Raspberry Pie for $35 and a $5 USB dongle and stick it in the side of it. So for $40, I have a fully working Linux machine with Wi-Fi. Why is it a $60 upgrade to get my $2 AVR chip to speak Wi-Fi?

Huang: I think part of it just speaks to the oddness of using an AVR as a platform.

Osborn: I mean this is pretty true for most microcontroller platforms. I guess until you start talking about ARM—even if you look at ARM, if you're not running Linux or have some real-time OS, you're going to have to license the driver for like $40K or something.

Huang: Yeah, that's strange, but it's right. There are a lot of artificial barriers in the Wi-Fi space, for sure. Any time you go into these wireless spaces, it seems like you run into these massive artificial barriers, artificial cost barriers, and regulatory barriers that serve to protect existing monopolies and hegemonies of different technologies. I think it really defeats innovation and it really deflates entrepreneurs.

I think one of the scary things going on in the United States is that the moment you're remotely successful, you're getting your ass sued off. The whole Apple versus Samsung thing is setting a terrible precedent for people. It's like, "Great. You've become successful. You can now challenge the incumbent." Guess what? You're slapped with a million-dollar lawsuit.

Like Formlabs, those guys are building 3D printers. They're awesome. They've got great technology. The incumbent tries to sue them out of existence the moment they ship.[12] What innovation ecosystem does that salvage? It doesn't even make sense anymore, right?

When you raise money from VCs, you have to reserve half of it as a legal defense fund. Is that a good expenditure of money? Is that how entrepreneurs should be thinking? Should we always be living in fear of lawsuits and trying to design around patents? Or should we just be focusing on making things better for consumers?

Honestly, one of the things that happens out here in Asia, is that when people build stuff, they don't give a damn about IP laws, and they're chastised for it, and there are problems with "the lack of respect of IP laws." On the other hand, they're not shackled by it, right? They just do it. These people just do. And then they figure it out later on, whatever happens. The government doesn't really care or enforce things too strictly there. The fact of the matter is that the people there just don't worry as much about these kinds of things, and that makes things a lot easier as a maker.

Osborn: Unless you raise like a billion dollars from a VC, half that fund is not going to help you if you're a small start-up and some billion-dollar company wants to sue you. When a billion-dollar company is suing somebody like Formlabs, they don't even care if they lose the litigation because they're just going to drag it around for years, and a small company is going to run out of money before then.

Huang: Also, who is going to invest or acquire a company with a lawsuit pending? It kills valuation. It distracts the founders. Even if it's completely false

---

[12]http://wired.com/design/2012/11/3d-systems-formlabs-lawsuit/

and was unjustified, the fact of the matter is, the plaintiff bought months of time for them to come up with a competing product. Lawsuits are completely valid business strategy in the United States, and it's respected and honored by all of the systems and considered to be sound. That really heavily favors certain classes of companies, right?

Osborn: Even if you win the battle, you lose the war through legal fees. Maybe large companies that file lawsuits and lose should cover the legal fees of people that they tried to sue.

Huang: But that doesn't buy back the time and the opportunity cost. I've been through lawsuits, and it is draining. It is a huge, huge mental exhaustion and lawyers can be total assholes. They can really make your life hell.

Osborn: I see both sides. I have a friend whose dad is an electrical engineer in India. He jumped through all kinds of hoops to make it hard to look at it and figure out what he was doing. He was grinding off the tops of chips, and then turning them over upside down, and then designing his boards where the chips were soldered on upside down, things like that. So that if somebody gets a hold of it, they're not able to easily clone it and make five thousand of them the next week.

Huang: I hear you. That is definitely a problem in China, the whole cloning and copying aspect of it. There are pluses and minuses. I think me, being a small entrepreneur—I would be blessed if someone copied my idea because that means somebody actually cares. Nobody copies shitty ideas.

Osborn: I think just the insight I got from you about manufacturing in China is pretty interesting for a lot of people. A lot of folks are launching Kickstarter projects, and then realize—you already mentioned this—anybody can build one of a thing, but when you try to scale, things get hairy.

I guess the worst thing that can happen to you on Kickstarter is that you sell half a million units, because then you have to go build half a million units. A lot of people go out and hire Dragon Innovation[13] or something like that. I mean, not really to knock on them, but now you're paying them half of your income just to guide you through manufacturing things in China.

Huang: That's absolutely true. It is one of those things where if you do a Kickstarter and it really knocks out of the park, you're screwed, because a lot of the guys aren't really ready for that. They're like, "Oh, I soldered one together at my house. It was great." Then they have to solder together a thousand at their house, and they're thinking, "Shit. I'd rather be watching TV, or walking my dog, or hanging out with my kids and my family than slaving away in my office building things for Kickstarter, which I didn't expect to

---

[13]www.dragoninnovation.com

happen." They say, "Okay, let's go to outsource." They find there are all these problems and troubles with it.

There was a period of time where every couple of days I'd wake up in the morning and there'd be an e-mail in my inbox from some guy who had a Kickstarter that just knocked out of the park, and they're like, "My God. What do I do? I can't handle this." So you ask them, "What's the status of things?" Then I'd say, "Oh my God. You Kickstarted that? It's a cool idea, man, but you're not ready to deliver on the schedule you said."

That's one of those things. It's actually a blessing to not know about the production side of things because once you get into the world of production, you see more of what's not possible than what is possible. A lot of what I do is, "You can't do that. That's not going to be producible. We can't build that." Then sometimes I'll be surprised, "Oh my God. They built that. That's amazing." I completely got it wrong, it's totally doable, and the fact they could do it made that project just outstanding.

To some extent, from a newcomer's eyes, everything's possible. They don't know any better. If they just do it, maybe they tank, but sometimes they win, right?

I think that's one of the great things about people on Kickstarter and guys who aren't inhibited is that they come with really innovative ideas. Maybe it can't be made, but they're going to try anyway. You know what? Sometimes they really come up with things that are really awesome. I would never have seen it, right? I can't knock them and say, "Oh, let's do your homework before we build it," because if they do, then everything would end up being a square black box, because those are easy to make. The world would be very producible, but not really very innovative.

Osborn: There are a lot of stories like that. The Sifteo guys decided to change the type of glass on top of the Sifteo cubes, and it ended up being this ten-week process or something like that. Because they had to change a millimeter here or there, how the glass set in the device, and things like that.

Huang: I'm actually intimately familiar with that because I'm an advisor for Sifteo and I helped them with that process. That was an exciting time. I was actually trying to help them move to a completely different design—it didn't work out. My path didn't work out, but at least I helped them explore a different thing. They didn't have time as a company to explore, but that's fine.

Osborn: That's cool. I like David a lot.

Huang: Dave's a good guy.

Osborn: Hackers in general are easy to get along with. I think understanding how the electronics industry is and has been striving in China is going to be key for companies and engineers in the US, and you have a great insight there. Thanks for sharing.

Natan Linder

Founder

Formlabs

Natan Linder is one of the cofounders of Formlabs (Formlabs.com)—makers of a 3D printer called Form 1. Natan is also a PhD student in the Fluid Interfaces Group at the MIT Media Lab. His work fuses design and engineering to create novel human experiences. His background is in computer science, product design, and entrepreneurship. Before Formlabs, he worked for Sun Microsystems and Samsung. Natan holds a bachelor's in computer science from the Interdisciplinary Center (IDC) in Herzliya, Israel, and a master's degree in media arts and sciences from MIT.

Steven Osborn: Why don't you start by telling me a little bit about yourself and your background, your education. What got you interested in building things and being an engineer?

Natan Linder: As you get from my name, I'm originally from Israel and I've been around computers from a very early age. I guess it was a very classic story of a kid who learns to program early from his dad—the classic engineer story. My dad had a Sinclair ZX81 PC he taught me on. That's my first experience with computers.

I also come from a home where my grandfather had a carpentry shop. So I got to play with big, dangerous toys, like saws.

My dad built our house at that time with his own hands, even though he wasn't an architect or a builder or anything. That was a good background for someone interested in computers and physical objects.

So then, fast-forward, I was always interested in entrepreneurship. I don't know why, but I started my first company when I was seventeen and never stopped.

Then I spent three years in the Air Force doing intelligence work. I can't really share a lot about that, but you learn a lot in those types of environments.

I finished a BA in computer science/business administration/entrepreneurship at the Interdisciplinary Center at Herzliya. I was just trying to do things differently. I got two amazing scholarship to the school, the first from the late Efi Arazi, who was an MIT Grad that built Scitex, and the second from Sam Zell.[1]

At the time, Efi Arazi was looking for people who had good potential for entrepreneurship and leadership in tech. So that empowered us, my partner to be and myself, to go all the way to the dean and ask to do the final project in the first year of college, basically. The dean threw us out of his office until he figured out we were not going away.

My partner and I ended up working at Sun Microsystems doing this cool project that enabled dynamic application content creation for mobile as early as 2001. The project caught the attention of the Samsung people in Israel. It was early to talk about how mobile was going to change the world, but still, my partner and I were doing some work. We ended up taking a deal that sold a bunch of IP to Samsung, and we ended up starting an R&D center for Samsung in Israel.

I grew that operation from four people to well over one hundred, and we shipped a lot of software on several Samsung handsets. I guess the point is that Samsung was a really good school for consumer electronics software, embedded technology, and manufacturing—all of that together in a very tight economic environment was a good learning experience. I guess I've seen the whole spectrum, from whiteboard to factory floors, and that was a pretty amazing experience. I did that when I was twenty-five. I'm thirty-five today.

Osborn: At what point in there did you end up at the MIT Media Lab?

Linder: After almost five years at Samsung, I felt that I had achieved what I started, what I wanted to achieve. I think I felt, "This is getting too cool for me." And deep down inside, I'm much more of an entrepreneur, so I decided to leave. I ended up joining a VC out of Jerusalem—Jerusalem Venture Partners—and working on a new company. Then my wife told me one day that she got accepted to MIT. So that was a no-brainer. In a big step, we ended up moving to Boston, and she started at Sloan.[2] I thought, "Gee, what am I going to do now?" I knew a little bit about the Media Lab. I had been there

---

[1]Sam Zell is the US billionaire head of Equity Group Investments, which has holdings ranging from real estate to media to healthcare.
[2]The business school at MIT.

once before. So I started going to the lab and talking to people, and I ended up meeting my current advisor, Dr. Pattie Maes. She sees hundreds of people who want to come into the Fluid Interfaces Group every year and she said something like, "I think there's good potential, but I don't know. Let's keep in touch." I applied anyway. At the same time, she introduced me to Rodney Brooks—are you familiar with Rod Brooks?

Osborn: I'm not.

Linder: Rod used to run CSAIL, the Computer Science and Artificial Intelligence Lab at MIT. He was cofounder, chairman and CTO of iRobot. You know, Roombas, Packbots and all that. In 2008 he started Heartland Robotics.

Rod was looking for a design engineer-type of person to work on the user interface. I ended up being employee number ten and the lead user interface guy, at what is now Rethink Robotics, on the product they now call Baxter—but which at that point in time didn't really exist. Well, it existed in theory, I guess. Heartland was starting to build it, which was pretty exciting.

From that point on, I wasn't sure if I would end up at MIT, but it didn't matter because I was doing pretty cool stuff with Rod. Pattie did end up accepting me. So I went to MIT because I thought there would be plenty of time to start companies and not so many opportunities to go to MIT. I thought it would be a nice break. Little did I know that this would start eventually the Formlabs rollercoaster and some other cool projects that I'm working on right now. That's the short version of how I got to MIT.

Osborn: Did Formlabs come out of MIT? I guess you are working with people you knew there?

Linder: No. So Formlabs is not a spinoff from MIT research work. The cofounders, Max [Lobovsky], David [Cranor], and myself, we were all in the same class at the Media Lab and we met there. We went to the same famous "How to make almost anything" class that Neil Gershenfeld teaches every year.

There was a lot of discussion around things that could be done with personal fabrication tools, but really, Formlabs was started later. We were all into our second year working on our master's thesis and got together to work on something that would come after Max and David graduated. I did want to continue to a PhD, so I did both, but it was really an after-hours thing that took off after Max and David graduated and we all submitted our thesis for the master's. So that's how Formlabs got started.

Osborn: Can you tell me about some project that you saw, either inside the Media Lab or outside that somebody else was working on that inspired you or you thought was a cool project?

Linder: You mean that is related to Formlabs or in general?

Osborn: Just in general. When building something, whether it was software or hardware, some thing that you find interesting that somebody else is working on.

Linder: So there are so many examples that come to mind immediately. You know that problem, right?

Osborn: Were there other 3D printer projects that got you interested in it?

Linder: Well, the first thing I did at MIT was build a CNC[3] milling machine. I was watching Jonathan Ward, who used to be Neil's student, and he was building his own CNC machine. I was like, "Gee, I would like to build my own." I was looking at his stuff, and that was pretty interesting to me. I'm not a mechanical engineer by training. I'm much better at the system-level software side of things. Max was giving me tips on the mechanical end, and I was determined to get it working. So I ended up building a machine myself. That was exciting.

Osborn: So besides 3D printing, what are some things you are passionate about?

Linder: My other passion was in the field of projected augmented reality. In that space, there were very old classic works by people like John Underkoffer, who built I/O Bulb, and folks like Pierre Wellner, who did the original first projected displays. I was thinking very deeply on projected augmented reality at the time. This relates to my current research project called LuminAR. I spent my master's thesis on it and I am still developing it. Basically, it suggests there's another form factor for a computer where the main interaction modality is augmented reality. That project became the center of my master's.

To put it very simply, I built a computer within a lightbulb. There's been tons of press about it and you can see some demo videos. The idea took off, but I'm still working on it. The gist of the project is this: imagine you have a computer that you can just screw up into any light socket. That computer is actually a pico projector, an embedded board sensor, a camera, and depth sensor that you can just screw into any light socket. And once you do that, you basically get an interactive projector display, but one that can not only display pixels outside the traditional boundaries of a display like a computer screen as we all know it, but that also can augment physical objects. It's also a computer that looks down. If you think about it, most computers look at us. So that was the gist of the project. It caught the attention of a bunch of sponsoring companies and they shifted some funds, so I've got a bunch of grants to build this thing.

Osborn: So your project is part of the Fluid Interfaces Group?

---

[3]Computer Numerical Control, or computer automation of physical processes.

Linder: Yeah, the Fluid Interfaces Group. My advisor, Pattie, is focused on this idea that there are other computing experiences that we should have by now.

All our experiences are display-centric if you think about it. We have this notion that there's a computing device and this device would have a screen, and this screen is a way of interacting. This is trivial even though it's new.

We're still pretty much relying on the keyboard and mouse. Not to say that this is an interface that should go away, but on the other hand, in the day and age of Google glasses and that stuff, the way that we interact with computing by and large changes. And we're scratching the surface right now of how user experience, and talking to computers and interacting with computers will actually come about in the next forty years to come.

One of the big things is how do we integrate what we describe as digital information and the physical world? Now, today, this is all done through devices, right? But there are other ways to do it. We talked about interfaces that are context-aware and just-in-time, and provide services and information just because you are in a certain location. You know, it's the stuff you see in the sci-fi movies.

Osborn: Like *Star Trek*.

Linder: Yeah, but they're becoming reality. I want to say my interest in this area had two big motivations. One—and this is specifically for my work on projected augmented reality—if you look at the history, you see the ideas were there for sixty years, and the technology keeps getting better and better, but it's not put together into a form factor that is compact and simple, and that lets you just plug it in and it will work.

All the projector camera systems that you see out there, or the interactive projectors that you see out there, are pretty much the same. You need four engineers to put together and calibrate them, and stick a supercomputer next to them so that something will happen. I thought that was the totally wrong approach to do it. I thought we have enough technology in mobile devices today that we can use interaction to make those devices actually meaningful. The other approach is if we want people to adapt new types of technology, we need to package it up in a form factor that would be appealing and clear and simple. This is where the metaphor of a lightbulb or just a simple design object like a task light comes into play.

So, I started to build exactly that. I build interactive projector camera systems that fit into a lightbulb, which are carried by this arm that looks like an Anglepoise lamp. This was an embedded system that has a simple front end that effectively is a web browser. You can write simple web applications for it.

The promise of it is turning light into an interface. This has a lot of advantages over existing interfaces. Although it does not negate the need or the use for them, this computer that I'm talking about coexists with other devices that we have.

Osborn: This sounds a bit like David Merrill's story. He also went through the MIT Media Lab. He built the Sifteo Cubes.

Linder: Yeah, Sifteo came out from my group. I know Dave really well. He took a traditional display and broke it up into smaller pieces and created a new type of tangible interactivity with it.

I'm saying a simple thing like, "We can actually take light and make it a valid medium for interaction." And when you're talking about light, you're talking about the footprint of the interface is something different. Light can go away, disappear, and the interface can disappear by blending the physical and the interface in a way that we simply don't have today. All of a sudden you can think, "What is an application?" Because our applications, if you think about them deeply now, they're virtual objects that have a metaphor.

You know, you say, "Oh, I'm just going to use my stopwatch application," and then you get this thing projected on your wrist. We used to have real stopwatches, right? I'm not saying those should come back, what I'm saying is imagine a world where a physical object could become a part of your digital life in a way that makes sense.

You pick up a book and this computer sees the book. It may augment the actual book, and it may provide you more digital content in your earphones as you're glancing over the pages of this physical book or magazine. Basically, this is the promise of ubiquitous computing. It has been promised for the past thirty to forty years, depending on how you count it, but it hasn't been delivered. I argue that part of the fact that it's not delivered is just because there's no form factor to do it.

Mark Weiser, if you follow the famous Xerox PARC guy, used to say, "We'll have different displays with different sizes." Basically, that's the world we live in today. And I'm saying that there's another step to it.

Osborn: The flexible-display technology is pretty interesting. I think that will open up some new possibilities.

Linder: You combine that with what you see today. Five years ago, if I would talk about gesture-control and things like that, the world was freaking out basically.

Osborn: "That'll never work."

Linder: But today, it's like, "Of course." Gestures and touch are trivial. For kids growing up today, it's like the computer mouse. I remember growing up, the point in time where my dad brought in this thing and connected it to the computer. We used to have a computer without a mouse and that was computing. Then we had a mouse, and we never looked back, right? I think a similar thing is happening with gesturing technology—you see it with all those products and sensors out there. And this is just going to become so natural for us, right?

Osborn: So this is your PhD work at MIT?

Linder: Yeah, that's still my PhD work.

Osborn: Are you able to get your PhD while building Formlabs? I would imagine that's a lot of obligations to juggle.

Linder: You can add that I have a one-year-old baby.

Osborn: I've been there. It's pretty exhausting and exhilarating at the same time.

Linder: We all work three hundred percent nowadays and we never stop. I know it sounds like a lot, but that is my way of doing things. I'm always involved in more than one or two things. Otherwise, I get bored and I'm not feeling happy.

I'm an early-stage, fire-starter animal. I live for the thrill of being there when things start and then doing it again, I guess. I am trying to finish this PhD, but you never know. Sometimes you plan and then something else comes up. As Lennon said: "Life is what happens while you are busy making other plans."

Osborn: Tell me how you got from working on the augmented reality to Formlabs. Can you go into what Formlabs does and what the Form 1 is?

Linder: Sure. This might be surprising to you, but what I'm trying to do with augmented reality and creating new form factors is not that different in principle from what the Form 1 is doing. The Form 1 is a new form factor 3D printer. It's trying to offer a new design, both in the product design sense and in the usability and the technology, making high-resolution 3D printing affordable and accessible for designers, engineers, and makers right on their desks. While that has been a promise, it's yet to be fulfilled despite the fact there are now some successful venture companies and lots of projects in that space that we now call the maker community. From Formlabs' perspective, the promise of routine 3D printing that can help you realize projects in 3D form has yet to be fulfilled.

What we've discovered is that on the price-point side and usability side, users of this technology—which we like to call *prosumers*, who are people like you and me who have dabbled in design or design and engineering—in their line of work, they need certain things from this as a tool for them to adopt it. The Formlabs rollercoaster so far has proven, and I believe will continue to prove, that people want the ability to take a design on a computer and just turn it into an object, and then just do it again.

The key use case there is classic rapid prototyping and product design of use cases, but there's lots more—from architects to jewelry makers, to educators to a lot of other niches, more vertical areas, such as medical usage, and so on and so forth. To achieve that, we had to think about 3D printing from the point of view of 3D printing users.

In a way, the Form 1 is the first 3D printer that has been designed by users of 3D printing, not by makers and not by the engineers who invented the field. That is a fundamental difference and approach. That is what I believe puts Formlabs in a very different, unique position to become a serious force in this emerging market. We've just started, right? We're coming out of the gate with this product, and we still have a lot more work ahead of us.

Osborn: Tell me, from a technology standpoint, what makes the Form 1 different from the popular, more common ones using a filament-deposition method? I have an Afinia[4] printer in my garage printing some things for my Shapeoko[5] right now. What makes it different from that? What do you see as a key differentiator in the future?

Linder: So the Form 1 is a stereolithography machine. Stereolithography is a thirty-year-old technology or so, and it's been around. It's is the gold standard of 3D printing in terms of quality.

It's basically a laser that draws layers a pool of liquid plastic, a photopolymer resin. Wherever the light hits the resin, it solidifies. Then you repeat this process layer by layer. This way you're getting a solid object at the end of the process. And we've managed to do that using inexpensive laser components and control systems packaged in a very usable, appealing design that people find very slick, modern, aesthetic and most of all easy to use.

From our point of view, we tried to generate a tool. The Form 1 has an enclosure that allows you to see the object you're forming from every angle. That's not a coincidence. That's design. The Form 1 has a single button to operate it. It's not coincidence. It's design. Design is how it works. And the way it works is that it lowers the complexity that comes with 3D printing, because 3D printing is not as simple as printing, which you don't even think about right now when you hit Print on your computer.

Osborn: It's not today, but at some point, I could see my grandkids taking for granted that they just push a button and a new toy pops out.

Linder: I agree with you, absolutely. But again, remember I said that we are thinking about this technology differently. Part of that is how we think about the end-user experience. Nobody is doing well enough yet at what we call one-click print. You don't have that experience. So you have to set up a print, you have to generate the supports and make sure it makes sense, and then you print. Sometimes it works and sometimes it doesn't. This is even with very expensive machines that are mature products.

---

[4]www.afinia.com/
[5]www.shapeoko.com/

So we're trying to address that from a different perspective. We're also trying to address the postprocessing part of the 3D printing process. So we provide this finishing kit and work through the process. We try to celebrate it. Many people were making molds before the day and age of injection molding, right? They were artists and that's what they were making. And they had a whole set of tools for that. We're trying to celebrate postprocessing, in fact.

Of course, there are two additional aspects. One is software. Good software provides you with the interfaces to get what you need done. So you can think about our software as a very advanced print dialog. The other is the materials that allow you to generate the actual object and the properties of the materials used in printing. The combination of all these together is what makes Formlabs and the product, the Form I unique.

Osborn: Can you tell me a little bit about the 3D printing landscape and some of the interesting things you've seen people doing with 3D printers? What are people using these for now? What are some unusual examples of how people are using 3D printers?

Linder: So people have been using 3D printing from the point they were available to do product design and rapid prototyping. That's the key use case. You also see companies like Invisalign that have a whole process of creating a dental solution based on 3D printing. You see companies like Nervous Systems[6] that have jewelry lines. You see service bureaus like Shapeways making 3D printing available and different types of processes to basically print whatever.

Then there's the long tail. A lot of people have little uses for 3D printing, but there's this big bright future where people talk about 3D printing as a replacement for manufacturing. There are companies doing that as well, and those processes are still very expensive, but they're making commercial parts for airplanes with 3D printers. More and more car manufacturers are considering adding 3D printing to action-manufacturing processes.

While I personally think that's indeed going to happen in the future, I think we're still quite far from the high-end, from that experience where you have just machines, that are part of a manufacturing process. But at the other front, the home front or the personal front, I think 3D printing is going to potentially change how we consume things and how we design things for our own— customize them.

The IP of an object is not just what comes from the factory and what the manufacturer/designer decided that we should have, but it's people who are versed with the Internet that are capable of some design. Maybe they're not professional designers. Not everyone is a web designer today, but almost anyone can put together a web site. So we can see that happening.

---

[6]www.shapeways.com/shops/nervous

On the other hand, the difference is that not everyone wants to design physical things. That's also true, just like not everyone wants to build a web site. Even though the technology exists, if you really think about it, there are more people who don't design web sites than people who do. So it's really hard to say what would be the killer app of 3D printing—and I don't pretend to know. People ask us this a lot. Honestly, we think the more interesting thing is taking the existing use cases—and maybe that makes us different in the landscape—and making them available to designers and engineers everywhere.

Osborn: It seems like, as you said, designers and architects and have been using this technology forever.

Linder: But just a really small number. It's just starting to become affordable and widely available with products like the Form 1.

Osborn: For me as a hacker, what is interesting is that this technology's really available to me. Before, there was no way I was going to buy a $20,000 machine and I probably didn't even have access locally to one. I might be able to use Shapeways, but even Shapeways is expensive.

There's a project called OpenRC, where you can download basically a whole RC car. So if that's your hobby, you can build and design new RC cars and print new parts.

I've also seen a tile-based board game. A couple guys came up with the idea, but now there are half a dozen designers who have made their own tiles and their own figures and added to the game.

There's also a cool project that basically takes the Erector set, and LEGOs, and Tinkertoys and makes pieces that allow you to bridge those. It allows you to use Erector set with LEGO because it has some pieces that are made to connect with both. It is just guys like me, hacking in their spare time in their garage.

Linder: Those are what I call the "long tail," and I think we're people like that, so we're biased. I see these kinds of things in the lab every day, and I think they're great, but they're still a small number of people.

What I was trying to tell you before is that there are about thirty thousand 3D printers in the world right now and about ten million people who can use CAD professionally. So when you think about those numbers, you're saying, "Whoa. What if a million people who use CAD print?" That's pretty phenomenal when you think about it.

We're thinking of a professional tool, and you mentioned the price. I think you're right. That is part of being accessible to bigger audiences. This is discretionary spending, right? You don't need to explain to your boss why you're buying a new Mac. It's obvious—you just need it. But if 3D printing is $20,000 or $50,000 to get what you need, that's going to be a bunch of work just to get it through. So guess what? You're not getting a printer. And if you're getting a printer, it's probably going to end up sitting in a workshop. It's not going to be available to you. You need to go through someone who runs the machine for you. So you don't get to use it with your own hands.

I think although those amazing use cases you described would jump out as soon as you put it in their hands. I think there are just so many things that people will do. All those cool projects that you described, we see all of them. We see all kinds of people making all types of things. People even make sex toys with them.

Osborn: I think I saw a company that was doing that in a TechCrunch article or something recently.

Linder: But even great things like personalized hearing aids and shoes that fit you exactly because they scan your feet to make a sole that fits you perfectly.

Osborn: A lot of these things were multistep molding processes that needed a skilled worker, but now you can have anyone with a scanner and printer do it.

Linder: If you're in design or engineering, you know that everything around us came through a prototyping process. So, yeah, if we can democratize that, it would be terrific. We've just started.

Osborn: Tell me a bit about the Form 1 from the hacker's perspective.

Linder: I'm running the betas for the Form 1. There's a guy using it to do 3D markers. You know, think about a QR code. Think about the 3D version of the QR code on a physical object. Imagine an elephant model, and that elephant has also a 3D QR code embedded into it. When you scan it with a camera, you can get some information and that information can come from three dimensions when you're scanning the object, for example.

There was another guy who is building a new type of—think about the Sifteo Cubes, but he's only building it with a cube, literally a cube, six displays, six sides of a cube. So he needed a special rig, and he designed the charging base for it. He told me that for the stuff he needed, he had to wait like four months for Shapeways because they were so backlogged with work that they couldn't deliver earlier. And in a day, less than a day, I can print the whole batch of first parts for him right on my Form 1. I personally, in my work, used to create rather complex parts where you have air ducts that have intakes and flow out of air, so parts with complex geometry with some piping and stuff like that, things that lower-end machines simply cannot print. You have to go to better machines to get a part like that done. Or there are groups that do a lot of microfluidics.

Microfluidics is basically trying to do interesting stuff with fluids, so imagine how many pipes, and different nozzles and junctions, and all sorts of different little bits that you need, and you need to customize them. So people are printing their own little microfluidics solutions on their 3D printers. We even have an example of that in a video. So there are so many, so many different examples of what you can do with this.

Osborn: You launched the Form I on Kickstarter. It had a lot of success there. I know there are a lot of makers right now interested in Kickstarter. It is possible to test the feasibility of something, the commercial viability of something right out the gate, without having to ship it first and take a huge risk or liability up front.

I was wondering if you had any advice about Kickstarter or had any interesting experiences with them, or anything you could share?

Linder: As you know, our Kickstarter experience was pretty amazing. Above all, it was pretty humbling because what Kickstarter does—it is this amplifier for early adopters, for lack of a better description—and sorry it's a little bit clichéd, but it's true. It's people who care about what you do and they're willing to risk a lot of money for something that wasn't done before, but they're willing to do it because they want it to exist.

There's tremendous value getting exposure to these early adopters and having them become the base of the community of future users. My biggest recommendation is to be super-honest and open about what's good and what's bad with your community and take their feedback. You don't need to completely abide by them, but you need to be very open and work with them. If you do that, then amazing things happen.

We've had a tremendous experience. First of all, we didn't know that the response of the community was going to be so great. We had no idea. We thought we had something great, but it took this campaign to actually help us understand what we've actually created and it was great. We saw our own brand forming in front of our eyes, and we saw this amazing response that caused us to change plans because suddenly we had to gear up for a much greater production run. It's amazing. What can I say? I feel very lucky and humbled by that.

Osborn: So what stage are you guys at now? Are you working at manufacturing?

Linder: We getting ready to ship, as we published on our blog. It's going to happen very soon.

Osborn: So you had some experience with design-for-manufacturing prior to Kickstarter?

Linder: Yes.

Osborn: So you knew where the surprises were and how to get things through the pipe. I think a lot of people in the Kickstarter projects run into some issues because they have no design-for-manufacturing experience. Do you have some advice for somebody who's thinking about launching a Kickstarter project or has launched one, and has had some success on how to get a physical product out the door?

Linder: Well, the first advice is to start design-for-manufacturing very early. Understand the cost side but also focus on your critical path.

What's not going to scale if you're trying to move from a run of ten to runs of hundreds and thousands? Identify and define supply chains early and validate them. Work very hard on quality control components early on and make sure they're actually giving you what you believe it should be.

Osborn: Have you run into some speed bumps along the way through the manufacturing process?

Linder: Yeah, for sure. We specifically work with contract manufacturing, and we have a supply chain that comes from multiple sources, so there's a lot of cat herding there that needs to get done.

Osborn: Can you give me an example of something that went awry or was unexpected and you had to work out?

Linder: For example, we worked very hard to get our transparent case that has a very distinct shape, with a curvy, rounded, direct-angle design, and that is not trivial to do with this acrylic. We had to identify a bunch of suppliers and make sure that they had the right way to do it and that we could ship it. That it doesn't break in shipping and things like that. That's just to name one example.

To do this right in a product as complex as the Form 1, you need a multidisciplinary team that works very closely early on. So we all sit in one room, with no overhead on interfaces, and everybody knows what's going on. We are very lean and mean, as you can imagine. So that agility is in the DNA of Formlabs now, and hopefully we can preserve that in future products as well. But that, I think, is very typical, and not something that we invented at all. That's how—if you think about it—many of the great hardware products that you are familiar with came about.

Osborn: For somebody who is really interested in 3D printing and wants to get started maybe doing 3D design or CAD design, what do you recommend? How does somebody get started? What are some materials to read or some program that you should check out? Do you have any pointers for somebody who's interested in 3D design or 3D printing?

Linder: There are tons of different resources online for people who do 3D design and there's open-source software available. SketchUp is a good example and there are all sorts of programs like that that are pretty good. I think even AutoCAD by now has a bunch of free tools that are appealing to people who are just starting to learn more about CAD and things like that.

On the software side, you can spend so much time just doing tutorials and whatnot online. But on the printer side, there's lots and lots of 3D printing projects out there, and some of them are for the do-it-yourself type. People who just want to learn about the process of 3D printing. And if they just want to do that, then you can get a kit, an FDM[7]-type kit, for $300, and you build your own printer and learn about the process.

If people want a tool to produce parts that are of quality, then I think the Form I is a very interesting and not that expensive a machine to get because it's going to be available very soon. We're planning to launch it with a community web site and a bunch of tutorials. We plan to improve it and try to make 3D printing and the process of 3D printing accessible by providing resources to do that. That's my personal hope for the Form I.

As for taking it to the next level, look, it's like anything. If you spend time learning the tools of the trade, you will figure out even when the Form I capabilities are not enough for what you're trying to do. For example, in Shapeways, you can print in metals and stuff like that, but that's a very expensive process, so you may want to use Form I to try it out first. Do you know what I mean?

Osborn: So you can prototype it at home, hold the thing in your hand and make sure it's exactly what you want to spend $800 on.

Linder: That would be my personal hope and desire. That the Form I would be the best machine in its class to do so for you.

Osborn: Awesome. I'm excited to see you guys get this out the door. I've thought about the different 3D printing methods and I'm making some assumptions about the future of the 3D printing technology. I'd like to hear your opinion on some of my assumptions. It seems like the filament-extrusion thing will only get so fast and it's going to hit a wall.

You can only extrude this filament so fast, and it will never compare to the speed at which you're able to project light. I think by using a different chemistry, you'll be able to improve over time—to the point where it will be much faster and a higher resolution, where the machines that are using filament will never be able to compete.

With stereolithography, I assume the big factor is how fast the material cures under the light?

---

[7]Fused Deposition Method, an additive manufacturing method used in hobbyist 3D printers that utilize ABS or PLA filament.

Linder: So there are many different processes, and they all have pros and cons. I agree on your analysis of the FDM.

So just so you know, in full disclosure, I'm not a 3D printing process expert. It's not my key contribution. I'm a product guy who cares about user experience. I'm a software system person who brings that perspective. But my personal take is that stereolithography—and I agree with what you said—can have a very interesting range of materials going forward. And that space, as far as I can tell, is moving very quickly, and many new opportunities are emerging there as far as what new materials you can do that you couldn't do before. That said, there are other processes that are interesting as well. You can imagine how we can do something similar to what we have done with stereolithography in other processes. Specifically, what I mean is taking them down market and simplifying them to a point that they're affordable and accessible to everyday users. And that's very exciting to me. What exactly that process would be, it's a little bit too early for us to say. But there are many options.

Osborn: 3D printing is a really exciting space in general, it's exciting to see so much great innovation and competition in this space. I'm excited about what you guys are doing and suspect you'll do very well.

Ben Heck

Host
The Ben Heck Show

Benjamin Heckendorn is the host of The Ben Heck Show (revision3.com/tbhs), sponsored by element14.[1] Throughout his career, Ben has been a graphic artist, video editor, pinball machine designer, book author, console modder, and hardware hacker. Most famous for turning regular console gaming machines into portable versions of their former selves, Ben finds creative new ways to reinvent and repurpose hardware. In true maker fashion, he is also the only person I interviewed who paused on occasion to grind on the project he was working on.

Steven Osborn: What got you into console modding? Did you just wake up in the morning and say "I think I'm going to cut up an Xbox and stuff it into a laptop today."?

Ben Heck: I used to be a graphics artist many years ago, so I didn't come from an electronics background. That surprises lots of people. That was about thirteen years now. Time flies, even if you're not having fun, it flies.

Osborn: That's true.

Heck: I was just doing my normal work stuff as a designer, and I wanted a cool, fun project to make for myself. I could remember the old Atari video game console. That was a fun thing. I was a big fan of Atari. I had an Atari computer back in the day. It was my first computer. So I thought it would be cool to make a modern project that honors that old Atari stuff, you know, like a throwback to that era. So I dug up this old Atari videogame console, the 1980 version of the Atari 2600. I was like, "I know what I can do. I'll make this thing portable." That was my big plan.

At the time, there wasn't even a backlit Gameboy. This was like the year 2000. There wasn't nearly as much stuff as we have now. But I think I was at a movie and I was completely bored by it. I'm in the theater and I'm like, "I wish I had a Gameboy or something I could play, but it's dark. I wouldn't even be able to play it." So my train of thought was I should build my own portable gaming system. I was into electronics when I was a kid, back in the eighties, but I didn't keep up with it as a hobby. I got sidetracked with things like making my own independent films, which is a terrible hobby in comparison, but I wish I didn't know now what I didn't know then, as the song goes. So I decided to get some stuff together and get back into electronics as a hobby. I got a console and I started hacking it, seeing what I could do, adding screens and batteries.

Ten years ago, the maker scene was not even remotely like it is now. There weren't all of the resources we have today. You had to do a lot of stuff by hand or by scratch. The resources weren't as prevalent as they are now. But I managed to get something together, a working unit. As a graphics artist, I was able to make it look really cool because of my graphics art background, and my mechanical design and CNC experience, so I was able to make something that looked really neat. I call it the "Brittany Spears effect." You know, "Make it look good on the outside. It doesn't matter what it's like on the inside as long as it looks shiny and cool." So I made a portable Atari. And I'm like, "Cool, great, but who cares?" So I made a little Geocities web page. Remember them?

Osborn: Yeah. They finally took it down. And it made me a bit sad, to be honest, for sentimental reasons.

Heck: They finally pulled the plug, but it had a good run. But anyway, I had a Geocities web site for my Atari portable project, and then, before I knew it, Classic Gaming or Gamespy did a story about it. People were talking to me about this story they saw about my Atari, and I was like, "Oh, I did that." It just exploded from there. I was getting eighty e-mails a day asking about it. I just could not believe how much love there was for these old game consoles and how excited people were about seeing something new.

There were a few emulators back then, but we didn't have all the different consoles and portables we do now. There certainly were not cellphones you could play games on. If you were fortunate enough to have a mobile phone, it wasn't a smartphone because they didn't exist. It's a different world now. So I was surprised at how much people liked the idea.

So that motivated me to build more. I started buying and modding more consoles. I made a Nintendo and a Super Nintendo or two. I've modded almost every console that existed at the time. I did that for a couple of years.

Then in 2004, I was on TechTV, where I made this video. They had me on talking about what I did, but I also edited the video myself, which was cool. I'm like, "Yay, I get to edit a video. Finally, my video editing experience has a use!" So I made a video that was going on cable television. Then a publisher, Wiley Publishing, saw my video. The guy saw my video on TechTV and thought it was really well done. So he asked me to write a book about hacking game consoles.[2] So I started doing that and left my job at that time because writing a book took quite a bit of time, the editorial process, making sure you hit the milestones. Plus, I was building projects that were being featured in the book. I was designing these game consoles, writing them up, building them, and submitting them, so it wasn't the easiest thing to do.

After that, I figured I was done and would need to go work for "the man" again, but instead I just kept getting requests to build custom things. People kept asking for stuff. That was nine years ago. I'm still just doing prototypes. And then in 2010, I was approached about doing a show for element14, an electronics supply company, on Revision3 Internet television.

Then I started doing *The Ben Heck Show* for element14, where we build things on almost a weekly basis. I still build prototypes, although these days, I don't build things so much for individuals, but I do a lot of stuff for larger companies and game-industry stuff just because they pay better. That sounds horrible, but making portable things—I mean, that market's gone. With smartphones and the tablets, the portables market is dead, so it's good to make new stuff. My new hobby that I've turned into a job is designing and manufacturing pinball machines—that's my new job. The market is surging right now. That's my other silly endeavor, but I guess I've learned, you can take silly projects and turn them into money.

Osborn: So there is a resurgence in pinball machine sales?

Heck: Yes, quite the resurgence! We've gone from only one company left in the business to two large ones, and several boutique small run companies all over the globe.

Osborn: I could see every software start-up in San Francisco and the Silicon Valley wanting a Ben Heck pinball machine, so I think you've got some time to ride that wave. It sounds really cool. I haven't seen one of your pinball machines, but I'll have to check it out.

Heck: I have YouTube videos[3] on the one I'm designing. One of the boutique new companies is owned by a friend of mine, so I'm like, "Hey, Chuck. My game's almost done. Your game isn't yet. We should build this game to get some cash flow." So that's the plan. Actually, he's coming tomorrow. We're going to work

[2]*Hacking Video Game Consoles: Turn Your Old Video Game Systems into Awesome New Portables* (Wiley Publishing, 2005).
[3]www.youtube.com/watch?v=mQMZC-ZPjWo

on the bill of materials. So that's kind of where I'm at. The portable gaming stuff, that market's gone or Apple and Android have eaten it, so I'm interested in pinball, because I've always liked videogames, but I'm not a very good programmer. Pinball's a game that I can make. I can't make Contra, but I can make pinball machines.

Osborn: So when you edited or modded that first Atari, did you have any electrical engineering skills, or did you just figure it out as you went?

Heck: Mostly, I had to figure it out as I went. My knowledge at that point was very rudimentary. But I was lucky. I was able to build it without destroying much. Later, when I would make subsequent versions, I was very aggressive with what I was doing and I would ruin a lot more things. But I learned a lot more that way. A lot of it is just being careful and taking things apart carefully, putting them back together the right way because you're not engineering the system. You're just redesigning how one's put together. Since then, though, I've made much more complicated projects. I design my own circuit board systems now.

The advice I always like to give people: if you're interested in something, if there's a project you can do that you're interested in, it's a much better way to build something because you need to learn in order to make your project a reality. And that is a great impetus for learning. It makes you want to learn. I've learned a lot just based on my own drive.

Osborn: So your recommendation is just pick something that you want to build and start building it, and learn along the way.

Heck: Right. The fact that you want to build something will drive you to learn.

Osborn: Do you have all of your own CNC equipment or do you just design things and have someone else machine the parts?

Heck: In those first few years, I made less money than I did before, but eventually, that changed. So once I became more successful, I started buying my own equipment because that way I have control. That way someone else isn't in charge of getting the parts, although I still obviously need outside help. I don't have that much equipment. I try to buy one big thing a year, you know, like MakerBot. I don't know what I'll get this year. Did you see that Formlabs[4] thing? They got that thing Kickstarted. I think that's kind of cool.

Osborn: There are a lot of people right now that have projects they're making in their garage. There seems to be this kind of movement or at least buzz around personal manufacturing or short-run manufacturing.

---

[4]http://formlabs.com

Heck: The future of manufacturing or whatever, I just saw an article today about that.

Osborn: I was wondering what your thoughts are. Do so see things going in that direction? Do you think with 3D printing and technologies like it will become practical means for manufacture?

Heck: This is going to be the same book as you interviewed the MakerBot guys, right?

Osborn: Yeah, but you guys don't have to have the same opinion.

Heck: I'm sure we don't. I love 3D printing. I go to Maker Faires and a lot of the conventions. I guess for me that's my vacations. I saw 3D printers years ago. They pretty much just made little bottle openers and keychains, so they were cute and everything. But only about a year ago, I started using them more for my own prototyping, specifically the pinball machines, which is both my hobby and job. And I was like, "Oh my God, this is a killer app for me." 3D printing—physical things I can stick in a game and bash the hell out of—it's amazing. Yeah, it's slow, but you just do something else while it prints.

I have designed entire mechanisms and 3D-printed them for the pinball machines. So I think for prototyping, it's great. Obviously, the economies of scale have brought the price down very low. A couple of thousand dollars is pretty reasonable for a company or even individuals like myself. As far as your wife saying, "Oh, honey, we need an extra spoon," and you go push a button and it comes out like on *The Jetsons* or *Star Trek*, obviously, that's a long ways off, and in the grand scheme of things, I'm not sure if it's that practical. Most people aren't that creative. They don't want to design something. They just go off to Thingiverse,[5] find what they want and print it.

Osborn: I've done plenty of that. Just spend a whole day printing random stuff off Thingiverse. It's fun.

Heck: Oh yeah, definitely, but I like to think of it from the energy and time standpoint. A factory making shower rings can churn out ten of them in one shot using injection molding, versus using two hundred watts of power over three hours to print them using a 3D printer. Right now, 3D printing can't really replace it. And, yeah, sometime in the future, maybe we can say, "I'd like some Earl Grey tea. Hot," like they always say on *Star Trek*. I think that's a ways off. And the majority of people are still in this consumer mindset. They'd rather buy something than build it. I even tell people who e-mail me these crazy ideas and requests that if you can buy something, it's always going to be cheaper and faster than making it yourself. I know that's kind of a curmudgeon attitude, but I find myself giving that advice many, many times.

---

[5] www.thingiverse.com

I'm not convinced we have reached this whole revolution in printing power. I guess it doesn't pass my "Mom litmus test." Is my mom, who doesn't know anything about technology, going to use it? Probably not. There's a lot of people like that out there. My mom buys new SD cards when they get full. She doesn't even know how to copy to the computer that I bought her. So you've got to have a technological advance. Maybe after enough time passes and we have all these kids who have grown up with all this Einstein-like stuff they have access to these days. It's going to take a while.

Osborn: My two-year-old knows how to work the Netflix app on his iPad, no problem.

Heck: That's insane!

Osborn: He can't read, but he knows you have to press the red button, because the blue button just adds it to your queue. He knows he can smash these buttons, and move around, and find the show he wants.

Heck: That's a testament to the UI.

Osborn: And in the same vein, you give him a nine-piece puzzle and he'll get really frustrated with it, not because he doesn't know where the pieces go, but because he doesn't have the mechanical development or patience to rotate it in place and get it just right, so it doesn't fall into place. But he has an iPad game where the pieces kind of snap in place, and he can do a two hundred–piece puzzle with no problem.

Heck: That's interesting.

Osborn: So it's just kind of matching his mental capability and his physical capability.

Heck: I'm sure the researchers have done something, some research. They probably already know. Maybe the kids are hindered by their physical capabilities and their dexterity, more than their intelligence. That's exactly what you just described.

It's just like the newspaper today, as soon as everyone over fifty is dead, the newspaper is gone. It's the same kind of thing. The population changes over and we have all these whiz kids, maybe they'll be a 3D printer home culture then, but I think it's a ways off. The thing is, not everybody needs one. I always bring this up.

I saw a perfect comment on an Engadget article. It was about a new MakerBot or new 3D scanner and someone commented—because I love reading the comments. I know writers don't like to hear that, but I love reading the comments on articles. I think it's more interesting than the articles themselves. And someone said, "Why do I need a 3D printer?" And another person responded, "If you have to ask why you need one, then you don't need one." And that sums it up perfectly. It's not an insult. It's true.

Osborn: Well, I recently got a 3D printer and people ask me, "What are you going to do with it?" And I'm like, "I don't know, but I had to have one."

Heck: But it sounds like you do things with it. You download things, right?

Osborn: There is a project called OpenRC,[6] so I've been working on building an RC car out of 3D-printed parts, which is pretty cool.

I want to segue a little bit and have you tell me about your podcasts—what they are, and what you talk about on them?

Heck: I have web shows, not podcasts.

Osborn: Sorry. I'm dating myself, I guess.

Heck: I get that a lot. It's like the people who still call videogame controllers "paddles." I mean, it still happens.

Osborn: Do you call it a "vlog"?

Heck: What's a "vlog"? I've never heard of that. Is that like verilog? I'm confused.

Osborn: I've just heard people calling their video logs "vlogs," and it always makes me cringe.

Heck: Oh. I've never heard that, actually. But now I can't unhear it.

Osborn: I'm sorry.

Heck: [Grinding sounds and a short silence while Ben is working his project.] Man, construction of this controller is labyrinthian. I think Ouya spent more money developing their controller than their console. The tooling was definitely a lot more expensive to make the controller.

Anyway, so web shows, we have *The Ben Heck Show*, and we shoot that about two and a half days a week on Mondays and Tuesdays. Today we just shot two tutorials, and then we edit it, and I have an assistant that helps with it. And then it is edited and distributed by Revision3 out in San Francisco. It is sponsored by element14, which is an electronic community and web store for electronics. They're changing their name from Newark, probably so they don't sound like an airport. That's the main one that we do, and that's something I do as a job. I post videos, sloppy cellphone videos, to YouTube, basically of my own stuff. So that's pretty much it. I used to do a BenHeck.com podcast. I'd talk about stuff, but we haven't done that in years. One vlog is enough. We do a fifteen-minute web show every week.

Osborn: You can shoot sloppy cellphone videos as long as you do them in landscape.

---

[6]http://plus.google.com/s/openrc

Heck: Right. How much effort does it take to hold the phone sideways?

Osborn: That's a pet peeve of mine. There's a good public service announcement somebody did on vertical video syndrome.[7]

Heck: [Laughing.] I've seen photos on forums like that all the time. "Sorry about the orientation." Yeah, just don't hold the camera that way. I totally get it. I'd love to do a public service announcement about e-mail etiquette. I get these e-mails that are a Stephen King–novel in length, and people expect you to read them. It's like, "What the hell?" I always tell people, "Three lines: who you are, what you're doing, what you need. The end."

Osborn: If you are interested, then you'll ask them for the rest of it?

Heck: Yeah. If had one wish: that people learn that. Sorry. We got off topic there.

Osborn: That's all right. One thing I wanted to know about is one of the more challenging or unusual projects you have worked on. I know you have done a ton of different projects over the years, but what was the most challenging or interesting?

Heck: Well, another one of these e-mails I always get is all these kids want N64 to be portabalized. They're like, "I've got to do N64." I'm like, "Don't do it!" It has four different voltages. You can fry it by looking at it sideways. It takes confidence. Unless you know what you're doing, do not even touch it.

Osborn: That was a great console, though.

Heck: It is. I have nothing against the console. I'm just saying, when you start hacking it, it dies. It's like this turtle with a disease. It just falls over and dies. I made a project with an N64 years ago. I think I fried three consoles building it, which is really bad for me. I'm usually more careful than that. And everyone that works with it, too—people on my forums, are like, "Do not use it as a first project."

The first time I made an Xbox 360 laptop, it kicked my butt, but it was still easier than the N64. It kicked my butt, but it gave me a whole new legion of fans, and it got me into modern consoles stuff. So I started to get jobs like developers and promotional people, and doing controllers with monitors for videogame companies. So it was tough, but it opened up new avenues, which is another piece of advice I can give. No project is worthless. Even if you think an idea is silly, try it because someone might want it somewhere, and you never know what it might lead to. Put it on Geocities, you know?

Osborn: Do you get a lot of comments saying, "This is stupid. Why would anybody do this?"

---

[7] www.youtube.com/watch?v=Bt9zSfinwFA

Heck: On YouTube or something, you mean?

Osborn: Just in general. YouTube comments are worthless to the universe overall.

Heck: Alyson [Herreid], my video producer, used to have to go through the YouTube comments. They're the armpit of the Internet. YouTube is great, but the comments are another world. People don't realize a lot of the stuff I do is kind of boring. It's not necessarily on the web site. No, I don't usually get too much hate mail. I mean, I'm sure not everyone likes me. I don't care if they do. I think I'd rather get hate mail than the insane tsunami of stupid ideas I get sent.

So I like it when I get original ideas, even if it's a crazy idea. The one I always bring up is from joystick.com. Six years ago, one of the editors was like, "Hi, I want to play Uno on my Xbox while using my rowing exercise machine. Could you build me a rowing bar controller system?" I was like, "Yes! That's cool. I will build it."

So I love cool, crazy ideas, and I will build it, but nine times out of ten, it's the same thing over and over.

Osborn: You've done a lot of pretty wild things, things people wouldn't ever consider, and that's great. But I wonder if there are any projects that other people are working on that you think are interesting, or things you've seen other people build that are cool?

Heck: Gosh, there's tons of things. That Oculus Rift guy, Palmer Lucky, he used to be on my forums actually, so it's pretty cool to see him succeed. I'd love to try that thing. Have you tried it? Is the field of vision really awesome?

Osborn: I haven't, but I saw a video about it this week, and I was like, "Man, I have to touch one."

Heck: How much is it going to be? Is it going to be somewhat affordable maybe down the road?

Osborn: I thought it was a couple of hundred bucks, but I might be wrong.

Heck: I think it's more than that, but that would be awesome.

Osborn: I can't help but have Virtual Boy flashbacks. It's got to be better than that, right?

Heck: I worked at FuncoLand, which was a precursor to GameStop, when that thing came out. That thing was like atomic turd sandwich. I think it's kind of funny. I see all these young kids today, who all love Nintendo, and they don't realize Nintendo can do stupid things, too, like the Virtual Boy. I think it came out in August, and by Christmas it was on clearance for twenty-five bucks. Atomic bomb. It was kind of neat, and the controller was pretty innovative obviously. They used that design on future systems.

Osborn: The Power Glove was also an atomic piece of crap.

Heck: Well, that wasn't Nintendo. That was Mattel, but yes.

Osborn: Oh, Nintendo didn't make that?

Heck: No, I'm pretty sure that was Mattel. I think the Power Glove used acoustics to sense direction and position, so that's pretty cool. But it was still a turd.

Osborn: I did what every other kid did and saw a movie called *The Wizard*, and then it was like, "Oh, I have to have it." And it was just so bad. You flung your arm to the left, and that was a left jab. And then you flung your arm to the right, and that was a right jab or something like that.

Heck: But, you know, with this motion-controlled stuff and putting a sensor bar on your TV, back then, I was like, "This is bullshit." Then the Wii sells a hundred million units. I mean, it's still flailing-your-arms-around crap, but eventually, it works—hence my point. It was a good idea implemented poorly way ahead of its time.

Osborn: I remember seeing the Wii video for the first time with the new controller, when they were still calling it the Wii Revolution. I remember just thinking, "Oh man, Nintendo just gave up."

Heck: Yeah, yeah, everyone thought that.

Osborn: But it turned out to be this amazing experience. The picture of playing tennis in your living room just totally captured people's attention.

Heck: Nintendo decided to go for a different market and it worked wonders for them. I think it's going to backfire because that same market has moved on to tablets and smartphones, but the Wii had a good run, when it did. It was a disruptive technology, certainly. It was an atomic bomb of destructive technology.

By the same token, don't we all wish we could back to 1997 and buy as much Apple stock as we could get? Turn the time machine into gold. You never know. There's probably some company out there right now, like in ten years, they'll be atomic superstars, you know?

Osborn: I still claim Amazon is going to be the first trillion-dollar market-cap company.

Heck: Amazon? Really?

Osborn: Everything I buy is through them. It gets delivered to my door in two days. I run my business on their servers. It's like they own everything. One day I'll just get my paycheck in Amazon dollars.

Heck: Huh. Wait? They're not even close to a trillion. Even Apple. They probably won't get there soon.

Osborn: No. I'm talking about a long-time projection.

Heck: You're talking about more like in the distant Jetsons future kind of thing?

Osborn: Yeah, I'm talking about the same thing you're talking about in 1997, if we would have all bought Apple stock kind of thing.

Heck: Yeah, okay. Yeah, it could be. Well, who knows? Not Google or some other company, though? Amazon?

Osborn: Well, that's my prediction anyway.

Heck: Interesting. It's very bold. I bought like two things on Amazon today, so it's obviously awesome.

Osborn: Thanks, Ben, for taking the time to talk to me today. I'm sure you're dying to dremel something, so I'll let you go, but it's been a pleasure talking to you.

Heck: Oh, I love dremeling on things. No problem. Good luck.

Becky Stern

Director of Wearable Electronics
Adafruit Industries

When it comes to wearable technology, **Becky Stern** *is paving the way. Her work at Adafruit Industries (*`adafruit.com`*) melds wearables and fabric with the world of electronics. As the director of Wearable Electronics, Becky produces a lot of unique wearable projects, which she shares with the open hardware community. With the video and web content that she creates, Becky enables hackers and students to learn sewing and electronics in fun and innovative ways.*

Steven Osborn: Hey, Becky. What got you interested in making things?

Becky Stern: Well, I'm the director of wearable electronics at Adafruit Industries. I make tutorial projects incorporating electronics components into wearable things, like scarves and bags. I teach people how to make them with videos online. So it's kind of an amalgamation of a lot of different things that I like to make.

At a young age, I was making a lot of videos. I liked to edit videos and film things. I learned video editing at a pretty young age. At an even younger age, I learned to make crafts. My parents are both very crafty in various ways. My dad loves to cook, and my mom does knitting, quilting, embroidery, and all kinds of sewing. So I learned those things from them. I got my first sewing machine when I was thirteen. I filmed my parents framing an addition on our house, when I was five-and-a-half, with our giant VHS video camera. So I started those things very young.

Then in college, I got into electronics. I went to Parsons School of Design here in New York City and started hacking toys and making my own toys with simple electronics inside. For instance, I made a glowing plush nightlight. So I got really interested in playing with LEDs and basic programming. That's about the time that Arduino came out, when I was in college, and I started making fun Internet toys.

From there, I was always putting my projects online and sharing tutorials, because I liked to write. My father's a lifelong newspaper editor. So I would share all these tutorials about how to make these projects that I was doing for school. I was doing documentation on our class blogs and on Instructables. My projects kept getting posted on *Make* magazine's blog until I eventually got offered a job there writing for their blog and ultimately making videos about various DIY projects related to crafts or electronics, or things like that. That's how I got here, I guess. I've always been interested in fashion and making things by hand, and teaching other people how to do things in open source, and making weird electronics gadgets.

Osborn: So you made an interesting transition from crafts to electronics, which is pretty unique. Would you say your parents inspired you to go down this route or did you always have a natural curiosity for things?

Stern: They were always teaching me how to do things and had an interest in showing me the things that they were interested in doing and making. They just happened to be making a lot of things. They did encourage me and buy me all kinds of tools. A few Christmases in a row, I was on a big baking kick, and so I got a Kitchen Aid mixer and every cookie cutter there was. I was encouraged to make a lot of things. Then my dad always liked to use my gear. My mom gave me half of her knitting needle collection because she had three of every kind. And I got a sewing machine for my thirteenth birthday.

Osborn: So what got you interested in electronics?

Stern: I was in school and I wanted to try out whatever was going on. I liked exploring new things I hadn't tried before. I took a class at Parsons called Making Wireless Toys. It was by Professor Yury Gitman, a toy designer here in New York, an electronics toy designer.

We were given these interesting challenges like, for example, to make a plush nightlight or a simple switch. We figured out ways to do those things with very limited knowledge—basically just a circuit with an LED and a battery.

I like to make—reconstruct—3D objects, so making plush toys is a natural extension of that. I used to clone my Beanie Babies when I was a little kid. I would take the duck, and I would figure out what shape the fabric needed to be to make a new duck out of new fabric. So it was something new. It seemed fun and new.

We started out programming PIC[1] chips. It seemed hard. Before that, I had only coded web sites in HTML, and so being able to code physical actions and make sounds and lights happen based on sensors seemed really fun and exciting. There was a support group at Parsons—lots of students and teachers who were also interested in that kind of stuff and helping get new ideas. It was a really fertile, creative environment there. It was a good time.

Osborn: When you were getting started, can you think back to any interesting projects or things you saw other people doing that were interesting or that inspired you?

Stern: There were a lot of professors' projects that inspired me, like a giant plush pillow that has a beating heart inside it with a simulation of a beating heart with vibrating motors. It was a toy for relaxation. You can hug it like a pillow and it can start to affect your own heart rate. That's interesting because it's a commercial product, but it's a boutique commercial product.

Seeing my professors as entrepreneurs was really inspiring. It was before Kickstarter and all that stuff, so launching your own product and sourcing manufacturing and being actually able to ship things was really interesting to me. I felt that way about publishing. I liked to publish lots of things as often as possible just to get practice and feedback from community. I was really inspired by the people that I met on the Internet who were sharing, who were really interested in my projects.

That's how I got hooked up in the FAT lab, Free Art and Technology group that I'm a part of. It's a bunch of people who know each other from Parsons or maybe Eyebeam, which is an art and technology center here in New York that has residencies. So it was a natural extension of the Graffiti Research Lab, if you've ever heard of that, which explores open-source culture and open-source technology for interacting with the spaces around you. The FAT lab is this international group of twenty-five artists basically connected over an e-mail list who all have a similar sense of humor and publish projects on a collective web site that we might not be able to publish elsewhere.

I met a lot of my friends who are in FAT at school, so after we weren't together anymore, we still wanted a way to express ourselves, even outside of our professional careers, either as artists, or writers, or scientists, or graffiti writers. We had a place where we could kind of get our jollies in a specific way. We just had a really cool retrospective show at Eyebeam not too long ago, back in April. So that kind of started when I was in college, and I'm glad to still be working with those people today.

---

[1]www.microchip.com/pic/

Osborn: All of these groups you've mentioned are based out of New York. Is that right?

Stern: The FAT lab is all over. We have a lot of members in New York, and then some in California and all over Europe—Germany, Sweden.

Osborn: I just asked because there seems to be a very dense amount of maker culture in New York.

Stern: That's true.

Osborn: In the software world, the start-ups that come out of New York are more financial or enterprise, and not usually the grassroots-type start-ups. But in the hardware world, it's becoming a hub of innovation. It's not quite Shenzhen, but it's as close as I think you can be in the United States that is not Silicon Valley, where people seem to almost believe all technical innovation comes from.

Stern: Sure. There's lots of businesses we've seen come through and get funding, and have different business models. At Adafruit, we're buddies with a lot of them, and we all support each other and hang out. It is a really fun community to be a part of.

Osborn: I guess the question in all that is why do you think that is? How do you think that came to be? Is Parsons and FAT lab a big part of that?

Stern: I think it's because New York makes media. New York is a media town with a lot of advertising and TV and movies. So when we make hardware, whatever we choose to make, we are able to communicate effectively to a broad audience. The Internet really spreads messages fast. So I'm going to say it's because we're good at producing media. But really, it has started to have its own gravitational pull. Lots of makers are inspired by local New York businesses. There's a lot of entrepreneurial history in New York, not just in tech. Then we see more businesses popping up because they see that it's possible to get funding and to grow, and to make a lot of great stuff on Kickstarter, for example. The Internet is helping that happen too. They're here also, by the way.

Osborn: What's that?

Stern: Kickstarter is in New York too.

Osborn: Well, I guess I can't say all cool software start-ups are on the West Coast anymore.

Stern: Social software start-ups.

Osborn: It's an odd environment when you go to the Silicon Valley, and you're in a coffee shop and everybody's having a conversation about his or her company's valuation.

Stern: I know.

Osborn: It sounds like there's a private mailing list maybe for you and some friends who have kept in touch and do new maker things, but what if I'm just average Joe and I don't know anything about e-textiles or maybe I know just enough to know that I want to get started or build some project, but I'm stuck? How do I find somebody or some group or people to share my passion to learn?

Stern: There are lots of databases for getting in touch with local groups online. There's a hackerspaces list, a wiki, where everybody lists all their hackerspace info so you can find places near you and then join up with their lists. We publish a new wearables tutorial every single week at Adafruit, and that's a complete tutorial, step by step, and a video with all the tools, supplies, and techniques you need to build a project. Then we have forums where people who are building a project can post up if they're having trouble, what their particular symptoms are. Or they can post their finished projects.

I'm a bit of an inside type. I don't necessarily go out and join physical groups or go and craft with others. I was never a member of any knitting circles. So I really found a community online for the stuff I was making. And although I had a local community at Parsons at the time, that wasn't permanent. I was really connecting more with people on the Internet who were sharing my vision because I was at school with a diverse group of students who were focused on lots of different things, not just physical computing and putting LEDs in plush toys, so they didn't always get it. I liked to find people who did online.

I think if you know just enough to know that you're interested in getting started, you can look through the Adafruit Learning site at learn.adafruit.com. There are so many tutorials for not only the wearables projects that I write, but also Raspberry Pi projects and basic Arduino projects, and also really fun Halloween costumes at all skill levels. We pride ourselves on having the best documentation possible, with very clear photos.

We try to make mistakes for everybody first, and show how to avoid them so they can have a fun time making projects. Then they're confident to go build more. Then we provide a forum for people to show off their projects every week on Google+. So Google+ has these cool hangouts on air, where you and up to ten people can all join in on a video conversation online. We think it's a really great forum for a show-and-tell. So people show up and they show off their electronics projects, and we all talk about them. It's a really fun community to be a part of, and people can ask questions, and you feel like you have a community there online.

Osborn: Awesome. I've asked that question to a number of people, and Adafruit Learning System has come up more than once. I think you are doing some great things with that. It seems to be the most concise and well-thought-out collection of resources available. There are a lot of tutorials on the web that are like, "Here's some code that doesn't compile anymore and a schematic I drew on the back of a napkin. You should be able to figure it out."

Stern: We're not immune to those symptoms either, but we try to keep things updated.

Osborn: I guess my point is, for a lot of people who are really beginning, even if they find some resources online, they still end up overwhelmed. It's just kind of deflating. I think you guys do a great job of having not just low-level projects, where people can blink an LED, but then go and build some confidence, which is great.

Stern: Well, thank you for saying so.

Osborn: It wasn't just me, I promise you. So tell me about some of your favorite projects or a wacky project that you've built that maybe got some attention—or that you are just proud of.

Stern: Well, lately we've been doing some really great FLORA projects. FLORA is our Arduino-compatible wearables platform that you can easily sew into clothes and other things. It's round and flat, and has these big pads for connecting stainless steel thread, which we use to compose most of the circuits. So recently we made a skirt that lights up when you dance. It has an accelerometer in it. It senses movement, and when it detects movement above an adjustable threshold, it tells the LEDs that are in it to flash in whatever color.

We really like playing with and modding things that people already have or can find on a rack in their clothing store today to make these projects. So we take some skirts that have an overlay kind of thing. One was a sheer overlay on top of a solid-color skirt and another one was a laser-cut overlay over a slip, so this gave us a substrate on which to compose the circuit that was then diffused through a different type of fabric. With the laser-cut one, you can see the light coming out behind the cutout design.

It's really fun to play with aesthetics and technology in this way, and kind of ignite some kind of passion in people who might otherwise not have been drawn to electronics. So they might like the way it looks and want to wear that to prom, and so they decide to make their own light-up dress based on their interest from a different place. So that's the Sparkle Skirt. I think it's really cool. Teenagers like that one.

We hope we can draw in a wider audience of people to get interested in technology, because we want people to learn programming languages in school. And we want them to learn how to write the systems that control the world around us and control our ultimate technological destiny. And the younger we get them started, the better.

I'm proud of boosting our number of female viewers on YouTube for electronics projects. We did a color-changing scarf. One of the FLORA sensors is a color sensor, and you point it at a thing that's a color, like your blue jeans, or an apple, or your handbag, and then lights inside the scarf change to the color of the object. So you can match your scarf to any outfit, and it's diffused through some ruffled knitting. It's both crafts and electronics. Here you can use a reclaimed sweater to make this cool scarf and embed electronics in it and have it change color. So you're learning a little. For the electronics nerds who want to learn the electronics, we sneak a little crafting knowledge and craft/sewing instruction to them. And then to the crafters, we sneak in a little bit of technology to achieve a desired aesthetic effect.

Osborn: I remember seeing a tie with the LEDs.

Stern: Yeah, that's a really fun project. The tie is a volume meter. It has a microphone amplifier at the very topknot of a Velcro-on-breakaway tie, and then a line of our color-changing LED pixels, and then FLORA at the bottom controlling the lights. So when you speak or music plays, the lights light up like a volume meter. It's really fun.

Osborn: I thought it was really unique. Just last week I saw the Kraftwerk video. Apparently, I'm way behind the times—like over thirty years behind. So I was like, "Oh my gosh! They just copied Kraftwerk's video."

Stern: It was inspired by the Kraftwerk.

Osborn: I was like, "Aha! I found where they got it." I thought it was just so smart. Then I realized I was probably the only one that didn't notice it to begin with.

Stern: We're good at media, and that's probably why you saw our project, but there have been lots of DIY Kraftwerk ties that have big old circuit boards inside the back of the ties, and they just weren't as media-genic or easy to construct as ours. We stand on the shoulders of giants. Sometimes we'll see great projects and work with the maker to make it its best version of itself. We're inspired by *Tron*, too, in case you didn't notice. We added a little extra color too, for sure, but that is a Kraftwerk tie.

Osborn: I think I lost some geek points there. Most people probably recognize that out of the gate.

Stern: Or not. It's all right. Recently we did a *2001: Space Odyssey* project. A colleague of mine made this little HAL replica with one of our gigantic arcade buttons that looks like the HAL light and a little papercraft stand that looks like the console. And when you press it, it talks to you. It says sound samples. It speaks to you in kind of an insulting way. It says quotes from the movie. And so many people on YouTube don't get it because they're not old enough to know the movie.

Osborn: I don't really remember that one either, but I've seen it enough in pop culture. Just like I've watched just enough Monty Python to understand the jokes. Otherwise, I get left in the dark.

Stern: Well, we all have holes, right? I'm missing all of *Doctor Who*. I've never seen it at all, ever, but do you know how many *Doctor Who* scarves I have blogged? Probably a dozen. You just have to learn that stuff. Wikipedia.

Osborn: You've made a lot of cult projects. Can you think of some other projects people have made that just blew you away or inspired you to go make something else?

Stern: We have Wearable Wednesday on the blog. Oh man, someone just posted some wearable LED suspenders. That's my project for tomorrow. It's okay. They're different than mine.

Osborn: Is that like wearing the same dress to the prom?

Stern: Kind of. These kids are definitely going to prom too. That's so funny. We all contribute to the wearables category, right? It's not just me. LED suspenders—they look great. Okay, great, they're in. So my project may be a hit tomorrow. We made these suspenders that have a Pac-Man animation running around them. That's a sneak peek for tomorrow. I'm working on that. Tuesday is my video-editing day. I spend all day quietly in front of the computer.

Osborn: That's a cool project. What about other projects people have made?

Stern: A great project that I love, that really inspired me and I haven't made something like it, of course, but the thought just like blew me away was this engagement ring with induction coil and LEDs inside it, backlighting some stones in a CNC titanium ring. When his fiancé puts her hand near the inductor—there are several of them, placed in different strategic locations— the LEDs inside her engagement ring light up.

Osborn: Wow. Is that safe? That's amazing.

Stern: Yeah, it's really fine. It's just a little LED-style thing. The craftsmanship is amazing. He CNC-ed the ring and then went through lots of iterations, and then set the stones, really tiny, and put this tiny little induction coil circuit inside the band of the ring. It looks incredible. So I thought that was super touching. He wrote a big story about making this epic project for the love of his life—"project longhaul," he called it.

Osborn: That's pretty cool. I understand the induction and wireless charges, but it still freaks me out. Even though I understand it, it's still just magic.

Stern: People are making some really cool 3D fashion these days, printing large sections of garments and then attaching them to each other. Let's see. There are also expressive wearables that are more like costumes than functional garments.

Recently, I saw a hat that looked like it was full of light-up water. A Japanese woman made a cap with LEDs all over it. When she moves her head, the LEDs—it has an accelerometer or a gyroscope that senses the position of the head—make it look like it's filled up with a sloshing around fluid because it knows which way is up. It looks like a bubble level, but out of lights. It's a very attractive and creative use of technology that's really just for the visual effect alone. We're seeing lots of celebrities pick up couture wearables made just for them. U2 and OK Go had these video jackets that either say their logos or react to the show. It's really fun to be able to bridge the gap between these amazing things that are made in complete secrecy for celebrity clients for thousands and thousands of dollars to a project that you could make—to be able to think that you could make that same look at home with products and projects that you make by looking at Adafruit stuff. So we see a lot of customer projects that are like riffs on our own tutorials.

Osborn: I've lost count of how many *Iron Man* arc reactors I've seen.

Stern: Yeah. There are some cool GPS shoes. I've always wanted to do shoe projects, but I don't know how to actually make shoes and there are a lot of specialized tools and equipment. Somebody made these really cool shoes, worked with a shoemaker to put GPS and LEDs in the shoes while it was being made so you could run the traces under the sole, and that kind of thing. They have lights in the toes and are beautifully crafted. They are supposed to be inspired by *The Wizard of Oz*, so when you click your heels together three times, they show you which way is home.

Osborn: That's pretty awesome. I saw some 3D-printed shoes the other day, and I was like, "Oh, that's cool," and then I realized they were basically 3D-printed Crocs. I was like, "We can do better, people!"

Stern: I know, come on. But, no, these are beautiful wingtips.

Osborn: Out of college, you worked at *Make* for a while?

Stern: Well, I went to grad school first in Arizona. I dropped out of a PhD program, and I dropped out of an MFA program, and then I moved back to New York. During that time, I was working at *Make* freelance and I kept doing more and more stuff for them that, by the time I moved back to New York, I was working full-time for them remotely.

Osborn: So what drew you into Adafruit? Was it just that you wanted to be back in New York? Or that you wanted to work for them?

Stern: I wanted to work for them. So the creative director at Adafruit, Phil Torrone, is partners with Limor Fried. He was the senior editor at *Make* magazine for a long time. He is the one who offered me the job at *Make* in the first place and was my boss there for a while, for a long time, until he stepped down to only editor-at-large to go help Limor run Adafruit. So I stayed at

Make for a while, and I was their senior video producer. My specialty was wearable electronics.

Oftentimes, my project would use a lot of Adafruit gear and *Make* sells a lot of Adafruit gear in their e-commerce store, the Maker Shed. My job description didn't change a whole lot when I came over to Adafruit, believe it or not. I was still making tutorial projects about wearable electronics, but just in a more direct way. So really, I just did what I wanted to do. I knew they were developing FLORA and they brought me on as director of wearables to sort of spearhead projects that people would make with the FLORA, and to help work on it late in its development there.

Osborn: There seems to be a lot of interest lately—I think it's more buzzword—in the whole "Internet of Things." I was wondering if you've seen some projects that are interesting or that incorporated some wireless technology or biosensing that is interesting?

Stern: So my favorite biosensing Internet of Things project is the chair that tweets when you fart.

Osborn: Of course.

Stern: That's by my friend Randy Sarafan, who works at Instructables and is also a member of the FAT. He put the methane sensor in the chair and the Arduino in the XBee and the other part of the XBee that connects to the computer and used the Twitter API, and all that kind of stuff. Of course, there are other ones, old-school ones like the Botanicals, the plant that used to call you on the phone, but then ultimately turned out a tweet to let you know that it needed water.

Osborn: I remember something about the chair. I thought it would be really awful. And if you could deploy a whole stadium full, it would either be so embarrassing that you would have to leave immediately or it would become this sort of contest.

Stern: Come on. I don't think that one fart in the stadium—if it were being done with everyone, you're part of a collective of farts. You know, everybody farts. And you can't say that if there's a stadium full of people that it's not going to happen. So I think it would quickly become a contest. Are you kidding? There's beer and hot dogs involved. Thanks for the project idea.

Osborn: I guess that was my bigger fear—that something like that would happen.

Stern: I think they're going to do it just for that. If there's going to be another reason to put a methane sensor in a chair, make that be the fun side effect.

Osborn: Oh man, I don't want to take that any further.

Stern: You might have seen Internet of Things printers. We have one for Raspberry Pi and Arduino. Those are really fun, just little a receipt printer that prints out whatever you want—like the weather. It's really fun when it's just sitting on your desk and it finds a tweet about you and prints it out. So instead of having to check my tabs with all of my Twitter tools in it or whatever, it just sort of prints them all out. That can be fun.

Osborn: So let's see. There's the Internet of Things. There's 3D printing. You do a lot of work with wearable technologies. Is there any other vertical or category that you think is interesting or you've seen starting to take notice lately?

Stern: There is Arduino and Raspberry Pi stuff. The Raspberry Pi stuff, we know it sells very well, so we know a lot of people are interested in making projects with it and we offer lots of cool accessories to extend the Raspberry Pi. I think we're seeing a lot more single-board Linux computers, right? Beagle Bone just came out with a new version. Everybody wants to make this kind of stuff so people can do more, so that the Linux programmers can finally get into physical computing. It's no longer just the electronics and electrical engineers. You can really come at it from a programming standpoint and not much else. It makes them really powerful and cool—Internet-connected or just computationally complex projects with cameras, and USB devices, and Bluetooth, and all that stuff. I'm more of the basic electronics camp because I come from this entire other, sort of crafty side. And I do know a little bit of programming. I'm more into graphics programming, so big matrix displays. I never did a whole lot of Internet communication coding.

Osborn: I know you guys are a big proponent of open hardware. Do you use a standard license for your hardware, or is it just kind of whatever fits the project?

Stern: There are many parts of a hardware project. It's comprised of many layers. I'm sure you've heard that one before. And we do have some consistency across the things we release. For our board files—which are like an image if you know CAD files—are distributed under a creative commons attribution share license. We don't bar commercial use of producing our boards, but we do enforce our trademark. So if people want to print their own versions of the PCBs we make, they can. And they can sell them, but they can't have our logo on them.

Osborn: Is the schematic underneath the same license?

Stern: Whatever licenses we use, we use pretty consistent licenses. Like for code, we'll use one license, and for image things, we'll use another license. And usually, we allow people to redistribute our work commercially, provided they aren't infringing our trademark—because in a hacker space, they might want to etch their own boards. They want to be able to make their own boarduino or whatever with one of our products that we released the schematics and circuit board files for, so that they can learn from the process and have a fun time.

Osborn: The only reason I ask about the schematic is because I've heard different things about how the board file can be considered a work of art, whereas a schematic is considered a technical drawing. So maybe the same license doesn't really work well for both.

Stern: Right. That's why we release it as creative commons. We have a suite of licenses for all our different kinds of intellectual property. You know that fashion designs can't be copyrighted either, so that turns into an interesting part of my job.

Osborn: I didn't really think about that.

Stern: We like to release as much as we can and as openly as possible, and we try to use licenses that are appropriate for the media that we're distributing.

Osborn: Well, good stuff to keep in mind. It seems like the open hardware space is still pretty young and it will probably take some time to figure these things out. Adafruit is certainly doing their part to share with and build a community around hardware.

Eric Stackpole

Cofounder

OpenROV

Eric Stackpole has a passion for exploring unseen worlds. His mission is to make new discoveries using robots controlled from afar. Before finishing college, Eric was already building space satellites. Shortly after graduating, he was invited to work on satellite technology for NASA.

More recently, Eric's passion has moved him to discover new worlds here on Earth. Eric and a friend started a project called OpenROV[1] (openrov.com) to explore the depth of the oceans with a new type of robot that he designed as open hardware to share with the world.

Steven Osborn: So Eric, start by telling me a little bit about yourself and how you got started in engineering.

Eric Stackpole: I guess I've always been kind of a tinkerer. But many young boys, I think, are tinkerers. It would be hard to find someone who as a kid did not have LEGOs and played with them regularly. In fact, most of my friends I think played with LEGOs as their main occupation when they were not in school. I suppose, like many people, it would have to start around that time. I remember being maybe eight or nine, and starting to realize that I could build anything provided the right tools and the right parts.

When I was a kid, I wanted to be a pilot. I really thought that being able to fly in the air was cool. It wasn't until a Boy Scout camping trip that I first had

---

[1] An ROV is a remotely operated vehicle, particularly an underwater vehicle.

the first notion that, "Hey, maybe I could be an engineer." That occurred when I was on a Boy Scout camping trip way out in the middle of nowhere, miles and miles from any other civilization. We had set up camp on a big granite outcropping on a hill. There we lay in our little sleeping bags, looking up at the most brilliant night sky you could ever see. I remember looking up at the stars, and then someone noticed it, and we all started to see it.

There was what looked to be a star steadily moving across the night sky, among the stars, this little light that was just slowly moving across the night sky. Our scoutmaster described to us that what we were seeing was a satellite. That star was actually a manmade device that engineers had created, and it was orbiting around the earth. And as I learned more about satellites, I realized that that speck we were seeing above where we were, in the middle of nowhere—this was a representation of what mankind can build, and in forty-five minutes, it would be on the other side of the earth. That was just fascinating.

So eventually, it came time to pick a school and pick a major. And I decided to choose mechanical engineering at San Jose State, because when I took a tour of San Jose State, they had a satellite that they were building. There are all sorts of subtle details and stuff, but long story short, because of a political drama going on at the school, I wasn't able to work on that satellite, and so I just started my own club to build a small spacecraft. From there, I got an internship at NASA Ames. At NASA Ames, I built small satellites— small CubeSat satellites. They said that I ought to go to grad school.

Osborn: The CubeSat satellites? Was that part of a group you started, or was that part of NASA?

Stackpole: So I started this club at State to build satellites because I wasn't allowed to as a mechanical engineer. I would have had to be an aerospace engineer, which was frustrating.

CubeSats were just becoming popular at that point. They're these little Kleenex box–sized spacecraft. And so I formed a club called CubeSat Team SJSU. We started putting together this design for a little satellite that was going to be essentially a communication satellite. The premise was you'd be able to send a voice or digital message up to it, and then when it flies over a different part of the Earth, someone would retrieve that message—kind of an answering machine in space.

So I went to a conference with some people in my club, a CubeSat conference, and that's where I met these people from NASA. At the end of the conference, they ended up giving me a job offer. They said I could come intern at their Small Spacecraft Division at Ames Research Center. So I did that for a few years.

The biggest project I did at Ames was I designing and building a passive aero-dynamic de-orbiting mechanism. It was this little device that had two metal plates and some material between them. When the satellite was released from the launch vehicle, this thing would expand by spring power and increase the surface area of the satellite, which would change its ballistic coefficient so that its orbit would deteriorate faster than normal. And thus the satellite wouldn't become space debris and get in the way of future spacecraft.

So I guess I digressed a little bit, but that's what I was doing at Ames. And around the same time, the people at Ames were suggesting that I go to grad school. They suggested Santa Clara University because my group already had a relationship with that school. So I went there, starting to work on satellites, but the lab I was in, the Robotic Systems Lab, also had ROV submarines, and that seemed really cool. I remember always peering into the door and thinking that the people who were working on those devices really had a cool job.

I remember—you know, all these things have turning points. I had always been interested in engineering, but the moment that I saw that satellite during that Boy Scout camping trip when I was—I don't know—eleven or twelve, was when it became conscious in my mind that, "Hey, maybe I could be an engineer." And just like that, when I was at Santa Clara, I was using the bathroom one day. It was one of these public linoleum tile and tile bathrooms, and my shoes squeaked across the floor, kind of like how basketball players' shoes squeak on the court. It kind of makes this [whistle] sound. I don't know if you can hear my whistle. That reverberated off the walls, and it sounded a lot like one of those old-school submarine sonar pings, that kind of echoing.

So maybe this is too frank. But as I was sitting on the pot, I was kind of whistling that sound and hearing the echo. You know, the greatest influences on my life have always been things where it's not logical, where for whatever reason, it just kind of moves. You know those things that you have? There's no reason specifically that you're excited about it. It just seems cool.

What was going through my mind, what I was picturing as I made this whistling sound in the bathroom, was an ROV, maybe like the ones that I had seen at Santa Clara, with its lights on, descending through the deep abyss, as it just goes deeper and deeper into the dark unknown world. And it occurred to me at that point that all this work I had been doing for space exploration, which I was thought at the time I wanted to do for the rest of my life, all of that could be done without needing a government and a whole lot of money.

You know, the frustrating thing about space exploration is that you need a rocket to get there, and you can't do that as an individual. You can't rove around on the moon without a huge amount of resources and thousands of other people involved. But all you need to explore the deep is a shoreline and some curiosity. And it occurred to me that the underwater environment is just as mysterious.

While we're trying to find alien creatures from some really distant land in space, you know, these species that have never been seen before, that are participating in processes that have never been seen before in places that have never been seen before, are all happening right here and it's accessible.

So it was at that point that I decided to start—just as a hobby, as a way to procrastinate from my studies—to design a robotic submarine that could be manufactured very easily at a low cost. The general premise was that I had been hearing about these laser cutters where you can essentially just press Print and it will make something out of acrylic. It seemed to me that that would be the tool to use. If I could create something like an ROV that would be built with a laser cutter, then I could very rapidly iterate on the design. And in my engineering experiences thus far, I realized that being able to rapidly iterate is a really important way to develop things. So that essentially gets us to the beginning of what became OpenROV.

Osborn: I remember as a kid, maybe in first grade, I think we took the whole class to the library, and we sat and watched one on TV. I think it was called Jason.

Stackpole: Yes.

Osborn: It discovered the *Titanic* and they were doing a live exploration of it on TV. My school brought everybody into the library to watch basically live TV of people discovering the *Titanic*.

Stackpole: How did you feel when that happened? What was that like?

Osborn: It was almost like they had both discovered a new world and traveled back in time.

Stackpole: Our parents' generation, everybody remembers the moon landing. That was the big thing. What is there like that for us? There hasn't—I mean, what you've described is about as close as I could picture what a young child has seen.

Osborn: I remember that well.

Stackpole: Something that actually influenced OpenROV as well is MATE.[2] You know, when I was in high school, I took part in this thing called the MATE competition. I think it stands for Marine Advanced Technology Education. And we had to build an ROV to go accomplish a task.

Osborn: My dad is a scuba diver and I've talked to him about ROVs before, and he was just kind of like: "Why would you build that when you can just go down there." But an ROV can certainly go places humans can't, and stay underwater for much longer.

---

[2]Marine Advanced Technology Education (www.marinetech.org).

Stackpole: There are the four Ds of robotics: If it's dirty, dangerous, dull, or distant, it's better to send a robot to do it. I heard that somewhere.

Osborn: That's good.

Stackpole: But there's a big thing that people underappreciate. I think they don't really consider how much better a job you can do exploring a place if you're comfortable. A lot of people kind of have this view, "Oh, well, I'm strong enough." It's almost an ego thing, where they're like, "I can explore just as well, even if it's cold. It doesn't bother me." But, honestly, if you can sit in a nice, comfortable chair and sip a hot chocolate as you look at a large, wide-screen view of what you're looking at, the decisions you can make are going to be a lot better than if you're struggling with a leaking water valve in your dry suit or whatever other issues there may be.

Osborn: The last thing you want is your dry suit leaking.

Stackpole: No good.

Osborn: I know you guys launched on Kickstarter and did pretty well. I was wondering why the decision was to launch it there, what you got out of it, and what your experience was like. I think a lot of people are interested in building a project and using Kickstarter as a vehicle to get traction.

Stackpole: Maybe I can just describe everything that led up to Kickstarter, which might give a background of how we set up this situation and what led to it being a success.

Where I left off is wanting to build this ROV on my own. To abbreviate that chapter, I started doing that. I had a concept. I had done most of the drawing and design work in margins of papers that I was supposed to be taking notes on in classes. For some reason, listening to boring lectures was probably the single greatest thing that could have happened with me coming up with new design ideas. So I have pages and pages of sketches of an idea in margins, and then scratching that idea out and coming up with a new idea. Four or five iterations of a design in one classroom sitting. Eventually, they started to converge on an idea I liked.

Then I got a TechShop membership and built it with a laser cutter. I had been moving at that time. I was moving around between summer and school year. I was living at the house of a friend of mine from NASA. He had another friend, Josh Perfetto, who was working on this OpenPCR[3] machine, and he also ended up taking a sailing lesson from the guy who ended up being my cofounder, David Lang. Josh introduced me to David via e-mail after talking to David and saying that he knows this guy who's building ROV submarines.

---

[3] An open-source thermocycler.

You know there's that YouTube video of viral dancing, where there's one guy dancing ridiculously on a hill? Then a second dancer comes up and joins him, and then a third, and people start to notice? And by the time it hits four or five, it becomes a thing, and then the entire crowd starts dancing ridiculously.[4] A guy did a TED talk using that as an example once.

I was doing my own dance at the time, and I was having a great time, but it was my dance. What David did is he came to the scene, and he ended up being that second dancer. He said, "Look, we can make this a thing." I had already had the idea of maybe making this a business and making it something that anyone can build, and so on. But he said, "Look, let's make this bigger. Let's make a community around it." He was really interested in what Chris Anderson was doing with DIY Drones at the time. So he and I formed a web site. I came up with the idea of calling it OpenROV, basically as a combination of what we're trying to do and web site URLs that were available. At first, it was just me and him talking back and forth on the forums, but eventually we started getting more people. There's a big aspect of this, too.

Osborn: That's great. It's always good to have that validation and someone else to keep you focused.

Stackpole: So right after I had become interested in ROVs, I was asking around to see if people knew cool places to explore, because it's much easier to design around an objective than to design something completely open-ended. I had heard about this cave in Northern California called the Hall City Cave.

The story goes in a very brief way that there was a gold robbery in the very early 1800s. Native American guys robbed two settlers, trying to discourage them from moving in, and stole an estimated one hundred pounds of gold. A sheriff's posse was gathered to chase after them. They're on the run. The gold was weighing them down. They ditched it, the posse caught up with them anyway and said, "Tell us where you hid the gold and we'll spare your lives." They said they hid it in a cave called the Hall City Cave. Despite the posse's promise, both men were hanged on the spot. The posse goes to the cave, finds the cave, but doesn't find the gold. All they find in the back of the cave is a puddle. In the back of the puddle, as they report, a perfectly circular, six-foot-diameter hole that goes straight down into a water pit. Presuming the gold was thrown down there, with no technology to explore it at the time, they give up.

Fast-forward to the mid-1980s. A treasure hunter tries exploring the cave, doesn't make it to the bottom, and almost dies. Another report in the nineties of cave divers going in and not finding it. So I wanted to build this ROV to explore this underwater cave that happens to be close to where I grew up and my friend told me about.

---

[4] www.youtube.com/watch?v=hO8MwBZ1-Vc

Anyway, I told that story to David. We eventually met up at the Fisherman's Wharf Youth Hostel, which is where I was staying, and I told him the story. So we planned a trip to the Hall City Cave. A year later, after we had developed the design and changed the design through many iterations, we went to the cave with an ROV that hardly worked. We didn't even have live video feed from it yet. We went down and saw with our lights that several channels in the cave connected. We found the cave, first of all. That's a whole other story. It turns out that it actually does exist and just like in the story, there's a six-foot-diameter hole. And then we went a second time several months later, with a live video feed, even though it didn't work very well. It ended up landing us a story in *The New York Times*.

So that whole work-around thing that I just blobbed out to you, that's all to set up that we got this story in *The New York Times*. And, of course, once that happens, all these other press groups pick it up, and we had a large group of media centers that were giving us attention. And that was driving traffic to our site.

We weren't selling kits or anything like that yet, but we knew we'd want to at some point. David was the one who suggested doing that through Kickstarter. So we set up an e-mail list. We said, "If you're interested in being notified once we start selling kits, probably through Kickstarter, sign up here." And we ended up getting over a thousand people signing up, a thousand e-mail addresses of people who were interested. Also, around that time, we were presenting at Maker Faire and adding to the list there. So this is step one of what would end up being the Kickstarter project. We got a lot of people ahead of time who were interested in what we were doing and wanted to be a part of it.

More time goes by and we were developing the rollout. We were now rounding the corner where it seemed to be mostly working. NASA, as part of their Nemo 16 Aquanaut Training Program, then invited us to the Aquarius Undersea Lab in Florida. Basically, Aquarius is a lab that was run by NOAA.[5] It's an undersea base. It's about twenty meters, or sixty feet, under the ocean floor off of Key Largo, and aquanauts, as they're called, live there for ten days at a time. They invited us to fly the ROV there as part of this NASA Open Government Project. We got some great footage of the ROV driving around there, and we personally got some confidence in the ROV being capable of doing what we wanted it to. So after talking about it a lot and making some videos using footage from that and some other things, we created a Kickstarter video and decided it was time to launch. We launched Kickstarter, and the rest is history.

---

[5]National Oceanic and Atmospheric Administration.

Osborn: So when the Kickstarter happened, there was already a lot of interest in OpenROV. What made you guys decide to do this as open source?

Stackpole: There are several aspects that factored into it, and I can address that on different levels. One of the levels is ideological, which is, what good are you going to produce for the world? And by making something open source, everyone has access to it. I have a personal mantra and OpenROV is a tool to help fulfill that mantra, which is that I believe telerobotics holds huge potential as a tool for exploration. I feel like it's my duty to help the world realize that potential. And that specific thing has been a very important driving force. Even before OpenROV, I was building telerobots with the same intention: to popularize telerobotics for exploration. So by making it open source, I think I am able to affect more people.

Look at how Arduino works. There were plenty of microcontrollers before it, but because everybody has access to Arduino, suddenly they can create a much bigger thing.

The second perspective or way to tell that story, the open-source story, is from an engineering standpoint. Someone once said, "Everyone is smarter than anyone." And I appreciated you saying that you've been interviewing smart people and including me in that category. But really, I'm not. I'm passionate. That's I think my biggest asset. I really like what I'm doing. But if I want to make a robot that's going to be able to do really capable things, I need experts and I need their advice. And the best way to do that is to crowd-source the data.

Right now, if I'm struggling with some sort of an engineering decision and I'm losing sleep over it, using my phone I can go onto the OpenROV forums and describe the problem I'm having, and as I doze off to sleep, the problem's going around Europe. People in Europe are looking on the forums. And the people who are the highest paid in their fields got that way because they're passionate about what they're doing. They're the type of people who for fun would love to log on and solve these problems. So by the time I wake up, there may be two or three solutions to the very technically challenging problem I had. And as I'm having breakfast and lunch, it's going across the United States, and I might get another three or four ideas. Within twenty-four hours, I can have a handful of very valid, very good ways of solving a problem that if it were just me doing or if it were just a small team that I had hired, we wouldn't have been able to accomplish. You know, it's a lot of different perspectives from different people who have different histories and educations. So that's an engineering reason for doing it.

Then the third and last one is the business reason, which is, okay, what does it really mean to patent something? To make something closed source? It doesn't mean that someone can't use your idea. It means if someone else uses your idea, you can sue them. Well, first of all, there's not too much that's really patentable about OpenROV. For the most part, it's cleverly misusing already off-the-shelf parts. The second thing is that patenting stuff is really expensive. Generally, it costs on the order of $10,000 to patent one thing. I didn't have that money at the time. I still don't really have that money. And even if I did—this is the third part—would I actually want to sue someone who's using the idea I had? I mean, what we found out so far, and this has been a great thing, is that honestly, I think we're moving too fast to patent. The ideas we're creating are getting us to the next level, and then we move on to the next thing before that even has a chance to mature. The technology that we have right now, any of it that might plausibly be patentable, I imagine will be surpassed by the ideas that we have in another few months.

Osborn: Especially when it takes three-plus years to get a patent issued.

Stackpole: Exactly! I mean, two years from now, the ROV won't even look remotely like what it looks like now. And I don't think we're slowing down. In fact, I think we're speeding up at the rate that we're innovating.

Osborn: Can you talk about some missions you've been on with the ROV or some things you've found?

Stackpole: Sure. Well, before I was even working on OpenROV, or before it was called OpenROV, when it was something that was just a hobby, I had talked to my advisor in the Robotics Systems Lab and expressed my interest in doing robotics rather than spacecraft design. By showing that interest, he let me start to work on them and I went on a few expeditions with Robotics Systems Lab ROVs.

We went to Lake Tahoe, and I got to be the pilot for the ROV and the person in charge of that expedition. Our objective was that we were flying around Emerald Bay, which is in South Lake Tahoe, and we had a scientist with us, a geologist, and he was looking for certain geological features.

One thing that was striking to me was that within moments of hitting the bottom of the lake, we started seeing manmade objects. Every time. Within minutes, we started seeing sunglasses, and pocketknives, and things like that. It was amazing to me how much stuff is down there. It's just sitting on this big empty plane, just waiting to be picked up. It's like trash on the side of the freeway, but instead of being light, not valuable stuff, this is all stuff that's heavy and not retrievable, and often has a lot of value. Doing that was one of those things that just clicked. I could feel that this is something I could do the rest of my life. It was really cool to be exploring things in a different place, you know. Telerobotics exploration, which has been my mantra. It just reinforced that that's what I wanted to do.

Certainly that trip to the Nemo 16 and Aquarius in Florida was amazing. I didn't even get to go into the water. We didn't have live video for that. But driving the ROV around in these crystal-clear waters with all these crazy fish, even sharks and other creatures around, was an amazing experience.

Going to the Hall City Cave was really awesome in several aspects, for several reasons. One was that we were exploring something that I was genuinely curious about and that I had spent months and months researching and learning about, and then to be there in person and see all the things that I had heard about and things I had seen images of, and now all of a sudden see that thing. That was cool. The first mission we had there, like I mentioned before, we didn't have live video. We just had the lights on the ROV. From an earlier trip to the Cape, we had wanted to see if two underwater tubes connected to each other, and so we drove the ROV down what was a kind of perfectly circular, vertical shaft.

Our objective was to see if we could see the lights from the ROV coming through the other shaft. So that was the first time that we used OpenROV to discover something that we wouldn't have been able to find out otherwise. That was a really cool experience. And there have been a few other times when we've driven the ROV around, but honestly, it's only been the last few months that the ROV's actually been fully capable. It's been in development up until then.

I've also driven an ROV in Antarctica, as well as OpenROV in Antarctica. That was recently.

Osborn: So what was the reason for that trip? Was it just pure curiosity?

Stackpole: The first time I was at Maker Faire was with TechShop. They had invited me to show off what I had built at that point, which was completely different. Someone came up and said, "Hey, this is really cool. I have a robot that I'm going to take to Antarctica and drive under the ice. Are you interested?" At that point, I had just gotten into grad school, I was working at NASA, my loyalty was to my employer, and so I had to turn it down. I referred a friend, the friend went and then the next year couldn't go, and so he referred me, and that was just last year.

I was pilot and mechanical engineer for a ROV named SCINI.[6] SCINI is a tube-shaped robot. It's about a meter-and-a-half long by twenty centimeters in diameter. It's tube-shaped so it can go down bore holes in the ice. We were going out to the Ross Ice Shelf, or the Ross Sea, I guess. The ice sheet on top of the Ross Sea. We were drilling boreholes with a Jiffy drill and deploying this robot under the ice, towing an acoustic instrument. We were doing these transects back and forth with the ROV, with the objective of detecting various life forms, such as fish, krill, and other plankton to see what the food web is like under the ice. The idea is to see how it's affected when the icebreaker comes to deliver supplies to McMurdo Station, if the food web changes there. And how algae blooms affect the food web, and stuff like that.

---

[6]Submersible Capable of under Ice Navigation and Imaging.

I was down there between October and January of last year and this year, respectively. Piloting this ROV back and forth for three months. I also brought an OpenROV while I was there, and I only got to fly it once under the ice. But through a hole we drilled, I drove the OpenROV around, and that was a really cool experience.

Osborn: Tell me about some of the technical challenges you've had to overcome or maybe talk about some ongoing technical challenges that you're still working on.

Stackpole: Any maker will tell you that things don't ever work right the first time. The ongoing challenges with OpenROV are figuring out how something should work, how to get it to work right to start with. It's kind of hard to articulate. We often come up with how it theoretically should work. But actually implementing it and fixing all the little bugs that we didn't think of ahead of time—that's the real challenge.

Right now, what comes to mind as being our biggest breakthrough was communicating through the tether. We knew that we wanted our OpenROV to be fully digital, so the tether was relaying digital data rather than analog video. And also, through that same digital channel, we wanted to send commands down to the ROV to control it. It had taken us a long time to figure out how to do that through a long tether without losing the signal. Also, we wanted the tether to be very thin and small.

In my experiences with ROVs up to that point, the tether had always been the hardest point to manage. It's this big, cumbersome, thick thing. If you don't have flotation, it will sink the ROV. It will pull the ROV down. So you need to add flotation, which makes it really bulky, and then that makes the ROV not as agile. Instead, what we wanted was to have our power onboard the ROV so we could use a very thin wire going to it, and maybe just the tether that was only two conductors. That way it could get to be very thin and low cost. Recently, someone in our community found that a HomePlug adaptor, a device I had played with before, but didn't think was a practical solution. A HomePlug adaptor is something you plug into your wall and allows you to connect to Ethernet through your AC line. We hadn't used those before because it would be dangerous to send sixty-cycle, one hundred twenty–volt AC through water. But a person in our community happened to find one specific version of it that you can remove the power components and only use the communication bits. And that allowed us to talk more than one hundred megabytes through this thin, twisted-wire tether. So finding parts that are off-the-shelf to give us those capabilities has been the main challenge of developing OpenROV.

Osborn: Does this plug use a proprietary protocol, or are you going to be able to replicate that? Or are you just going to continue using a hacked version?

Stackpole: I think we're going to continue taking the actual, finished, off-the-shelf product apart and using what someone else has already developed. HomePlug adaptors use IEEE standards, an IEEE protocol called IEEE1901, which is a closed protocol, but we can still use the system as a black-box solution.

Osborn: I'm really interested in electrical engineering. It's not really my background, but understanding the systems is interesting. I have a tendency just to take things apart and try to figure out how they work, so I kind of want to go get one of those now.

Stackpole: It's on our forum. You can find out how to do it.

Osborn: What are your next steps as far as the project, and even next steps for exploration?

Stackpole: That's a really good question. I'm really glad you asked that, because I think that's a good way of summing up what we're all about. The next step for us right now is creating a platform where anyone can explore, whether or not they have physical access to an ROV. What I'm talking about is Internet control.

Throughout high school and college, I know more people who dropped out because of video games, *World of Warcraft*, than sex, drugs, and rock and roll combined. They were spending hours and hours a day flipping bits, and it was just wasted time. I'd love to make a platform so that instead, those people could flip rocks. That the things they were spending all this time doing could be done in real life. I see OpenROV not just as a platform for seeing what's in the water that's right next to you, but as a broad exploration tool. The time and interest resources that are being committed to video games to me seem to be this extremely untapped resource that could be used for a better purpose. If we can democratize ocean exploration, so instead of it just being one specific place explored as a result of one specific research grant, if we can have random acts of curiosity in many places across the world, I think that there's a lot of good that can come from that. So technologically what we're developing right now is a way for people to control ROVs all around the world through the Internet. And I think that has profound potential that is not yet appreciated by the world.

Osborn: What are the places that you really want to see?

Stackpole: There are a few places that I think are really interesting that I've read about, but I think for me, seeing something that's never been seen by mankind is at the heart of what drives me personally. I'd love ROVs to be able to explore the deep ocean telerobotically. I'd really like to learn most about the things that we've never seen before. In other words, I don't want to know about a specific thing. I don't have specific questions. I don't think you need questions necessarily to get answers. I want to look in places that have never been seen before, and see what comes up.

Osborn: What is the deepest you've had the ROV at this point? I guess it's probably the length of the tether, but I'm not sure what that is.

Stackpole: No, actually, these HomePlug adaptors, which we're now using, are capable of talking over a distance of about three hundred meters, which is three times the maximum depth of the ROV. The depth that we're limited to now, one hundred meters, is that way because of a failure mode of the main pressure vessel in the ROV. There are actually two failure modes that happen at around the same pressure. One is that the end caps push into the main tube. The kind of lip [or flange] that holds them in place fails. And then right after that is the buckling mode in the main tube, which means the tube would just implode. So that's our depth limit right now. However, one hundred meters, I think, is still quite a good thing to be able to achieve. It's deeper than most scuba divers can go. It's most of the Continental Shelf. It's dark. You see species you wouldn't normally see, so one hundred meters to me is a very good starting point, but certainly not the end.

Osborn: A lot of people would not have expected you to accomplish what you have with off-the-shelf parts. With the cost of electronics declining, I could see this becoming more and more accessible and affordable.

Stackpole: There's three focuses of what we're trying to do with OpenROV. In kind of a corny way, call them AA, DD, and II. AA is "accessible adventure." That means that you can have an adventure very easily, like your Internet control, by just logging into your computer. DD is "daily discoveries," which is like instead of it being one expedition that happens once a year and returns awesome results, it will be like when YouTube first came out and all this crazy phenomena happening around the world was coming up everywhere. I want there to be so many ROVs that almost on a daily basis, you can see something that's never been seen before. And the last one, II, is "intense innovation." In the same way that daily discoveries can happen, thousands or tens of thousands of people around the world contributing and being a part of this.

I think the rate of innovation we can achieve is going to be tremendous, where on a daily or weekly basis, new ideas are being tested that revolutionize how underwater exploration is done and what maybe exploration in a broader sense is.

Osborn: Awesome. Well, I definitely learned a lot. Thank you for your time.

Eben Upton

Founder
Raspberry Pi Foundation

Eben Upton holds a PhD in computer science from the University of Cambridge. In 2006, while working for Broadcom and teaching at Cambridge, Eben noticed a sharp decline in qualified engineering candidates. This insight was the driving force for a project he started to work on at night and on weekends. Eben has a vision to provide the world with a $25 hackable Linux computer that enables students to learn computer programming and engineering in their bedroom. This effort later became the Raspberry Pi Foundation (`raspberrypi.org`), which is already making an impact on education in computer science and serving as a tremendous catalyst in the hacker community, as well as in the maker economy, where the Raspberry Pi has been well received.

Steven Osborn: Hey Eben, tell me a little bit about yourself before we get too much into the Raspberry Pi. Just your background and what you were doing before you started the foundation.

Eben Upton: Let's see. I did a PhD at the University of Cambridge. I was a compiler researcher, so I was working on research for optimizing compiler technology for C-like languages. I was also working as a director of studies, which is a junior teaching role that involves organizing undergraduate teaching and also arranging interviews and doing interviews with high school kids who wanted to come to Cambridge. I finished my PhD eventually, probably after longer than I should have taken.

Then I spent a little bit of time working on motor controllers, the kind of motor controls that go into Robot Wars robots. I spent about six months working on that and, really, I haven't an electrical engineering background. I have sort of a computer science engineering background. I'd never really done a lot of electronics. So I found myself building really interesting mixed signal analog and digital PCBs.[1] One can go bang if you screw them up, because you have one hundred fifty–amp motor controllers with big TO-220 MOSFETs.[2] And you kind of bolt them down onto these aluminum baseplates and stuff. It's quite common. For somebody like me who has come from a software background, it's kind of cool to get involved in building these kinds of things. If you screw up software, for example, you get a crash. No big deal. If you screw up these things, you get a big bang.

It was kind of fun. I kind of conquered my fear of electronics, too. It's easy to get stuck in software world. We were using AVR Atmel microcontrollers. I think those chips are a great bridge—for someone like me who was a software guy—into the hardware world, because they turned a lot of hardware problems into software problems. They let you do this very rapid development. You can choose the behavior you want to circuit without doing any soldering, which is kind of cool. So I did that for a little bit.

Osborn: So you were building those for Robot Wars, did you say?

Upton: I was building them for a company called 4QD, based near where I live in Cambridge now. Their market is wheelchairs and golf buggies. Robot Wars was a big thing in the UK. It's less of a big thing now, but it was a big thing that was a big part of their market because they were able to sell these very robust controllers to the Robot Wars community. And so they did a lot of that stuff. I did that for about for six months because I was getting kind of burnt out for my PhD. I did a lot of software and thought I would do something else.

Then I eventually joined Broadcom. All this while, I was still working at the university, still teaching. I joined Broadcom in 2006. I was originally an integrated software engineer, but I moved very gradually across into doing more and more hardware-type work, this time ASIC-level work, designing chips, rather than the electronics, soldering all of it together, designing the guts on chips, which then get fabricated. So I wasn't that far removed, really. I started doing more and more of that, and all the while, I was still teaching at the university as well.

While I was doing all of that I found that we have this problem of having fewer and fewer people applying to study computer science. At the same time, in my experiences at Broadcom, I was starting to see these chips that we thought we could use to build some sort of computer that we could give to kids, to give them a chance to learn to program. That was it, really. I've been at Broadcom ever since. And then I did the Raspberry Pi Foundation. I stopped doing university stuff in 2008 and then at the same time started the Raspberry Pi stuff

---

[1] Printed circuit boards.
[2] A transistor that amplifies signals.

as my nights and weekends project. I started Raspberry Pi in the evenings and weekends in about 2008, and then kept just plugging away at it for about three or four years until we got a prototype that we could bring to market.

Osborn: So the Raspberry Pi was started as a way to build a teaching tool for children?

Upton: Yeah. It was supposed to be your TRS-80, right? It was supposed to be your Commodore 64, the machine you have in your bedroom to hack on every night.

Osborn: What made you decide to solve that problem instead of pursuing something else?

Upton: Well, I guess I've always had this penchant. That I'll do something for charity, so I can't get any money out of it. The UK is screwed as a country, right? The developed world is screwed if it doesn't keep generating more engineers. It's a national emergency. Cambridge would traditionally be able to rely on there just always being this stream of bright kids who had been training themselves in computing since they were eight. So we probably saw it more than anyone else. We saw this very early on, that as the supply of kids like me, who grew up hacking on computers, went away. We at the university were some of the first people to see there was a problem because our applicant numbers went off the cliff, and the sorts of things our applicants knew how to do well went with it. They're still bright kids. They just haven't spent ten years learning to hack before they came in the door. So you see, I'm motivated because it's a problem. It's a really, really, really desperately serious problem for the university. I believe it's a really desperately problem for society, for our countries. Plus it is nearby, and I have the tools to tackle it. So, yeah, I'm sure there are other problems, but this is the nearest to me.

Osborn: Fair enough. It sounds interesting. There's definitely a shortage of engineers. I certainly see it in my work, but sometimes I appreciate it, too, because it means that I'm really overvalued.

Upton: There is always that. I sort of look at my paycheck, and I think, "Wow, I'm being pretty well paid for this. Do I really want to create more engineers?"

The problem is that there's a critical mass. A tipping point. I mean, we already see it in the UK. We used to have engineering everywhere, all over the country, and increasingly as the engineering, especially the electrical engineering retreats, the skills base contracts. Previously, there were people doing electrical engineering everywhere. Increasingly, the stuff is retreating back into the Cambridge area, the London area, the Bristol area, sort of west of England— retreats into these little clusters because that's the only place you can sustain the density of engineers, the density of engineering firms required to make it economically viable. On some level, I saw engineers, individual engineers, get a bit of negotiating power when negotiating for jobs, and I've certainly exploited that in the past. Below a certain point, the industry just collapses. And then there's no work for engineers.

Osborn: So, can you tell me where the name Raspberry Pi came from?

Upton: We just wanted some kind of fruit in the name for nostalgia. Computing has a history of great devices named after fruit like the Blackberry or Apple. And Pi just comes from Python.

Osborn: One of the things that created a lot of buzz for the Raspberry Pi was the promise of a twenty-five-dollar Linux computer, which was just unheard of at the time, still unmatched today really, to have something with that kind of computing power and capability at that price. I was wondering how did you guys even arrive at that price initially, and what was driving that?

Upton: So we had the price before we had anything else. I think we had the price in 2006. The whole original idea was that it had to cost as much as a textbook, a schoolbook. That's the big motivation. Often, many schoolbooks are more expensive than that, but the idea was, if we're going to build for kids, if we're going to ask them to buy a kit, it couldn't be $100. It's unrealistic to ask every child to buy a one hundred–dollar computer. So it was just this design. We looked around at what you can ask kids to buy. So you can ask kids to buy a textbook, and most kids can afford it, and the ones who can't afford it, there aren't many of them, so you can afford to help them, and the amount of money is fairly small, so you can afford to subsidize. So that's originally where it came from.

And we had that before we had hardware. I was hacking our hardware for this in 2006. It was based on Atmel stuff. It was actually quite Arduino-like. So we had the price before we had anything else, we kind of designed the platform to the price, rather than designing the platform and then pricing it.

Osborn: You just had the vision and did whatever you had to do to get where your vision was?

Upton: Yeah. And, of course, even after we launched—we launched the thirty-five-dollar one. We launched the Model B first. It was a year and a half later that we launched the Model A, the twenty-five-dollar one. And I think the thirty-five-dollar one is actually the one that most people want because they want networking and the extra USB. The vision for the thirty-five-dollar one was that we kept pitching a twenty-five-dollar computer, but people kept coming to us and saying, "Look, the first thing we're going to do with this twenty-five-dollar computer that has one USB port and no network, is we're going to stick a hub on it and then a network adapter." Well, you know, if that's what everyone is going to do, then why don't we try and build one that has the hub and the network adapter integrated into the device? That's really where the $35 came from because it would cost twenty bucks to add those features to a twenty-five-dollar computer, so if we did it for an extra ten bucks, everyone wins.

Osborn: It's gotten incredible uptake. The hobbyist community freaked out. I think I might have three of them by now. I'm not even sure. I think I have every revision.

Upton: Well, thank you.

Osborn: This week, or maybe it was last week, I saw a 3D printer on Kickstarter at a three hundred and fifty–dollar price point, and the guts of it are Sanguino[3] and a Raspberry Pi. I think it has a five-dollar Wi-Fi dongle for wireless networking.

So people are using Raspberry Pi to build products and DIY media centers. I'm wondering if there are any really interesting use cases that people are using the Raspberry Pi for now, which you hadn't considered when launching this project.

Upton: Well, I think the really exciting use cases right this second are going to be camera use cases. We've got a camera out now, and that really adds a whole new dimension to it. So I think one of the ones I saw that's been going around last week is the ZSL, which is the Zoological Society of London. They're part of the London Zoo and they've got a wildlife camera project going on. They've got several components. One of them is they're going to give these cameras to kids. So all kinds of kids can build a wildlife camera to put in their garden or on their windowsill to take a picture of the garden at night.

One really cool thing is that they're going take these and put them in Africa. They're going to hook them to Iridium satellite phones. That's what they do. They put them in the field in Africa, with solar-powered batteries and the Iridium phone. They take the infrared filter off the cameras, for a sort of night vision. And they use it to keep track of animals. And they use it to look for poachers. I think the things are going to have microphones, so they can hear gunshots. If you've got multiples of these nearby, then you can look at the time that the gunshot sound arrives and triangulate the location of the gunshot. So you can send rangers with high accuracy to the field to find and try and track down poachers in the middle of the night. I think that sort of thing is really cool. It's just using the Raspberry Pi as this piece of LEGO.

I always thought of using it just as a computer, as just a natural computing device. I'm a software engineer. My natural idea is just to write software on it. So we'll use it as a computer, just as naturally as you say, people are using it like a piece of LEGO to build all this hardware.

Osborn: When it becomes the cheapest and most capable device you can buy, it's just natural that you want to screw stuff on it, and solder things to it, and use it for a building block.

---

[3]http://sanguino.cc

Upton: And the multimedia stuff is already a really good one. The multimedia capabilities of the device are things like the media center. This is a device that started off as a Broadcom graphics chip. It is not actually a general-purpose processor at all. It's a graphics chip with a general-purpose processor bolted on the side. So it's got this kind of outsized amount of graphics performance, a PS2 level of 3D performance. It can play 1080p and high-definition video. So I think that's the closest use case we've got to my original conception of people using it as a software media platform. It's this XBMC[4] thing that a lot of people do.

Osborn: So have you got a lot of Raspberry Pis out to schools and universities? How is this working as far as the original vision? What are schools and kids doing with them?

Upton: I think it's the early days. What we're doing this school year is a fairly slow but steady deployment in schools led by pioneer schools. There's always a school that has a teacher that is particularly keen on teaching programming. So we're seeing those kinds of pathfinder schools doing really good work and getting through some of the lessons that we need to learn in order to make this effective in the classroom. We have to remember this isn't really about the classroom. This is about bedrooms. This is not supposed to be the classroom computer, because the schools already have computers. This is supposed to be the bedroom computer.

We're starting to see parents who are doing stuff with their kids along with technically enthusiastic teachers doing stuff with their students. We're starting to see a bit of it. I think what's going to happen this coming academic year and the academic year after that is we're going to see much more formal use of it in universities. I know a number of universities who have already incorporated it into their EE and CS classrooms just because it's a very cheap and standardized platform. We're going to start to see it in pathfinder schools more. Then the next academic year, the 2014 academic year, the government in the UK is revising their curriculum. It's got a new curriculum for computer science that has less emphasis on PowerPoint and Excel, and much more emphasis on computer programming.

Osborn: I wish I had something like this available when I was learning programming. I got my first PC when I was sixteen because the price tag back then was like two grand. My family just couldn't afford that type of expense, but I had a lot of interest in programming.

Upton: When I was a kid, I had to use old computers that I bought myself. I used to save up and buy machines. I had a BBC Micro and I had a Commodore Amiga. Each of those cost me about three hundred bucks, so about two

---

[4]XBMC is a free and open-source software media player.

hundred pounds. They plugged into an old TV, and those were just amazing and yet so wimpy and not powerful.

I remember we got our first lot of Raspberry Pis in March of last year. We had two thousand shipped to us from China. And they came on a little pallet, because a Pi is a little thing. The guy comes out of the back of a little DHL van and with a pallet jack, and jacks this little half-pallet of Pis into the garage. There were two thousand computers, and each of those computers was a hundred times more powerful than the one that I used to love as a kid. The computer was one of my most treasured possessions as a kid. These things were a hundred times as powerful as that. That was kind of a funny moment. And then we unpacked them. We unpacked a few of them out of the box. They all worked. It was quite something.

Osborn: You guys have done some great work, and the community has definitely taken hold of it. It sounds like everything's going great, but I wonder what kind of challenges you've had along the way, either technical challenges or challenges with manufacturing. Can you give us examples of things that didn't go quite as planned along the way?

Upton: We had a few. I mean, obviously, getting it down to cost was a huge challenge. Getting the billable materials down to cost was hard. And Pete Lomas, who's my colleague, did most of the hardware design. I think he struggled to get the cost of the device down. And then finding cheap manufacturing was a struggle. We took this around to ten different UK contract manufacturers, whom I presume are kicking themselves now, and they all just gave us these ridiculous quotes, like ten pounds, fifteen bucks, to manufacture the thing. It was just completely uneconomical—just crazy money. Kind of like they would give us a quote to just wish we'd go away, I think.

We were very lucky because we had a guy at Broadcom, a Broadcom employee in Taiwan who heard about the project. He said, "Look, let me try to find you a Chinese contract manufacturer." He found me this company who makes MP3 players for Wal-Mart. That's their main business. That was their main business before Pi. They gave us a quote, and it was a good quote. We had been struggling so hard to get the cost down to $35, where we wouldn't lose money, and they came in under $35, so we could actually make some profit selling these things.

They're based in Shenzhen, mainland China. We had to send them chips and we had to send them money. We wired them the money, and it was probably—gosh, it was probably $25,000 or something exorbitant to their bank account. And then we had to send them the chips for the Pis. But you can't send chips to mainland China because there's an import duty, so the way you get chips into China is to use a shipment point in Hong Kong. You take them across the border from Hong Kong into Shenzhen. That's a special transaction, because Shenzhen is still a special economic zone. And so we had to send these chips,

$25,000 worth of chips, to these guys at their trans-shipment point. And their trans-shipment point was an apartment. It was an apartment building. We sent $25,000 worth of chips to these guys at their apartment. I was kind of like, "Ehhh, $25,000 just blown away," you know?

And then there were delays, which made us worried that things had gone wrong. As usual, the guys in the manufacturing business gave us a slightly optimistic quote in terms of time scale. It was supposed to take three weeks. It took eight weeks. But like I said, it was a pallet of perfectly working Pi, so that was kind of cool. So that was a bit of a challenge.

Another challenge, I guess, was just from the point of managing the explosive growth. We thought we were going to build ten thousand of these things, so you can imagine managing what happens when that turns into a billion. Needless to say, we were very lucky we had these partners. We don't make Pis. We license the design to our partners. They make them. So we were lucky. That was a place where we would have been screwed if we tried doing this ourselves. But we have great partners, and our partners really helped us out. They helped us out so much, of course, that we were able to move the manufacturing back to the West. We moved most of the manufacturing back to the UK, where Sony builds it all on contract. Sony, who I didn't even know did contract work. We were so pleased with the Chinese guys that we actually gave them a license to build their own Pis. So they're now building these Red Pis for the China market, which is a nice little business.

Osborn: Cool. I've seen the Red Pis. I didn't know if those were a legitimate license or not, but it's good to know they are.

Upton: They're only sold in China to Hong Kong/Macau. They're completely legitimate, but they're designed to be distinctive. They're designed to be different so that we can check to see that they're not leaking into the West in significant numbers.

Osborn: So you started out with the Model B, and then you launched that, and more recently the Model A, and now the camera. I was wondering if you could tell me what else you have in the pipeline? What's next?

Upton: So we want to do a display board. We obviously have this other little connector that we've never used, which is for connecting a display. We would really like to do that. It would be a flat-panel display, and I think that would be quite useful for a lot of applications.

We're obviously going to do a revision of the Model B board. We've always said we're going to do that. It's just to improve the power consumption and characteristics along with a few little minor tweaks.

We thought we might do a night-vision camera because people have been taking our cameras and peeling the infrared filter off with a scalpel. This is kind of hard-core. Just the other day, we thought we might sneak in a cheeky product. We'll just buy some cameras without the IR filters for people to use. That might be a bit of fun.

What else? Lots and lots and lots of software work. And lots of documentation work to try to make the platform more attractive to users and trying to make it more comprehensible to total beginners.

If you've looked at our web site, you'll see that we've done some work recently. There's a program that we call NOOBS[5], which a simple out-of-the-box experience that makes it easier to get going with the Pi. You don't need to do so much if you can't program it yourself. You just drag files on the SD card and boot the Pi up, and the Pi does the rest. So lots and lots of little things like that to improve the user experience.

Osborn: Well thanks, Eben. I think my Pi camera is still on backorder, but I'm looking forward to getting it and seeing what I can do with it. For me it's more about the possibilities than really having a solid idea as to what I'm going to do with it.

---

[5]New Out of Box Software.

Catarina Mota

Founder

OpenMaterials.org

*As an extremely active member of the maker community, **Catarina Mota** is a member of NYC Resistor, research chairperson at OSHWA.org, a TED fellow, and founder of both OpenMaterials.org and EverywhereTech.org.*

Catarina has dedicated a lot of time to furthering open source through her academic research and by teaching workshops on high-tech materials. She is currently working on her PhD, researching the social impact of open-source practices.

Steven Osborn: Hi, Catarina. You're in New York now, but originally from Portugal. Is that correct?

Catarina Mota: Portugal, yes.

Osborn: Tell me a little bit about why you moved here, your background and education.

Mota: Well, that's a long and complicated story. I lived in Portugal until after college. As an undergrad, I studied communication sciences. So I went first for journalism, and then realized I was terrible at it, so I did a mid-course adjustment and turned to film. After graduation, I worked for a year teaching video and filmmaking. That year I accumulated all my vacation days and I wanted to use them to take a course in filmmaking. So that's what brought me to New York. I came here for a six-week film program, and fell in love with the city so much that I ended up staying.

So the next step was to find a graduate program. I went to Tisch School of the Arts at NYU. It's a really good film school. I got into the elevator to go to the film department floor, but was distracted as usual and got off on the wrong floor. Tisch is performing arts, so it's theater, costume design, film, that kind of thing, but there is one kind of odd piece in the building going on in the school. It's the Interactive Telecommunications Program [ITP]. ITP is a program focused on technology for people that do not necessarily come from engineering or programming backgrounds. Basically, you can make whatever you want out of it. You can leave the program being an expert in web design, or being an expert in electronics, or in anything.

So what happened was that I accidentally got off on ITP's floor, but didn't realize it right away. I went to the reception desk to ask for information, and they were starting to give me some information, when I realized I was in the wrong place. But they were so nice that I didn't have the courage to say I had made a mistake. I just looked around and then something really strange happened. I saw the work that the students were doing there, which was electronics and computer vision—this was back in 1998 and the web was still very young. We still used modems to connect. Basically, something clicked, and it felt like I had found my place.

So I never even applied to the film school. I actually never even went there. I basically went home, applied for ITP, and I got accepted. Luckily, I also got a scholarship because I couldn't possibly afford NYU otherwise.

ITP is a very special place. It started in the seventies as a program to explore interactive television and audiovisual systems. It has evolved way beyond that as technology changed. It was a couple years before the dot-com bubble bust, so there was this excitement about emerging technology. The web was still pretty young. We had video conference calls with the Media Lab at MIT, and it was extremely exciting that we could actually see each other over video. So there was this atmosphere of "anything is possible and we can make it."

Very few of us were actually engineers, so we were making it up as we went along. How do you teach people with no technical background how to do electronics or programming and all that? Well, we learned by first learning to learn. So instead of teaching us one specific programming language or one specific area of hardware or anything like that, we were given basic tools with which to come up with solutions. I think this resonates a lot with the maker movement because most makers are not professional experts in what they make. And that way they end up coming up with alternative solutions because no one told them "this is how it is supposed to be."

Osborn: So they just say, "Here's a problem, solve it"? Instead of giving you some instructions on how something works and then testing your memory of their instructions? Is that how I'm understanding the course?

Mota: No, they would give us the basics of working in an area. So, for example, they would give us the basics: "This is how electricity works. This is what a capacitor does. This is what object-oriented programming is." They would not usually give us the challenges. Usually the challenges were whatever we wanted to do. And because we wanted to do a certain thing, we would learn to do it, which means that our knowledge of the technology would be interest-based, although fragmented. For example, even now, I might know a lot about one specific area of electronics just because I had to work with it for a project, but absolutely nothing about the rest of the electronics world. So it was self-motivation driven. I have an idea. What do we want to do? What is the outcome? Usually, it's very much art-based, but it doesn't have to be, right? I want to create this installation that does this, and then I'll have to learn this to get there. So this is what I mean by a more unstructured learning environment.

Osborn: You get what you put into it.

Mota: Right, right. The idea was we would first come up with a human-level goal, like what is it we want to do? And then the technology would follow.

At ITP it was common to freely share code and schematics amongst students and teachers. They just circulated from one person to the next. Back then we didn't call it open-source hardware, but that's what it was. It was this culture in which it was very normal to share your work.

When I graduated from ITP I realized had been in school for most of my life, so I decided to go out into the real world and became a consultant specializing in information architecture. Along the way, I realized that the open-source approach we had gotten used to in school was not how the real world worked. So I became increasingly an advocate for open-source practices.

I worked as a consultant for several years but eventually realized it was time to go back to research, which is what I really liked. So I enrolled in a PhD program five years ago, and that has been my main job until today. I'm currently trying to finish my dissertation, which is on open-source hardware. The reason I decided to get a PhD is because it would give me the opportunity to spend more time doing research. At the time I enrolled, PhD programs were still very, very open. So basically, you apply, you get accepted, you submit a project proposal, and then you go work on your own for five years and come back with a dissertation. This means I had huge control over my time. Of course, I could do that because my program also came with a fellowship which basically allowed me to do research for a living.

A few months after that, I went to this three-week production workshop that takes place every year at MediaLab Prado, which is a media lab in Madrid. What they do at these workshops is bring people from all over the world, about fifty of us, to work on open-source projects. The project I worked on was led by Zach Hoeken from MakerBot. And we built the most rickety RepRap[1]. It kind of worked for a little bit. This was back when we had to source all the materials by ourselves. There were no kits. It was really hard and I think it took five or six of us three weeks to build a RepRap that worked for a couple hours.

---

[1] Open-source 3D printers (www.reprap.org).

Osborn: The newer ones are much better and more reliable, but they are still kind of finicky machines.

Mota: But nothing compared to that. Your perspective on what is a reliable 3D printer really depends on what your entry point was, right? So, comparatively, machines now are very efficient and easy to make. At that point, I was already interested in digital fabrication, but I hadn't had the chance to actually build a RepRap before. This was my first opportunity. And then, two other things happened at that workshop. One is I met Kirsty Boyle, and Kirsty and I went on to found OpenMaterials. Kirsty was also on the MediaLab Prado RepRap team, and we realized we wanted to collaborate on a project after the workshop that required several smart materials like muscle wire and thermochromic pigments. So we began working on that after the workshop and realized that the materials we wanted to use were not only extremely hard to obtain in small enough quantities, in maker quantities instead of manufacturing quantities, but the few that we could actually buy came with no instructions.

Up until today, I still have a material on my shelf called Expancel, which is a powder made of micro spheres that are supposed to expand to four times their size when mixed with paint and heated up. The problem is that there are no instructions as to the proportions, or what kind of paint or what temperature to use, so it's been several years and I still don't know how to make that material work. It's sort of a reminder of how things used to be and still are up to a certain point.

Because of this, Kirsty and I had to work through a trial-and-error process. We would take our best guess as to what the factors in the experiment should be and then change one at a time until we got the material to work. And we documented all of this. We also documented the failures. Since both she and I were open-source advocates, we realized we should share this for two reasons. One is so other people wouldn't have to repeat a process we had already been through, and the other one was so hopefully we could gather a community of experimenters around smart materials to exchange information and, of course, advance faster. So that's how OpenMaterials started.

Osborn: That started as part of your PhD studies?

Mota: No, nothing to do with my PhD. My thesis is on social sciences. I'm looking at open-source hardware and peer production in general and thinking about, first of all, how does it work? Why does it work? But, mostly, what does it mean for society?

Osborn: You call it peer production?

Mota: Peer production.

Osborn: Okay. I haven't heard that term before. That's a good term for desktop manufacturing.

Mota: This was a term Yochai Benkler used on the *Wealth of Networks*,[2] and it's a term many people use to describe horizontal networks of creators who get together to produce something in nonhierarchical systems.

I made time to work on all these other parallel projects at the same time as the PhD. One of them was OpenMaterials, which was and still is focused on smart and unusual materials, but also mixed with more traditional materials. For example, we're very interested in paper, wood, etc., and generally in reusing traditional materials in smarter ways and coming up with DIY recipes.

Osborn: I've seen quite a few different types of conductive ink projects. People in this community have quite a bit of interest in electronics anyway, so there's quite a bit of overlap. I've seen people with a lot of different conductive inks and transparent circuits.

Mota: Yeah, it's very exciting to see interest in materials grow. More and more, I try to encourage people to share knowledge themselves instead of sending it to me and having me process it. You'll probably see that there are a few guest posts on OpenMaterials. In the last few years, I also began teaching workshops, geared mostly towards artists and makers, on how to use smart materials mixed with electronics, paper, fabrics, wood, etc. And then last year, I taught an ITP a class called Tech Crafts, which is a variation of physical computing.

Osborn: Could you explain what Physical Computing is?

Mota: Physical Computing at ITP is the intro to electronics class. Many people in the program do not have a background in electrical engineering, so the class focuses on teaching students how to work with electronics, program a microcontroller, etc. The Tech Crafts class I taught, which could be taken after physical computing, focused not so much on traditional electronics materials and engineering platforms, like breadboards, perf boards, PCBs,[3] but on making your own. We made our own sensors, we made our own resistors, things like that, out of mostly raw materials, both smart and traditional. The idea was to take electronics out of the box and off the PCB.

By understanding how each of the components works, you have a lot more freedom to create.

For example, there was a group of students who wanted to make a rug that reacts when someone steps on it and decided to use pressure sensors since that's the most common solution available off the shelf. The pressure sensors were about an inch wide, so they had to wire a bunch of them together to cover the entire surface of the rug, which makes the process more complicated and expensive. Using smart materials, such as conductive ink or conductive

---

[2]http://cyber.law.harvard.edu/wealth_of_networks/
[3]Printed circuit boards.

fabrics, you can just make a single pressure sensor yourself in any shape. So that's what the class focused on. I am not a materials scientist. I knew nothing about this. I learned on my own and from other people. I learned a lot from Hannah Perner-Wilson, Jie Qi, and Leah Buechley. There are still only a handful of us working with these materials in Europe and in the US that I know of. But the number of individuals is growing as well as the number of universities. There are a couple of universities with materials science departments that are starting to focus more on simpler ways of making and using materials. They are publishing simpler formulas that don't require specialized equipment so they can enable makers. I did see a huge growth in terms of interest and activity in this area in the four years since we started OpenMaterials.

Osborn: Can you give me a couple examples of materials that you have on OpenMaterials? Maybe the ones that you think are interesting or popular?

Mota: One of the most popular is conductive ink, which is basically a black ink infused with graphite or some other sort of conductive particles. Conductive ink used to be really expensive because it was made of silver, so it was not accessible to most people. But now that they're making it with graphite, it's pretty cheap. People started using it first to make traces in circuits. Personally, I find that that is not necessarily the best use for the material, because copper is so much better for that purpose. In my opinion conductive ink is really good to make sensors in any shape that you want. You can apply it to any material. You can paint an area and turn it into a capacitive sensor, for example. Or you can make a touch sensor on a book without a lot of hardware.

Osborn: Turn surfaces into sensors. So when I touch the conductive ink it would sense the presence of my hand and the object can react in some way?

Mota: Exactly. That's one type of sensor that you can make with conductive ink. Another great property of this material that can be used for sensors is its resistance. It's significantly more resistant than copper, nickel, and other metals that we normally use as conductors. What that means is, if you paint a line of conductive paint, the resistance on one end is going to be different from the resistance on the other end because it gets increasingly more resistive. A lot of the sensors that we use are based on variable resistance. In this case, the whole material is the variable resistor so you can use it to make a potentiometer. I've used conductive ink to paint a circular sensor on paper in order to control the volume of a piezo buzzer for example.

Osborn: I don't know if I saw this on your site recently, but I saw a speaker somebody made out of a Post-it note and some copper spirals. It was pretty interesting. They just had a magnet and the Post-it note and they made a speaker, which was a pretty interesting way to learn about speakers.

Mota: That is the kind of work that Leah Buechley and Hannah Perner-Wilson, who was Leah's student at the High-Low Tech Group at MIT several years ago, are doing. They explore the intersection of craft and technology and came up with many interesting systems that have inspired the rest of us. The Pulp-Based Computing[4] group, led by Marcelo Coelho, is another group working on this topic at MIT. They mix paper and crafts materials with hardware. A few years ago, Marcelo wrote a paper about making speakers. And based on that, Hannah Perner-Wilson created a series of handmade speakers that use paper, fabric and magnets. If you go to Kit-of-No-Parts,[5] you'll see a lot of really interesting experiments in which she deconstructs electronics components and hardware, and then builds them from the ground up with unusual materials.

Osborn: At some point, you did a TED talk. Not just anyone gets to come in and talk at TED. I'm interested to hear about that experience and how you got invited. What was that experience like for you?

Mota: What happened was a bit of a network effect, I think. I didn't know this at the time, but I later reconstructed it. I did a talk, a materials run-through, at the Open Hardware Summit a couple of years ago. And there was someone there who was an advisor to the TED Fellows Program. So after that I got an e-mail from the TED Fellows Program saying, "We have this program. You should consider applying." At the time, I didn't really know what the program was, only that they bring fellows to one TED conference. So I thought, "Wow, cool. Free TED conference." I ended up applying at the very last minute of the deadline and didn't think about it again. And then I went through the process. It's a couple of interviews and references, things like that. A lot of people get super nervous with those interviews. At the time, I didn't because I had no idea what I was applying for.

Osborn: Nice. You were just cool as a cat.

Mota: It was just, "Oh, you know, no pressure." Eventually, I got the fellowship and with the fellowship comes the possibility of giving one talk. All the new fellows give one talk before the main TED program begins. That's already pretty nerve-racking. But then I got a call from the curator of TED Global—there are two TED conferences: one here in the US and another elsewhere in the world—with an invite to also give a main stage talk. So that's how that happened. I was flabbergasted. It was very intense, because for this one conference, I gave two talks on two consecutive days and TED conferences require months of preparations. In addition to that, I also participated in a parallel showcase, a sort of exhibition area at the conference venue.

Osborn: And then you went home and slept for days I imagine. That would be exhausting.

Mota: Right. It was a very, very, very intense week there. I think there are around six hundred attendees at TED conferences. And, when you give a talk at a conference, people will know who you are afterward and know what you

---

[4]www.cmarcelo.com/pulp-based-computing
[5]http://web.media.mit.edu/~plusea

do, so many will come talk to you about that topic. I think I must have talked to hundreds of people, which is not something I'm used to. It was amazing and very much a blur. That was it for the TED conference, but TED fellowships are sort of for life. We only get to go to a conference once, the first year, but the fellowship doesn't end there. It's an amazing network, an amazing, amazing network. There are, I don't know, three or four hundred fellows from all areas—scientists, artists, engineers, programmers, everything. So, basically, it's this worldwide network of people who really like each other and are constantly collaborating and exchanging information. Given what I know now, if I was applying for the fellowship today, I would be very nervous because I would be afraid of not getting it.

Speaking of networks and exchanging information, going back to OpenMaterials for a second, I just wanted to mention my criteria for selecting materials because that's very important to me. First, they have to be commercially available, so other people can buy them. I have no interest in working with a material that others can't get. Then, they have to be available in quantities and at prices that are accessible to most people. Finally, they can't require specialized equipment. So my criteria are all based on availability to others.

Osborn: Right, so that people can actually apply your processes. And it's unencumbered so that you don't have to pay a fat license fee for the privilege of mixing some chemicals together.

Mota: Exactly.

Osborn: So your transition from media to tech is interesting. When you were growing up, were you always naturally curious about materials or were your parents engineers? What did they think when you told them that you were going to move to New York to do media?

Mota: My parents are chemical engineers, both of them.

Osborn: Okay, so you had some background or at least knowledge.

Mota: Yes, yes. I remember my mom explained to me the theory of relativity and things like that. But they weren't makers. I know a lot of people in this community came from maker homes and they would make things with their parents, or grandparents, or siblings. That didn't happen in my home. We got the scientific theory and even a little practice, but we didn't repair our own things. My parents didn't have a shop in their garage. In a way, I kind of took on the role of fixer. I fixed appliances whenever something broke, just because I liked it, but this wasn't a tradition in my home. And then I think I went to social sciences and film basically because I was a teenager. My parents wanted me to be an engineer.

Osborn: You were just being rebellious?

Mota: I wanted to be something else.

Osborn: Your parents are relieved now that you're not in film?

Mota: I don't know. They still regret the fact that I don't have an engineering degree, even though I keep telling them that, at this point, given that I don't do any hardcore engineering work, I don't need it. When I went to ITP, that was the *only* way, the only way available to people with no engineering background to learn how to use and make technological devices. Things have changed a lot since, right? Nowadays, you don't necessarily need an academic degree to learn certain things, because you have hackerspaces, you have tech shops, you have online communities, you have fab labs. All these things that didn't exist back then.

Osborn: Just with the online resources, like Khan Academy,[6] you can learn basic math, from addition up through college-level calculus using online tools.

Mota: Exactly. But if this was fifteen years ago, going to school was practically the only way to learn those things. Speaking of hackerspaces, that was, for me, another important transformation that came out of the workshop in Madrid we talked about earlier. For a year before that, I had been trying to start a hackerspace in Lisbon but at the time I didn't know many people there—I had lived in NYC for several years before moving back to Lisbon—and just couldn't get it off the ground.

But at that workshop in Madrid, I met Ricardo Lobo and Tiago Henriques, also from Portugal. Several years before, Ricardo had started a hackerspace in Porto. He didn't call it a hackerspace, but that's what it was. And Tiago was also eager to start one in Lisbon. So together we launched altLab.[7] This was all at the same time as OpenMaterials, in May 2009, so I basically didn't sleep for six months, just getting these projects off the ground, and doing research, and taking classes, but it was totally worth it. So altLab is still there. One choice we made from the beginning was to, rather than creating an independent organization, join the Porto hackerspace under the same nonprofit. And then, three months later, a third hackerspace was also created in Coimbra under the same umbrella. So we're actually a network, under a single nonprofit organization. And that's something I'm particularly proud of, because it's very much in line with the collaborative approach.

Osborn: Hacker spaces seem to be popping up all over the place. There are quite a few in Portland, but they're all for-profit. They don't really seem to have an interest in being under the same umbrella or the same name, because they want to be *the* hacker space in town, which is probably working against their goal of openness and getting people in and out the door.

---

[6]www.khanacademy.org
[7]http://altlab.org

Mota: Right, right. The Portuguese hackerspaces are very close to the original hacker ethic and sharing. They're not for profit. But about a year after we launched, I moved back to New York—altLab has someone else as the chair now and he's doing an amazing job. But I needed to find myself a local hackerspace and since I had met Zach in Madrid, I was able to join NYC Resistor. NYC Resistor acts in most ways as a nonprofit, but technically we're also a for-profit organization. I wasn't a member when that decision was made, but I think it had something to do with the fact that it's much more complicated, from a paperwork point of view, to start a nonprofit.

Osborn: What's it called?

Mota: NYC Resistor. It's in Brooklyn, in the same building as MakerBot. Because of that connection, we have a lot of MakerBots round.

Osborn: The new MakerBot is a nice machine.

Mota: Right, much better than that rickety Darwin RepRap I helped build ages ago in Madrid.

Osborn: So let's talk a bit about your involvement in open-source hardware.

Mota: When I came to NYC, I ended up meeting many people from the open-source hardware community, mostly through NYC Resistor. And given that I'm very passionate about it, I became increasingly involved with open-source advocacy. As part of that, two years ago, I was lucky enough to join Alicia Gibb's and Ayah Bdeir's Open Hardware Summit organizing team. And then the year after that, since they wanted to move on and do other things, they passed the torch to me and Dustin Roberts. So we organized last year's summit. That was an interesting project. We're talking nine months of work putting together the conference. I learned a lot.

A little over a year ago, several people in the community began thinking that, in addition to the open-source hardware definition and the Open Hardware Summit, we also needed some kind of organization to act as a hub, a nonprofit to protect the practice and educate the public about open-source hardware. Alicia bravely led the effort to create the Open Source Hardware Association [OSHWA], of which she is now the president. I was on the board of directors for the first year and right now I serve as the organization's research chair. My role there is to help research and understand open-source hardware practices.

Osborn: What roles do you see open-source hardware having and its impact on society, as far as knowledge distribution? What are the economic and social arguments for it?

Mota: I think that, in order to get at that, we must first have a better understanding of what is happening and it seems to me that the growth of open-source hardware can be explained on a few levels On a first level, what makes open-source hardware possible is obviously the Internet, which allows people to share information easily and to connect directly with one another. Before the Internet, our options were the phone, which allowed only two or three people to connect, and mass media, which were controlled by private corporations, so the public didn't have access to broadcast systems. If you combine the Internet with the fact that people are inherently creative and inherently social—they want to share— you have a recipe that you never had before, which is a combination of those characteristics of human nature with a medium that enables them to go to heights they've never been before. It's not that suddenly we are all becoming sharers. We've always been sharers. We just didn't have a good medium to do it on this scale.

On top of that you have the technologies that actually enable the production of open-source hardware. We have the computers to design models, and we have the Internet to share them. But what does that mean if we can't make them? That is the importance of digital fabrication tools, more specifically, of open-source digital fabrication tools, like 3D printers, laser cutters, and CNC mills. We now have this really interesting feedback system because, on a simpler level, people are using computers to design things and then using the Internet to share them and then using digital fabrication tools to materialize them. So you design a tool on a computer, you share it with other people over the Internet, someone materializes the tool and then uses that tool to make more things that in turn are shared in the feedback loop, so that's really fascinating.

Why is this happening now? It's happening because the willingness to share, the desire to create is part of human nature. And we now have technology to both create and share on a large scale. Then there's also the impact of these practices on business. Although some traditional businesses see information sharing as a threat, a lot of research shows that, with the possible exception of some very specific cases, such as pharmaceuticals, intellectual property is not that important.

Osborn: Unless your business is extorting money out of other companies, then it is.

Mota: Unless you're a patent troll. Did you see that someone actually tried to patent being a patent troll?

Osborn: I saw that. That was brilliant.

Mota: I loved that. Intellectual property is more a construct than a reality. It was put into place because it was assumed that people would not create if they could not make money off of their creations and that they could not make money off of their creations without exclusive rights. But now open source—and all the sharing that is going on across many areas—is showing that we do not necessarily need that particular incentive to create. So the premise behind intellectual property was false from the start. But what happened was, once those laws were put in place, instead of fostering business models that were not based on exclusive rights, they fostered the emergence of business practices that took advantage of intellectual property mechanisms. And that's what we're talking about in the case of patent trolling, or secretive information, or traditional content, music, movie, and book businesses. These business models are based on the fact that the legal tools are there, so they use these legal tools to build their businesses.

When the underlying scarcity that gave rise to intellectual property disappeared—when we switched from actually having to buy or make physical CDs and tapes to just being able to share anything with anyone at marginally zero cost—those business models became endangered. There have always been other ways to make money that do not rely on owning information, and that's what people forgot. We got to a point in history where intellectual property is almost seen as a law of nature, and it's not. It's actually a social construct that comes from a very defined historical context. It just happened to be that way, and then it snowballed and turned into what it is now, but it's not the only way.

What this means is that open-source businesses compete differently. They compete on being faster, more agile. They compete on getting free R&D from their customers and from their competitors because everyone has access to the same knowledge. Mostly, they compete on offering the best products and services at the best prices.

Osborn: It's a social construct, and it's also different in different parts of the world, too. In China, the IP laws are much less strict.

Mota: Exactly. What you said is very, very important. The fact that something is open source or not doesn't matter. Everything can be cloned. So intellectual property is not even a very good protection, because if you make something here, how are you going to prevent people in China from copying it? You're not. It's just not feasible or practical. The other important factor is that there are advantages to the open-source model that the proprietary model doesn't have, and that's collaboration.

Everyone's building on top of each other so much faster because you can use your competitors' knowledge on your own products, and vice versa. You can also use your customers' R&D. And finally, you get free market research because your customers will tell you what they want and they will even prototype it and sketch it for you, so you don't need to spend a lot of money finding out what your customers want.

What happens in open-source businesses—I'm not even talking about very big ideas—in a very practical sense is that some businesses perceive these advantages as outweighing the advantages of intellectual property. They say, "Intellectual property protects me in some way, but it doesn't make me a better business. It doesn't even protect me all the way because everything can be cloned."

We have many native open-source businesses, businesses that were open-source from the start.

But now we're seeing some of the more established or traditional businesses also realizing that: one, they're getting cloned no matter what; two, they need to be competitive in other ways that don't rely on intellectual property. So my guess is that even though proprietary systems are not going away anytime soon, we are going to see increasingly more open-source production, based on its practical advantages.

In terms of what this means for society, I'd say equal opportunity can be a game changer. Making the knowledge of how things work and how things are produced freely available to everyone does not resolve all social inequality problems, but it is a big step in that direction.

Osborn: I think it does a lot to increase the speed of innovation because businesses are forced to be more innovative and open, whereas if they're closed, they can sit on their IP forever and not innovate, because there's no market competition. If the IP is out in the open, everyone is forced to innovate faster in order to remain competitive.

Mota: Yes, innovation has social value too, of course. So it works at both levels, business and social. On the one hand, faster innovation is beneficial to businesses. On the other hand, open access leads to more opportunities for more people, and in turn, more opportunities for more people lead to increased diversity. The production of both media and physical goods has been in the hands of a handful of corporations for a century now. And whether we like it or not, the content of media and the objects we use, the objects that are part of our everyday lives, greatly influence the way we live. If those objects reflect more perspectives, more diversity, then we'll also live in a more diverse world by extension. I think that's it in a nutshell.

Osborn: Great. That's a good perspective. I definitely think a lot of people are starting to agree with you. At least in the maker community, but I don't think most people have considered the larger implications on society. The effects are way more important than, "Oh, I get to see how this works and I can make my own." We're talking about a drastic increase in innovation based on the availability of information.

Mota: It's the aggregation of all the micro effects.

Osborn: Exactly. I think it's definitely something to think about. I love what you're doing with OpenMaterials. I looked at the site quite a bit last week and got some good ideas for things that I want to try out and play with.

Mota: That's great. That's what I feel a lot when I go to other materials web sites. To me materials are way cooler than kits, because a kit you can only assemble in one or two ways, but in general materials are just inspiring. All right, thank you very much.

Osborn: Thank you for your time.

Mota: It was nice talking to you.

Ward Cunningham

Inventor

Wiki

Ward Cunningham (http://c2.com/~ward/) *has made many contributions to software programming and the Internet. Ward laid groundwork that established design patterns[1] and extreme programming[2] as common practices in computer software design. His work on design patterns led to his invention of the Wiki, which has changed the way information is collected and shared around the world on the Internet. Ward holds a master's degree in electrical engineering from Purdue University.*

In addition to his notable career as a computer programmer, Ward is a capable electrical engineer who enjoys building weekend projects at home to share with the local Dorkbot group in Portland, Oregon.

Steven Osborn: So Ward, have you always had this natural curiosity for inventing things?

Ward Cunningham: Yeah, absolutely. I tell people I'm a child of the Sputnik era. The Sputnik era was when kids that showed any interest in math and science or technology were really encouraged, even if that interest was a little

---

[1] en.wikipedia.org/wiki/Software_design_pattern
[2] en.wikipedia.org/wiki/Extreme_programming

dangerous—playing with electricity, high voltages, throwing sparks, things like that. I would discourage my children from doing those things, but my parents didn't discourage me. I have an older brother who was really the kind of mad scientist personality in high school. He had friends that formed a network where they'd hear about things and do experiments, and I was the younger brother tagging along. But it kind of set the tone for the excitement of making something and seeing it work.

I remember one was very simple. It was a glass furnace. I had never heard of it. I'd heard of a blast furnace because I grew up near the steel mills, but a glass furnace is where you just run electricity through molten glass and it gets hotter, and hotter, and hotter. Glass doesn't conduct when it's cold. So you get a couple of electrodes and put some broken glass between them and heat it up with a torch. Once it's all glowing, you turn on the juice and start throwing in more glass. The vessel was made out of three steel mill–grade fire bricks, cut a hole in the middle one, stack them up, and that's a vessel that will hold lots of molten glass, and just hook that right up to the power line and run power through it. Pretty soon we had this boiling glass, orange turning into yellow. What do you do with that? Throw a penny into it and poof it's just gone. So that was neat.

Osborn: So that was the stuff you were doing as a kid?

Cunningham: That was my brother and his friends, and I'm there, "Let's try a dime." Experimenting. Another experiment was his building an oscilloscope from a kit, and then when it was finished, what do you measure? The idea was to measure the television. So we opened up the back of the television to see if we could hook up this oscilloscope and get a television picture on it.

Osborn: That's dangerous.

Cunningham: High voltage. But the problem was that the television picture wasn't uniform. It was squeezed on one end because it was measuring the voltage on the magnetic deflection coil. My brother and his friend were both two years older than me, so I was very proud of the fact that I was able to diagnose that. I said, "Oh, well, that's because the deflection in the beam is by the magnetic field, which is current, and you're measuring voltage." And the solution was to cut the wires and insert a resistor to measure the current, the voltage over the resistor. I knew Ohm's law by then. We did that, and we had this beautiful picture. But the fun part was, well, when we were done looking at a green little television screen on an oscilloscope, we had to put it back together, and we said, "Just for fun, let's reverse the wires."

Osborn: So it's upside down?

Cunningham: Yeah, so the picture's upside down. It just looked cool as hell to have that picture upside down. So we took the TV, and it was a big, heavy portable TV, but it was portable, so we took it back upstairs and put it where it belonged. We thought that Mom would be so proud of us for having figured out how to turn it upside down. It turned out she had been waiting all week to watch a golf tournament on Friday afternoon while we were still at school. Oh my gosh, she was outraged by the fact that she tried to turn the television over just to watch the golf game right side up.

Osborn: And how old were you at the time?

Cunningham: High school. I think my brother was still in high school, so I was probably a sophomore. He was two years older. I learned a lot of electronics just to understand what he was talking about. I got a book about how tubes work. I wasn't actually that great in school. I was always in the slow reading group, and it was a burden, but I was a good listener, so if I hadn't done my homework, I would sit there and listen in class. Sometimes I'd daydream, but I'd kind of follow along with what's going on in class.

So what I did learn I learned pretty thoroughly because I would listen ahead of the teacher and try to guess what he was going to tell us. And if he told us something other than what I had guessed, I would say, "Why is it different than I thought it would be?" It was a learning process that I took to college. I didn't take notes. When it was time to study for an exam, I didn't have anything to study, so I didn't study. I didn't get great grades, but I will admit that my college education, that there's probably hardly a day that goes by that I don't reach back to my college education and pull something and apply it. I think it's been fantastic. A lot of people will talk about college as a waste of time, but it certainly wasn't for me. And that's because what I did learn, I learned thoroughly.

Osborn: A lot of time students just write down the professor's slides as if they're just transcribing it, but not absorbing any of it. Just ask the professor for the slide afterward.

Cunningham: Yeah, and I figured it was my time to study. I was going to study by paying careful attention and thinking through as fast and as thoroughly as I could while it was being said. I still do, like in conversation. I learn more in conversation than I do in any kind of reading. I also find that I can apply this to computer programming—you know, a lot of people told us that to write a computer program, you should have a plan. Then you should just execute the plan. The program should be designed, and by the time you get to the coding aspect, you can turn your brain off and write the code that was asked for. And to my mind, it's much more like listening to my professor, only now I'm listening to my computer. I wrote this in and I thought it would do this and Professor Computer says, "No! This is what that does." And I think, "What does that mean?" So I'm having the same sort of hypothesis-driven mental process where I'm having a conversation with a computer.

I suppose just somebody who always took notes and in a sense never had a mental conversation with a professor wouldn't know what it meant to have a conversation with a computer, but I would often describe it as trying to feel what the computer wanted to do over anything else. To me, the computer is something you could touch—it's not nearly as abstract as most people would think of it, because you do something and it responds. That's touch.

Osborn: There's not that much magic there. It's a pretty simple machine when you get down to the bits.

Cunningham: Absolutely. We can layer, and layer, and layer, but if you only know a tenth of it, nine-tenths of it seems like magic. But all of it is knowable.

Osborn: It sounds like we're both lucky to have not killed ourselves growing up.

Cunningham: When I first came to Tektronix, there was an oscilloscope on my desk and no signal hooked up yet, so I just started probing the AC wall socket and was watching all the different noises floating around. A colleague of mine walked in and he was freaked out because he knew all the grounding circuits and how dangerous it would be if I touched any metal part in the oscilloscope. It was just a foolish thing to do, and I was told in no uncertain terms that I shouldn't be cavalier around AC power. AC power is a dangerous thing. And that's why I like the electronics of today. The chips are so easy to fool with now, and you do everything in five volts or three volts. You can burn stuff up, but it's so cheap that you hardly care and it's hard to hurt yourself.

Osborn: You have always had a curiosity of electronics and it sounds like you got a lot of that from your brother. Most people seem to have someone, maybe a dad who was into electronics who opened that door for them.

Cunningham: Well, it was my brother and his friends. I was just trying to know what they were talking about. They'd use these big words. I remember one was *selenium rectifier*. It was so many syllables. I'm a slow reader, so to be able to imagine a word that long was something. Oh my goodness, I had to figure out what a selenium rectifier was. Turns out it's actually a pretty crummy rectifier. There are much better rectifiers now.

The funny thing is I didn't much like school. I learned a lot, but I didn't like it because I always felt guilty for not doing the homework or finishing the reading, because I was a slow reader. But I ended up going to college just because my friends went to college. A friend said, "Go to Purdue. Here's an application."

So I applied to Purdue and I got into the program, and I'm reading the list with the courses of study, and my heart sank. Nothing looked any good. I didn't want to study something like history, the last thing I wanted to do was read more books, right? And I turned to electrical engineering. It didn't look fun either, but it looked less bad than anything else. I said, "Okay, I'll be an electrical engineer." It wasn't a lot of deep thought. I didn't really know what an electrical engineer was, but when I read about the courses there, I knew what the words were and I knew there was more that I didn't know.

Osborn: I think a lot of people have about that much sense of direction when they get into college. They have no idea what they're going to do.

Cunningham: Well, they were smart at Purdue. They said, "Well, you can't be an electrical engineer as a freshman. You can only be an engineer because you learn some math and you learn about all the different kinds of engineering." But I stuck with electrical engineering.

Osborn: Do you feel you got a lot out of it? Do you feel you learned a lot?

Cunningham: Well, for instance, I knew how a tube amplified. I could visualize it, with the electrons, but I could not understand how a transistor amplified. Every description would say, "Well, the way to think about a transistor is as two diodes." And I'd think about it as two diodes, and I just couldn't imagine any way that amplified. Now, remember, I knew what diodes do because I understood what a selenium rectifier does, and I knew that was not going to amplify. And it just drove me nuts. It wasn't until I think my junior year in college where I learned enough physics to understand how a transistor worked, and at the DC level, it is kind of like two diodes, but that DC isn't about amplifying. That's the analog characteristics going into it. So you can bias a transistor by thinking of it kind of like diodes, but it's a very sophisticated device. And electrical engineering taught me that.

I also I built a radio and thought a two-way radio would be neat. At that time, in amateur radio, a single sideband, an SSB, was new, and I thought, "What a crazy name. I knew about amplitude modulation because I knew what amplitude is, and I knew what modulation is, but what the heck is a sideband?" I just would read about it and it would say, "Every signal has two sidebands, but if you eliminate one, you have a single sideband." I said, "Wait a second. What's the sideband? Just answer me this: 'What is the sideband?'" Gosh, it wasn't until my senior year that I really got an intuitive understanding of what a sideband is. There's a lot going on when you modulate a signal.

I wasn't satisfied until I could get an intuitive understanding of that. Now, that insisting on an intuitive understanding actually distances me from a lot of what I call professional engineering because at some point, you don't have time to get an intuitive understanding. You've got to just work out the equation, get an answer, build or fabricate even. You've got one chance to make the chip, and it damned well better work. So that style of engineering, I've got a lot of respect for people who can do that, but it's not where I find energy. My approach is more like, "We don't have intuition to solve the problem so let's get an intuition, and once we've got an intuition, we'll be able to choose the best solution." And that's a good methodology.

Osborn: More of an artisan approach than a scientist's approach.

Cunningham: I think so. I'll let other people do the science. I'll read the science. I like to know the science, but mine is a practitioner's approach.

When I was starting my career in the computing industry, it was all about trying to be like another engineering discipline. They'd say, "Computers are new. We need to be like an old discipline, like civil engineering, and civil engineers won't start anything without blueprints." So after they made a computer, they took all that physical learning out of the process of writing a program. And I just thought, "Well, you're taking the best part about a computer and throwing it away. With civil engineering, you have a complicated scheduling problem, you'd better have the right steel at the right time or you won't be able to bolt it together or weld it.

Well, the thing about computer software is if there's ten pieces that have to work together, you can write them in pretty much any order you feel like. To get a feel for how that first piece works, you'll have to put stuff around that piece to account for all the other pieces that aren't there. But you can do that in any order. You have so much freedom to approach a problem, why not approach a problem in a way that builds your intuition as quickly and completely as possible, so that you can finish the whole project in a way that makes it look like you were really smart right at the beginning? If you have to make all the decisions when you're dumb, and then follow those dumb decisions, you'll end up with software that makes you look like you're dumb.

This goes back to this idea of having a conversation with the software. You say, "Software, do you want to do this?" The software says, "No, I don't think I want to do that." "Well, maybe this?" And then back and forth, minute by minute. It's obviously not a conversation in the literal sense—it's you learning as you go.

Osborn: I know you've done a lot of work early on with software design patterns. Can you talk about what design patterns are and why they're important?

Cunningham: My pattern work started at Tektronix. It turns out I was not alone with this idea of wanting to feel what a computer wants to do. Tektronix was filled with electrical engineers that worked that way. I liked to work with electrical engineers and do the software part.

Smalltalk[3] showed up in our lab, the Tektronix Computer Research Lab. It was about ten years after researchers started experimenting with Smalltalk at Xerox PARC. It was marvelous. But it was a challenge to figure out how I could put it to work. Not only was it a neat language that had some new concepts,

---

[3]A programming language developed by Xerox PARC, first released in 1980.

it was a neat graphics system that drew pictures, and it was also a neat operating system. I went to work listening to Smalltalk but it was slow going because it was so different.

Smalltalk was done in a clean and coherent way, just begging for me to take a hold of it and take it someplace. That excited me, but a lot of people were dumbfounded by it. They'd just say, "Well, how are you supposed to use this thing?" There wasn't an instruction manual that tells you what to do in step one, because it wanted to be different from all the methodology of how to put things together. It has a lot of faith in the ability of everyone—kids of all ages, you might say—to learn like kids learn, by touching and feeling things. So it was a really good fit with me.

Now, it turns out that since I was working in a research lab I had the opportunity to play with it a lot, and after a couple of months, I began to have a real deep respect for what was there. People would come into the labs and say, "We're interested in the Smalltalk you have here. We would like to use it out in the business units of Tektronix. How do you learn it?" And I'd say, "Well, I recommend two to three months of undirected exploration." And this manager would say, "Well, I was hoping for a two-day class." All of a sudden, I'd realize, of course, he can't take this to his staff and say, "Go play with this for two or three months." In fact, the labs probably shouldn't have even done that with me.

Osborn: He might, but it would be from seven in the evening until morning.

Cunningham: Right. "You can have Saturday and Sunday every week to go learn this stuff."

I was working pretty closely with Kent Beck, who's another guy who fell in love with it in the same way. When we talked to each other, we clearly shared in the experience and could talk about it. We weren't afraid to say how we felt when we were programming. So we just sat down and solved problems together. We'd watch each other work, and then all of a sudden, the ability to talk about our experience was magnified by ten times because something would happen and we could just, right then, talk about it.

So we would say, "Okay, well, how can we turn that into a two-day class? What are we going to teach in two days?" We didn't have an answer for that, but Kent was going through his stack of old books and came across one that described patterns as a way of understanding architecture or design processes. He brought it in and said, "This is the answer. Here it is, right here in this book." I read the introduction to the book. It was Christopher Alexander's thesis.[4] Some people say that he, in a sense, invented the formal design movement, but we were less interested in the process than in the essay style he

---

[4]Notes on the *Synthesis of Form* (Harvard University Press, 1964).

had where you could write about something that you knew worked. It was a structure of an essay that would take a page or two and could link together with other essays. He had a book that was a big set of examples, and he wrote another one that said, "Here's why these work." So we said, "We'll try writing that in software. Let's see if we can find the patterns."

And it turns out, it sounds easy, but that's like if I asked you, "Just make me a list of all the words you know," right? Well, what you know isn't indexed that way. You can't enumerate all the words you know, but when you need a word, it comes to mind because your mind is hooked together that way. Its how language works. And that's why Alexander calls his work a pattern language—because it's something hooks together design just like words hook together effortlessly. That was something that we were very keen on duplicating.

At the time, people were saying, "Gee, we should make software that's easy to use." Well, that's like saying you should make a house that's safe or fireproof. It's a criterion, but it isn't the thing you do. The question is, "What do you do?" Well, the answer turns out to be patterns. If you have patterns for easy to use software, you can make software that's easy to use, or if you have patterns for secure software can have software that is secure, but it might be hard to use. These are properties of the software and they are properties of the patterns too. Just like you could have patterns for a stairway that's safe and patterns for a stairway that's something else.

We set out to write the patterns and discovered making these sorts of design decisions were hard. We enlisted the help of others who had read Alexander's book and wanted to write patterns too. We taught classes on how to think this way. And it really helped. The first book sold really well. We had publishers coming out of the woodwork and saying, "Hey! Do you have any patterns? Do you want to write a pattern book?" And so lot of books were written on design patterns. And it has really changed how people talk about computer software.

Osborn: I've read that first one, the Gang of Four[5] book, which is still very popular.

Cunningham: Yeah, it's had a strong influence. One thing I wanted to mention is that I think of problems in terms of patterns, and do I know the patterns I need to solve those problems? And if not, what can I do to learn the patterns? Or I'll be talking to people and I want to say, "What patterns have you got?" They won't know what that means, like, "What sentence structures do you know?" What I do find that works is that I'll ask people about a project they've done, "Don't tell me about the whole project. Just tell me about something that you've learned when you made the project that you didn't

---

[5]*Design Patterns: Elements of Reusable Object-Oriented Software*, by Erich Gamma, et al. (Addison-Wesley, 1994).

expect to learn. What was the surprise or the delight that proved to be true?" And people can stop and they'll think, "Well, that's a funny question." Then they say, "Oh, I can remember the morning that I did something or other and I was so surprised."

The unexpected is something you do remember. And what they're doing is they're saying, "I had a problem. I discovered a solution that resolved the forces, and I'm going to tell you what it was." They tell me, and I say, "Ahh, now that sounds like a pattern. That is something that you'll hold on to for the rest of your life. You'll look for that. And you know what? I'll look for it too because you just told me." That is the stuff that makes software patterns worth talking about.

One thing we discovered is that Christopher Alexander said, "Well, here's the way to write these essays. This is the form."

Osborn: You found a pattern for essays?

Cunningham: Yes. And we found that it made for kind of dry reading. A number of people have written very good books by trying to write a pattern book, and then just saying, "I got to rewrite it and just tell the story, and I'll forget this form. I won't make the modularity so visible. I'll just—it was good for me organizing it, but I'll just write the book." And you can kind of see a style in those. It's sort of short chapters, and there are sections that flow in a surprisingly natural way.

Osborn: It's about telling the problem that the pattern solves and then the story behind it?

Cunningham: It's whatever the author feels is going to work for the reader, but I recognize books written from patterns because I'm seeing a solution every two pages.

I took a lot of calculus. Professors would say, "This week we're going to learn integration by parts." That's just a pattern. When you see something where you can integrate by parts, you apply the pattern for integration by parts. And a lot of doing your calculus homework is to learn a lot of patterns and to recognize when to apply them, and then apply them. So it works. Of course, Christopher Alexander was a mathematician, no surprise there.

So, a practical skill is having a lot of patterns. And one way to have a lot of patterns is to have a lot of experience, to face a lot of forces and overcome them, or balanced them, or find solutions. One way to have a lot of patterns is to work with a group that ships software and shares that knowledge freely. I'm a real fan of, "Well, let's look at the screen together and experience it together so we can talk about what's happening on the screen, and maybe both get the benefit of this one bit of programming."

At Tektronix I worked with people who were really good at electronics and I held up the software end on some pretty good projects. I learned enough electronics and I had studied electrical engineering, so I know the theory behind the circuits, but not the practical circuit knowledge. I needed the engineers and they needed me.

Today I find that the parts are so easy to use I can get them working by myself. Modern parts are so powerful. So I say, "Well, let me see if I can build something." And after I've solved a few problems, I discover it's actually the solving I like. It's learning new patterns to the point where I start making up new problems that I don't actually have, and seeing if I can solve them. If I'm not solving it, maybe I can pick a different problem. Maybe I don't knock myself out because I'm doing it for fun.

The other thing that really got me going was a get-together—a meet-up called Dorkbot—that meets in places around the world, including Portland. They love the making. They're dedicated to electronics or technology meeting art. And to me, the art means just that: that it doesn't have to go into production. If you build just one, that's enough. You've finished your art piece.

Osborn: It doesn't really need a reason to exist or solve a problem, it just is.

Cunningham: That's right. I have a lot of parts and I would think about something I could do, and I would say, "If I built this on Sunday afternoon, could I take it to Dorkbot on Monday, and while we're all sitting around and talking about different things we're working on, could I put it on a table, turn it on, and tell a story?"

Remember, I like to ask people, "What did you learn that you didn't think you'd learn, that you didn't expect to learn?" I'm going to make something that uses electronic parts in these little microcomputers in a way that when you look at it, you say, "Oh, that's the answer to the question, 'What did you learn that you didn't expect to learn?'" And I found that I could just do that on a Sunday afternoon. Now, you do that over, and over, and over, and pretty soon you've got a storehouse of things to do.

Osborn: Can you give me a couple examples of things you've brought to Dorkbot or that you built just for your own interests?

Cunningham: Well, one thing that got me going was this professor teaching robotics years ago. He showed how his students were developing software to move a robotic arm to solve the problems in manufacturing. But he also challenged his students to make the arm dance. He showed us the dance, and the arm just moved around in free space assuming postures. It was also very robotic. It was not artful at all. I thought robot dance was an interesting challenge, but they failed. It was not a dance. It was an awkward robotic motion. So always in the back of my mind I thought, "I want to make a robotic arm dance."

This thought came back to me after 9/11 when everybody's waving the flag. I thought, "I'm going to wave a flag in an artful way." And I just glued two servo motors together and I made this thing that would wave the flag. I made it wave back and forth, but that wasn't dancing either. So I said, "Let's see if I can make that perform something that is a joy to watch. What would be a way to wave a flag that's interesting?" I spent a few evenings. I would teach it to do something, like wave around in a circle or back and forth. I had a little plastic, polyethylene flag, and as I moved it really quick, it would make a snappy sound. I was getting somewhere. I ended up having five or six successes that were worth showing, so I just wrote the program that would do each dance in turn. A performance would last ten to fifteen seconds. Then it would stop to rest. I found that if it was just moving all the time, you got sick of watching it. But if you waited with anticipation for the next performance, it was fun.

I've had it now for over a decade. I bring it out on the Fourth of July. People look at it, and they get immediately that it's dancing. That it is not just a simple way to wave a flag. It's performing in some way. And after they see it a minute later do another thing, it really connects. It's silly in a sense, but it was probably my first success at making something like that that's fun.

Osborn: I think the first time I met you, you were telling me about some sensors in your yard. I think a creek sensor that just uses a ribbon cable maybe.

Cunningham: That almost worked.

Osborn: Almost worked?

Cunningham: Somebody gave me a digital thermometer, something that was accurate to a tenth of a degree. It sent a digital signal. I hooked it up to a computer, a little computer, and showed that I could read temperatures out of it. Then I hooked that to a server and started recording, just read the temperature every five minutes and write it into a text file. I let it run for years. That turned out to be interesting because then I had data about my own house, so I hooked up more of them. Then I thought, "That neat. What else can I sense?" I put a photocell on the window and watched the sun go up and down, plotted that in interesting ways." I noticed that, by looking at the daily signal, the way the brightness of the light in my backyard varied, I could tell latitude and longitude of my house.

Osborn: Just by looking at that wave?

Cunningham: Yes. I recorded the time of every sample. I could tell longitude from when the sun was overhead. And the latitude came from the shape of the curve. And, of course, you know you're up above the Arctic Circle if it stays dark all winter, for example. But I could measure all kinds of things with great patience, and that was cool. So I collected that data for a long time. I tried this with three photocells. I put colored filters over them so I could get a color signal, one color pixel.

Osborn: How did you do the color filter?

Cunningham: I bought them at a camera store. I bought red, green, and blue filters. They might have been five bucks apiece. I felt guilty paying $15 for this crazy experiment, but I wanted them. I was hoping that on blue sky days, I could get blue, but the way color happens and the way we perceive it is much more complicated than that measurement. Still, the experiment got me thinking. "I could just read any old webcam for color pixels." So I wrote a program that reads dozens of webcams. I could just pick the pixels out of the sky in the webcam, and I would get blue on a blue-sky day. I could read them every five minutes or every hour, something like that. I started collecting sky pixels for multiple years. I could see when and where it was getting lighter, and where it was getting darker. Hemispheres and all that.

Osborn: How many blue-sky days are there in Portland? Not many.

Cunningham: Not too many. Down in sunny California there are a lot more blue-sky days. I learned a lot about programming scrapers of the web by scraping these webcams. It was hard to make my software run every hour, 24/7. So I would just plot those out, and I would look at five cities and bands, and you'd get these kind of sinusoidal things. And it just looked good. Each city was unique. I'd been to Tromsø, Norway so I watched their webcam too. Tromsø ran a great webcam: solid data for two or three years, as long as I looked. There were good images and the data set looked beautiful.

I became interested in this idea of having a simple sensor and a computer, and the computer provides the persistence in recording. I wasn't interested in battery-operated things. I wanted things that when I turned the power on, it stayed on. I could record things for years. I really liked that.

Remember my brother got me interested in electronics? He's still as much an inventor as ever, and I'm telling him about this photocell. He says, "Oh yeah, I've got data that goes back two years before you were even recording it. I've got a complete data set." So I described how I was plotting the data and getting bands where I could see—I would plot twenty-four hours in one vertical stripe, and day, by day, by day, there would be new stripes, so I could see summer goes to winter, goes to summer, goes to winter. So my brother whipped up the same program and sent me images from his data.

I said, "Wow! You've got great data there." He had put his sensor out on a pole in the middle of his yard. I taped my photocell to a window, but he worked harder and had great data for the effort. Plus, like you say, there are a lot more sunny days in California, where he lives. When I looked at his image I could see his trees. We talked about which trees I saw and where they were in the picture, because the image was all distorted, based on the motion of the sun. He says, "Well, I can filter that distortion out." He wrote the program that took this data that he had collected over years and projected it into a panoramic picture of his backyard. The trees of his backyard appeared in silhouette as captured by his one-pixel camera and the computer that recorded it.

Osborn: So a photocell in the backyard got the horizontal scan line from the earth's rotation and a vertical one from tilt over the season?

Cunningham: Yeah, it was actually just using the orbit of the earth, rotating about the pole and rotating around the sun, scanned and, of course, the way it looked, it looked like this big swoopy swipe across the panorama. It got down close to the ground, as close as the sun does in the winter, and it got high in the sky, as high as the sun got in the summer because the sun was scanning, sketching out the picture. And, in fact, if you made a box camera or pinhole or something that was small enough and left it there for half a year, you'd get the same picture. We were just using a computer to do it. And, of course, because he had six years of data, he had twelve exposures. Every spring and every fall he'd get another picture and can rifle through them. He'd say, "Oh yeah, I remember that spring. Boy, it was terrible," because it was all blotchy because there were a lot of clouds that spring. So you got a little bit of weather in there, too.

Osborn: I think we'd do everyone an injustice if we didn't get to talk about your other invention, the Wiki. What problems were you trying to solve when you came up with that?

Cunningham: Yes, that's an important part of the story. Remember, Kent and I are trying to figure out this notion of patterns, and we realize that we maybe didn't know all the patterns, or we couldn't think of them in the right order, or we didn't know how to approach the problem, so we wanted to get other people involved.

We wanted to invent a new literature of computer programming. Not just to write a book, but also to create a new way of writing and get a lot of people to write in that form, so we talked about creating a new literature. It was a concept that resonated. So we talked about people like Christopher Alexander and his theories, and we eventually got a mailing list going and found the people who were thinking the same way, and we had a couple of retreats.

After the first retreat, I think five or six of us got together and talked about why we thought this was important and basically said, "Okay, how come nobody is doing it? How come it's not working? What do we have to do?" The decision then was, "Well, we need to have a bigger community. We need to have a conference or a workshop on this. Let's just have a workshop." A lot of things in organizing that workshop we did right. We decided we should hold the event at the Allerton House, which is a conference center, an old mansion near the University of Illinois that made it easy to hold workshop-type conferences, and Ralph Johnson agreed to be the conference chair.

Then my friends said, "Well, we need a program chair," and then everybody looked at me. I said, "Wait a second. I'm the guy who's a slow reader. I can't be the program chair." And they just said, "No, you've got to be the program chair." I don't know who it was that decided I should be the program chair. We had another couple of get-togethers to plan it and it turned out to be great.

We told everyone, "This isn't to present results, like traditional papers. This is to come and workshop your partial results. If you think you're doing patterns, let's get together." We borrowed the writers' workshop style that novelists and poets use. We got a hundred folks together at the University of Illinois to invent the new literature of computer programming. It worked.

I stuck around for an extra day to hang out with the graduate students, Ralph's graduate students, who really put on the event for us, to understand what they were up to. I was into Smalltalk and they were into Smalltalk, so we had at least that in common.

Brian Foote was one of those students then. Brian says, "Let me show you this thing called the World Wide Web." Mark Andreessen had worked on the browsers there at University of Illinois the year before. He said, "Hypertext was going to be important."

Brian told me, "Ward, I think this literature that we're making needs to be in hypertext on the World Wide Web, and I think you should do it." Again, I don't know why he thought I should do it, but maybe it was because I was the program chair—and I wasn't sure why I was the program chair—but I just said, "Okay, I'll do it. I'll figure it out." I had been given the charge of collecting together this new literature and making it available on the Web.

At the time I wasn't even on the Web. I was on CompuServe, but that wasn't the Web. So I ran into my old boss from Tektronix, who was now working with a guy who was setting people up on the Web. I asked him to hook me up." He brought over a little UNIX system that slipped under my desk. It made some touchtone sounds and I was on the Web. So simple.

I learned enough web technology that I realized HTML submissions weren't going to work. Instead I asked contributors to just send me text files formatted with a few simple rules." Even this didn't work. They would send me text files, but they could not follow my instructions. I'd say, for example, "Put a blank line in between paragraphs," because I was going to write a little program that would recognize blank lines and then put in the HTML markup. But they wouldn't do it. They wouldn't follow simple instructions.

After about doing four of those and doing massive edits, I said, "Let me take this new feature of the Web that had just come out." It was forms, markup so you could submit forms. And I said, "Let me make a form for submitting new patterns to the Web." I just started playing with that. The patterns all linked together.

The linking between patterns would map to the links in hypertext. So I came up with this real simple way of doing links. If my contributors didn't do a link right, it wouldn't make a link, and then they'd say, "Oh, I didn't do it right." They'd fix it, and they'd keep trying it until they got the linking right.

I'm just sitting there running this program on my little PC running UNIX under my desk. It was so fast and so easy. It was fun to write. I had spent a few months writing HTML, and that wasn't fun. HTML was powerful, I could tell it was powerful, but it wasn't fun, and this was fun. If you ran words together, it would recognize that as being something important. The idea is that the shorter it is, the more important. Really short words like "me" and "you" are short because we use them a lot. They're important. So I thought, "A word that is minus one, the punctuation where we take a space out, that's as short as you can get. That's negative one." And linking is what hypertext was about. So I could tell it was going to be important.

"Well, I need to give it a good name." I thought, "It's quick, it's fast, compared to writing HTML. I need to name it after that experience." I almost called it "Quick Web." I'm going, "Quick Web, Quick Web" But that wasn't special enough. I knew that "wiki" was the Hawaiian word for "quick." You double it for emphasis, so a really quickly web would be the "Wiki Wiki Web." I said that to myself two or three times, and I said, "That's it. I'll call it the WikiWikiWeb," but it was really just a way that I could get submissions to this body, this collection of patterns and it turned out to be fun.

As I'm sitting there, I thought, "Well, this is a little weird. People aren't going to understand it." I asked them to write a page about themselves first, so they'll feel ownership of one page. That worked. But I wanted people to improve each other's patterns. I wanted them to finish each others patterns. That reflected the way I'd been thinking about computer programming. I was thinking of Kent and me finishing each other's computer programs. That took some coaxing but I made it happen.

Every day I would come in to work and I would get on my computer and talk to my server and find out what people left me overnight. It was fabulous. It just kept getting bigger and bigger every day. Some people started writing in different ways. They were going to try different ways to write. But I had thought carefully. I had written the first hundred pages. I said, "Well, I kind of found the style of writing that fit with this notion of literature. Sure, you can write whatever you want on your own page, but when you're writing in these pattern pages, I want you to write in a way that's consistent with what would serve the purposes of this new literature."

So I became the editor. I edited aggressively. Nobody seemed to mind. Maybe they didn't even notice. But what happened is, over a year of that, there turned out to be hundreds of pages, many hundreds, and they all were edited into a consistent style. And then, pretty soon people would come and they'd read around and say, "Oh, I get the style here," and they'd write in the right way. Not only did I make the medium, I invented the style of writing in this form.

It's like an old house that you keep fixing. It just keeps getting better because you have the freedom to do that. Well, we had the freedom to do that because we had the freedom to improve something, to bring something personal to a body of work. I would tell people, "If you want Wiki to work well, you really have to consider the words you write a gift to the community. Don't think of them as your words anymore. They're our words, and if somebody changes those words to make them better and you feel insulted at that, get over it." People who understood that really made the Wiki great. I would find amazing things written.

Osborn: So now you are working on what you call a federated Wiki? Can we touch on what the difference between a federated Wiki and a traditional Wiki is?

Cunningham: I was just talking about sharing words. That worked then but less so now. You get into situations where you don't want the confusing ownership. You want people to use your words, but you want to have your originals for reference. These were the words as I said them.

Let me explain, really simply to start with, that what I made in Wiki is a way that we could put our words into a database. I made a web interface so that anybody could come in and edit that database. That's what I had: a database, a web interface, and people from anywhere in the world could come in and read or write on it. So the sharing happens in the database, behind those web servers.

Osborn: One thing that made it really interesting was the freedom for anyone to come in and make changes. Which seems really counterintuitive to a lot of people who want to have control over things, and that would be overrun, right?

Cunningham: Yeah, most people thought that. The fact is that I thought if it lasted for six months that would be quite an experiment. And it lasted for six years, but six years into it, what happened to it became so important. It became a place where people came and found things and trusted them. The site earned the attention of a lot of people. And eventually, somebody who wasn't of a giving mind would show up. And even though all of it was free and there was nothing to steal, they would come to steal attention. They could come in and they could write something that would cause people to think about them. Maybe it would be spam about new web sites or sex products or something like that. There were more psychologically disturbed people who would write stuff to create grief. Grievers, I think you call them in computer gaming. They were people who just wanted to hurt people one way or another. Wikis are very vulnerable to that.

Wikipedia survives because there's just enough continuous traffic and enough editors that when someone does that sort of thing, it gets changed back very quickly. They do battle. They defend that space. But after seven or eight years of Wiki, a lot of people had put up a Wiki in a quiet little corner of the Internet. But somebody would find it and fill it up with spam. It was really sad. Disgusted they'd say, "Well, I guess this Wiki is used up." A lot of Wikis were destroyed. There were a lot of other problems with that particular model. It was very successful, and Wikipedia's made me famous, there's no doubt about that, and they deserve all the credit.

But what I've done recently is make something that was like Wiki but one that didn't share just one database. In my new Wiki the sharing happens in the client, in the browser, so that you could be browsing along and it can hop from database to database to database. Everybody makes their own database. Everybody puts their words in their own database. If they like your words, they take your words and put them in their database, as their words, so there's this radical sharing, but the only place I write is to my database, and the only place you write is to your database. And we share because we set up our browser to read both at the same time.

Maybe you've got some friends that I don't know about, and I'm looking at your pages, and all of a sudden I learn about your friends because I follow your pages to their pages. And it becomes this giant gossip network, except it's better than gossip because it's digital. They don't get misunderstood in translation. In fact, if I'm reading about your friends on your pages and you're not really telling their story right. Well, pretty soon I'll be reading your friends' pages on their site, because if you take something your friends write and present it to me with your spin on it, well, I'll read that and say, "Okay, this is what you think your friends said, but let me go back and see what your friends really said." So there's always an ability to go back to the source.

This is made possible with this fabulous legal contract, the Creative Commons Attribution Share Alike. It says, "You can take your friend's stuff and call it your own, but you have to admit that you got it from your friend. And if he gave it away for free, you've got to give it away for free, too." The Wiki is designed to be a medium that embodies Creative Commons Attribution Share Alike.

The programming trick that makes it neat is to make this feel like a Wiki, not like a bunch of blogs. In a blog, everybody says their own thing. People go into their corner of the Internet and yell at each other. I wanted it to be a place where it feels like a Wiki, even though it was stored like a blog or a bunch of blogs. So that involves a lot of tricky programming. It took me months to learn how to actually make it feel that way, and I'm not even sure I have it yet. We're still doing a lot of experiments with it. But it wouldn't have been possible without the modern browser and the ability to do so much in JavaScript.

JavaScript is pretty fabulous. That's my new toy at the moment, the modern browser. I tell people, when I had Smalltalk on my desk, I could feel this tremendous jump in the amount of power I had. A lot of people weren't interested in it, but my friend Kent and I recognized, "This is important," and we figured out why it was important. I'm feeling a similar jump in the last couple of years and, of course, it's no surprise that the people who figured out how to make Smalltalk work really well are the same people who twenty years later are figuring out how to make JavaScript work really well. And they've done it. JavaScript is on the client and JavaScript on the server now, JavaScript everywhere. It's like Smalltalk was, except that it's global.

Smalltalk was cool on my desktop, but this is all over the world, and that's hard to ignore. I want to make the new browsers a place for people who want to create in the same way that we wanted to create our new literature of programming—change the way programming is done. Whatever the next problem is, I want them to find their voice in a Federated Wiki. The computers of the era are not like the computers from two decades before. They're very powerful and they're misunderstood. What I'd love to see is a Wiki-style conversation, but one that is global and about us collectively changing how we live.

Jeri Ellsworth

Founder

Technical Illusions

Since birth, **Jeri Ellsworth** *has been a maker, questioning the world around her and looking for creative ways to improve it. Over the years, she has built numerous gadgets, ranging from toys to race cars. Jeri is well known for her Commodore 64 joystick creation that included a large number of games in a small package and was a huge hit with hackers. More recently, Jeri founded Technical Illusions (*`technicalil-lusions.com`*), a company that is making amazing strides in augmented reality and the way we interact with computers and virtual worlds.*

Steven Osborn: Thanks for taking the time today. I've seen you in a lot of videos—not necessarily videos that you did, but videos of you and Ben Heck, or you and Becky Stern. It seems like you have your hand in a lot of different things. Could you start by telling me about early projects you worked on, your education, things that got you where you are now?

Jeri Ellsworth: I was raised in rural Oregon, in a little town called Independence. There weren't a lot of role models around, like maker types. I had a lot of interest in how things worked at a very young age. One of the things I vividly remember was my father being upset with me for taking everything apart. He would buy me these expensive toys, but I was more interested in seeing what made them tick than in playing with them. This is probably at the age of seven or eight—just about the age where I could start manipulating screwdrivers and prying things apart.

Eventually, my father got frustrated and quit buying me regular toys. He owned a gas station, and he put a box outside with a sign, "Bring your broken electronics here." His customers would drop off old VCRs and toasters, all kinds of weird stuff. Every few weeks, he would bring those boxes of stuff in for me to tear apart. It was heaven. I tore apart tape decks and learned how they worked, VCRs, all kinds of things. For many years, it was just taking things apart. I didn't like things being a mystery to me.

Then that morphed into wanting to make my own things. So I started modifying some of these devices to get them working again. I might change a green LED into a red one, and that was a big deal for me at the time. It progressed from there. I started learning more.

I started to find mentors in the community, mostly ham radio operators. They took me under their wing and taught me how to do electronics and mechanics in a more engineering-wise way.

So I got into doing radio transmitters and working with vacuum tubes, which was very interesting to me. This was the eighties, and transistors were well cemented into everything. But the old-timers, the ham radio operators, all their equipment was tube stuff. So they'd be talking about tubes. I had all these tubes that I had gotten out of old, broken radios and I started making transmitters with tubes, mainly because transistors were expensive to buy from the local Radio Shack. So I spent a lot of time working on radios.

My neighbor up the road was into electronics, so we started building transmitters and having these competitions where we would build AM radios. We would get on our bikes, and we'd have our little transistorized AM radios, and we'd ride as far as we could, and listen, counting phone poles away from our houses to see how far we could actually transmit, it was like an arms race. He'd make one that would go two or three miles, and I'd make one that would go four miles, then he'd make a bigger one. Pretty soon, it got to the point where these transmitters were so powerful that we were transmitting beyond what you could ride in an afternoon on our bikes. I'm sure it was very illegal, FCC-wise. So then we moved onto FM radios and other radio stuff.

I was really into exploring. I think that's part of my hacker background—"hacker" in a good way—being interested in exploring things. I was fascinated with phones early on. I made all kinds of circuits to do fun things on phones. My first telephone was actually one that I built myself because my father wouldn't let me have one. I took one of those electronic kits that you can get from Radio Shack and I figured out how to match the impedance and actually make a phone. I dialed it with a little Morse code key, and back in the days of rotary-dial phones, you would rotate it to the number that you wanted and then release it, and it would make and break a circuit to pulse in the number that you wanted. So I would call my friends via Morse code. My friends who had phone numbers with zeros in them were really frustrating because I had to get the timing just right, and I had to do a lot of pulses to send a zero. One was obviously just one pulse. With my first phone, I ran some wires outside and tapped into our phone line, and I was making calls at a pretty early age on my homemade telephone.

Eventually, I found a broken phone, thrown out alongside the road, and I fixed that up and got it working. Then I took the ringers out of it to hide it from my father, because he didn't want me having a phone. I got busted one time because he was in my room talking to me when my homemade phone started ringing. It still had this little solenoid that knocked back and forth between the two bells, but the bells weren't installed. It was a distinctive enough oscillation that he figured out what was going on. He was pretty cool at that point. He let me keep it, but I started pranking my friends with the phone, making circuits that would pick up the phone instantly when people called.

I had this Triac circuit that—as soon as a little current flowed in the line for the ring—would immediately pick up and turn an LED on so I could see that someone was calling. It would happen so fast that they would hear no ring on their end. I would prank-call all my friends and go, "Aaaahhh!" They would know it was me and try calling back. Immediately it would pick up, but they'd never heard the phone ring on their end.

I eventually expanded this, where I'd have automatic tape recorders that would play messages back. I would record various messages like, "Please deposit twenty-five cents," or "This phone line has been disconnected." I had my friends convinced that I had complete and utter control over the phones. I even found, by war-dialing the entire city one time with my Commodore 64 computer and a modem, a bank of phone numbers that were used for pay phones. There were all kinds of interesting messages, like, "To make an international call, [do this]," or "Deposit twenty-five cents." So I'd go over to friends' houses and I'd say, "Oh, I need to call my dad. Can you let me use your phone?" And then I'd call and dial one of these numbers that would return, say, "Please deposit twenty-five cents," and then I'd be like, "Hey, didn't you pay your phone bill? It's asking me to deposit twenty-five cents!" And then I'd hand them the receiver and they would hear the recording and go, "Whoa!"

Osborn: So they thought not only did you have control over your phone, but all phones.

Ellsworth: It was kind of a sleight-of-hand.

Osborn: I remember there was some number you would call and it would cause your phone to ring back, and I would do that to frustrate my mom from time to time.

Ellsworth: Local ring-back numbers for the line workers? Actually, I burned out our phone lines one time because I found that your normal handset can only get so loud because it just has a little speaker in it, but if you amplified the audio going into it, you could blast people's ears on the other end that you call. I had a CB radio that had a PA output and this echo mike—yeah, I was into CB radios. I admit it was fun. But I hooked the PA output to my phone, and then I would call my friends and just scream into it and blast their ears out.

I was doing that one time and somehow I fried our phone lines. They quit working. It was just this loud buzz when you picked up the phone, so I went to my father and said, "Oh, Dad, I don't know what happened, but the phone is not working." So he called from his work phone and had them fix it. But when they fixed it, somehow, it was slightly crossed with our neighbors down the road, and I didn't know who it was crossed with. Off in the distance, you could hear a little of them talking, and they could hear us. So I'd use the same amplifier trick and would talk to my neighbors that way. Eventually they figured out it was me and came and talked to my father. We never got that fixed, which was frustrating, because when I started doing a lot of BBS stuff with my Commodore 64, when they would be on the phone, that little bit of crosstalk would mess up the modem. Rather frustrating. So you pay for your messing around sometimes.

Eight-bit homemade computers were a huge influence on who and what I am today. The first computer I ever touched was at a friend's house, a friend of my father's. It was a TI-99/4A and I was completely enamored with it. I would sit in front of it for hours. I didn't understand how it worked. I had only seen movies about how powerful computers were and they were going to talk to us someday. I would type into the computer "draw house" and it would return "syntax error"; "paint house"? And I would just spend hours trying to type things in, and every once in a while, it would respond with something different, like "for without next" and I'd get excited, "Oh, it did something. It's responding!"

Those friends gave me a programming book and taught me how to enter a program, and I entered some Mr. Bojangles dancing guy into the thing. I was really hooked at that point. I pestered my dad, "I need a computer! I need a computer so bad!" So we started going to different stores and looking at all these computers. It was funny. They were all on big long benches with monitors hooked up to them or TVs, and they didn't have anything running on them. There were just BASIC prompts. So we were going down the line looking at the computers and I saw this VIC-20 and it had these really big letters. Most of the computers at the time had forty characters per line, this one had twenty-two characters per line, and that was the thing that I really wanted, the one with the big characters, even though it was less of a machine. It was funny.

My dad opted for the better Commodore 64 and brought it home, and he bought a couple of game cartridges and a disk drive. He bought this thing and put it in his bedroom, hid it from me. He was trying to go through the book to learn how to use it before giving it to me. Of course, me snooping around the house, I spotted it in there, weeks before he gave it to me. I'd sneak in there after school when he wasn't home yet, and I'd work on the C64. I was writing things to the disk. I was well underway before he even gave it to me.

Osborn: You were like, "Oh! Thanks so much. I'm so surprised."

Ellsworth: Exactly! I guess maybe to emphasize how little I knew about electronics at that point and how I learned about doing electronics and making things just by observations, it had a game cartridge that came with it. I plugged the cartridge in and played a game, and thought, "Well, this game cartridge has these gold fingers on the edge of it. It must be wire connections between those gold fingers that's causing this videogame to happen. And so if I can, in the cartridge slot, somehow get the right connections, then I can make a videogame show up." That was my thinking at however old I was, maybe eight. So I would take butter knives, forks, and jam them into the cartridge slot. I ended up frying two or three Commodore 64s like that. And I'd go to my dad, "I don't know. It just quit working for some reason." So he'd return it under warranty.

Osborn: I remember the old cable box that had switches on it, with the cord. You could do stuff sort of like that. If you smashed the right buttons in the right combination, you could get a pay-per-view channel that you weren't supposed to get. You could unscramble the channel just enough to see what's going on.

Ellsworth: That brings up a whole other area that I was really fascinated with, descrambling video. My father bought a satellite dish for us. In the beginning, almost everything on this dish was unscrambled. But they started scrambling things. By my teens, I was pretty good with electronics, so I started making my own video descramblers. The one I'm very proud of was this scrambling scheme where they just inverted the video and inverted the sync pulses, so that was easy to get the video. With a simple couple-transistor circuit, I could get the video recovered. But the audio—they would sample the audio and then take a one-millisecond clip of audio and bust it into several different pieces and reorder it, so it just sounded garbled.

As I was looking at the video signal, I noticed that there were some barcode-looking things up in the vertical blanking interval of the video, and it corresponded with this garbled noise. So, the echo microphone that I was talking about earlier, I ripped it apart because it had an analog delay line with multiple taps, and it was an analog bucket brigade circuit. You could feed it an oscillator signal and it would move analog values through the audio values. It's what I ended up using it for, and it would delay them. It had multiple taps, so I found that I could run the audio in and then I could rearrange the audio with this, and eventually, I got so advanced I made some PPL logic. It would go down and count the number of scan lines, go in, find these little barcode encodings, and then it would choose the correct audio delay to reconstruct the audio.

So to watch a movie, I would start this thing up and it would be completely out of synchronization. I had a button that would bump the oscillator which would shift all of the delay lines around. I would bump the oscillator until everything lined up and the audio sounded good. I'd watch the movie for a while, it would slowly drift, it would get a little more garbled, and I'd bump the oscillator again and bring it back. It was great fun. I had all of the first-run movies for free.

Osborn: I know a little bit about when you were a kid, you somehow got into dirt-track racing. How did that fit in with everything else?

Ellsworth: So the whole race car story—you have to take a step back and look at how kids treated me in junior high. I was this weird kid, into electronics, very nerdy, into the sciences. So I was in a really small town with a big football emphasis, and if you were a football player or a cheerleader, you were on top of the mound, and if you were a nerd, you were at the bottom. I was a very sensitive kid, and the jocks and the bullies found out that they could make me cry very easily. So they would constantly tease me. This started in junior high.

I was *the* one in the school that they would pick on. I became very reclusive, which just egged them to pick on me more. When I reached high school, it continued and got worse because there was a bigger population there. Then my freshman year—maybe it was my sophomore year, I snapped one day. I just couldn't take it anymore. There was this one bully that was always picking on me. I was walking in the front of a math class or something, one of these classes that had a really big, thick book, and he tripped me. With tunnel vision, I grabbed the book and swung it around like you'd throw a discus, and I just clobbered this kid across the head with it. He flipped out of his chair and fell to the floor.

The teacher had walked in behind me and saw me do this. He grabbed me by the arm and took me to the office. I remember feeling like my feet weren't touching the ground. He was so mad at me for doing that. And I got suspended because they had the zero-tolerance policy, which I found ironic because these kids would spit in my hair or shove me down all the time. They were more savvy about it. They wouldn't do it in front of teachers.

So when I came back to school after my week's suspension, the bad kids were like, "That's pretty cool. You stood up for yourself." And I found this new group of kids to hang out with. They thought I was all right for standing up. And I changed my whole personality. I found that the more edgy I was, the less these bullies would pick on me. So I started looking for everything I could to make myself appear more dangerous. I got in a lot of trouble with the police and got suspended all the time. I would vandalize things. This became part of my persona.

My father, when I was younger, had built this jalopy-type race car and raced it a bit. I saw that and thought that was really cool. We'd go to the track occasionally. I started going to the racetrack once I got my own car, and watched the races with friends. Within the first or second race that I went to, I thought, "This is for me. I'm going to do this." There were different classes of cars, and of course, I wanted to race in the fastest.

So I started asking around, how do people get into this? And I found that a lot of people built their own cars. I started asking my dad—at this point, I was working at his gas station. I was changing oil and pumping gas and doing all kinds of stuff. I had been doing that for a few years. So I started asking my dad to build a race car. And he'd say, "*Absolutely* not. There is no way I'm going to do that for you." I kept pestering him, and finally, he caved in. He said, "The only way you're going to get to race is if you figure out how to buy a car or build one yourself." And I thought, "Hey, I can make things."

So I signed up for welding classes in school. I went into the local machine shops and started talking to machinists. And at this point, I had already been working with ham radio operators. So I identified, "If I want to do something, I need to go out and find mentors, someone that knows what I need to know and see if I can establish some win–win relationship with them." So I found a machinist in town that would let me come in on Saturdays. He made me just schlep metal around and clean the bed of his lathe and do all his grunt work in exchange for spending an hour or two at the end of the day teaching me how to do some machining things. He would grab a piece of scrap metal and show me how to turn it on a lathe. Or he would grab the welder and show me how to do a certain type of weld. So I started learning how to do all these mechanical things that I needed to do.

I ordered some books on how to build a race car, from the back of a magazine. I got a video on how to do it and started doing research. I started building a car in high school shop. At the end of shop, I took what was left of this chassis—not complete—to my father's gas station. At this point, he's like, "She's going to do it. I should get involved to make sure she does it right." So he helped me quite a bit. He helped me build my first motor.

For quarter-mile dirt-track racing, it's an oval track. It's cars that you're racing at seventy, eighty miles per hour on this little tiny track right next to twenty or thirty other cars. You're constantly in contact with them because there's just not enough space. So I put this thing together and went out for the first time and didn't have any time to practice. I missed all the test and tune days. I did terribly, but I qualified. I felt like I set the track record. I felt like I was going so fast. I had this big ego, too, of course. I came in and found out I was the slowest time of the night, by a lot.

I went out for my first race. It was a heat race, and there were only five or six cars on the track at the time. I make it half a lap, I spin out, and there are cars all around me. One of them hits me head on. I'm just covering my eyes, "Oh my God." Then bonk, he crashes into me. "Hey, that's not too bad." I threw it into reverse, peeled my car off his, and took off.

It took me a long time to learn. I thought I would be able to learn very quickly, but it took me a while to figure it out. There's so much input and braking, and gassing, and steering, and stuff that you have to think about while you're racing. It took about a year or two into racing before all that thinking became muscle memory, and that's when I started doing really well.

Of course, I was always trying to innovate with my race cars. Everything I do, I always try to make it better. The first car I built off these blueprints I got out of the back of a magazine, but then one of the videos I got came from this guy in Florida. So I started calling him all the time, asking him questions, "How do you do this or that?" He was getting fed up with me calling all the time. He said, "I'll tell you what. If you just come out and spend a week with me and my wife, I'll teach you everything you need to know about race cars. You won't have to call me all the time." He was in Florida. It was the beginning of summer. Racing season hadn't started yet. I hopped on a Greyhound bus and drove four and a half days across the country. I was seventeen or eighteen years old. It was ridiculous. I got to Florida, worked with this guy. He became a really good mentor.

The first half of the week, he taught me how to do all the things—suspension, statics, dynamics of a car, setup. The second half of the week, he spent a lot of time talking about how to get into people's heads, which was as important as actually building a good race car, because the psychology of your opponents, as I found out later, can affect how they react to you when you're on the track. Much like being in high school, like trying to be the bad ass, if you're like really aggressive on the track and you don't let anyone walk on you, people will see your car and will move away. He taught me all these tricks. During a yellow flag situation, you're usually just driving around the track single file. He said,

> "Just bump the person in front of you. Just keep bumping them. Every once in a while just bump them, and then once you see their head start to bob back and forth, you know that you've flustered them and that they're not going to think clearly when the race starts, when they throw the green flag again."

Another trick he said was,

> "During these green flag situations, pull alongside them when you're on the back stretch or somewhere away from where they're cleaning up the wreck, and then out the window, give them a thumbs-up, just to let them know that you're there. And do that a couple times, but always at the same side of their car and give them a thumbs-up, wave. You can program them so when the race starts, in their mind they're going to think that you're going to go to the high side of the tracks. They're going to block you up there, so just be prepared to cut under them."

And, surprisingly, it works.

I kept innovating my car. I built a traction-control system. At this point, it was around '91 or '92, and a bunch of German cars were coming out with traction-control systems. I was like, "Wow, it would be really nice if I had a traction-control system on this dirt car, where you're sliding sideways all the time." So I started figuring out how to do that. I made this little 6502 board, this 6502 processor, a RAM and some ROM, various things.

I put a hall sensor out on the front wheel so I could measure its front-wheel rotation speed. In this type of car, we didn't have gears that you shifted. You put it in one gear to put your car in maximum RPM at the end of the straightaway. So I was able to look at the ignition pulse coming off the distributor and figure out how fast my rear tires were spinning. And then from the pulses coming from the front wheel and the pulses from the ignition, I could figure out how much my rear tires were spinning. So on my car, I had this ignition module that prevented over-revving. The way it did this was it had these chips you would put in. The chips were actually just a resistor at a certain value. And when your RPM would exceed a certain limit, it would just start cutting off the spark plugs. It wouldn't fire a certain spark plug. It would alternate them, so it would cut the power back. You'd still be dumping fuel through your engine, but you would cut the power.

I made a little toggle that would switch in my normal 8000-RPM rev limiter with one that was set to 3000 RPM, which was well below the normal driving RPM. So if my back tire started slipping too much, then the ignition module would start cutting power. I started doing really well with this thing because it made my car impossible to spin out unless I did some really bad steering, so I could go flying into the corner and press the gas until I'd hear the rev limiter kicking in, and then I'd go riding around the corner with no fear of spinning out.

It made my car very exciting for the audience because all this raw fuel was dumping into my exhaust. As the race would go on, the raw fuel would heat up my exhaust. Actually, the first time I ran it, I didn't have insulation on my exhaust, and it ran up and over the engine and out the passenger side of the car. It got so hot that it melted the paint on the inside of the cockpit. It was all scorched and melted. And it was *really* hot! I didn't think I was going to make it through the race. I wasn't smart enough to put a disable switch on it at the time.

Eventually, I insulated all my exhaust, and started running this thing, and all this raw fuel would be dumping out of the exhaust. By halfway through the race, there'd be these huge flames shooting out the side of my car. The audience loved it. I was winning lots of races, and making lots of money.

They eventually caught on to this and banned traction-control systems. The reason they caught on is because I was always an entrepreneur and I was trying to sell it. I was selling chassis at the time, and I was trying to sell this ignition module plus traction control, so word got out. I was making so much money racing cars that my motivation to continue in school dropped to zero.

I ended up dropping out of high school. I really wasn't fitting in there anyway. And I thought I was going to become this pro race car driver and chassis builder. So I did race cars for probably more five and a half years. I really got out of doing electronics at that point and was really into mechanics. I thought I was going to be a mechanical engineer.

Osborn: What did you do after you finished racing cars?

Ellsworth: I started to work on all of my bad attitude problems that I'd picked up in high school. All of a sudden, I didn't have this desire to go out and risk my life every weekend. So I was sitting with one of my friends who had made this computer room in his garage. We talked a wholesale vendor into selling us parts. So for a computer that would normally cost $1200, I built it for $500, or something like that. I was thinking, "Wow, that's a lot of margin, and you don't have to weld and burn yourself and lift heavy metal to do it. I'm going to quit racing. I'm going to sell my equipment. Let's open a computer store. We can sell these things." And so we opened a computer store and that's what I did after racing.

During that time, my attitude changed a lot. I learned how to deal with customers. That side of things. At the time, I was gothy. I was trying to run this computer store with my business partner, and I had a chip on my shoulder about the world. It was upsetting him, and I wasn't making the sales I could be making because I was swearing in front of customers and had this bad attitude. So he booted me out of the business, which was very frustrating after building it up.

I asked a bunch of people what I should do. My father's advice was, "You should go back to school. If you're not going to race cars, and this computer thing fell apart." I asked a few friends. They said, "Go back to school."

I was sitting in my apartment crying, "I can't believe this happened. He can't do this to me. I'm going to open a computer store and put him out of business." I was out for revenge. I called my landlord a couple of days later to ask what it would cost to get out of my apartment. I took the money that I had, which was about $1200. I had lost all my money in this fight to stay in the business. There were lawyers involved.

Then I found a little barbershop, a one-chair barbershop, and rented it. I took the barber chair out of this dinky space and threw it in the back alley. I opened up a computer store, but I didn't have any product to put on the walls. I'd spent all of my money to get the store fixtures put in. I was dumpster diving in my ex-business partner's trash to get the empty boxes he was throwing away. I would put them on the wall and make it look like I had something. So a customer would come in and he'd point to a sound card or something, and he'd say, "I want that sound card." I'd say, "Well, that one is already spoken for, but if you give me half the money, I'll get you one here in a couple of days," which half the money was about what it cost to get it wholesale. Or if it was something bigger with less margin, then I'd aggregate a bunch of different orders. I was just robbing Peter to pay Paul.

But during this time, across the street from my new computer store, was an insurance salesman who was a computer fanatic, so he would come over and hang out with me at lunchtime. He saw that I was starving to death. I didn't have money for food. He'd bring me lunch. He started mentoring me in business. He suggested I didn't swear in front of customers, and maybe I should change my dress to be a little bit more professional: instead of all black, maybe a business suit. I admired him because I saw him as successful, so slowly—it was difficult and painful to do—I started making these small changes to my personality and my image. Lo and behold, my business started taking off.

Eventually, the store grew and grew, to the point that it was just elbow-to-elbow in this five hundred-square-feet retail space. I moved into a bigger space, and then opened another store, and another store, and another. By the end of the nineties, it was '98 or '99, I had five computer stores up and down the I-5 corridor in Oregon. Things were going really good for me. I got back into hobby electronics and bought a bunch of different tools so that I could do circuit boards and FPGAs, these field-programmable gate arrays, and CPLDs were really new at the time. So the tools were expensive, but because I was making money at these computer stores, I could afford them. I started experimenting with FPGAs, just as a hobby.

In the '99 to 2000 timeframe, the whole computer retail business tanked badly. EMachines started coming out with very inexpensive machines that were $299, so my margins that were three, four hundred dollars per machine went down to virtually nothing. I started having trouble maintaining my business and eventually had to close some of my stores, lay off employees. I rode the business almost clear into the ground.

Our computer stores—we were very much like a family. We were all friends. We would hang out and do stuff. We were all fairly young. So we tried to make a go of it, but I ended up losing almost everything at this point.

So in 2000, I sold off my last store, and again it was another one of these decision points in my life: What do I do? Do I go back to school and try to get a degree? Or do I just try to blaze forward and carve my own path? I decided, "Well, I've got a little bit of money. I'll try to make a go of electronics. It's been my passion since I was a kid."

I started building little circuit boards that could show off my talent in electronics. I'd build these FPGA boards that could do video generation. I built all these boards and started going to different trade shows in Silicon Valley. I started off in 2000 by flying down to shows, and I would go in and try to meet every person I could and shake their hands and be like, "Hey, look. I can do electronics. Look at my projects." I got some interviews out of that, but I really wasn't making it very far. I don't think I got any jobs out of that. I started running out of money, but I knew I had to make the connections and get mentors.

So I started hopping on Greyhound buses again. I was riding down to Silicon Valley. I would go to a trade show. At this point I didn't have money to even stay in a motel, so I'd arrive in the morning, go into the trade show—sneak into the trade show—and then meet as many people as I could, and then jump on a Greyhound bus back up to Portland. I did that over and over and over again. I kept running out of money.

I took part-time jobs to try to keep myself alive. Actually, I took a job at an electronics retailer. It's called Norvac Electronics. It was like Radio Shack on steroids. I sold components and cables, stuff like that. Within the first few weeks that I was there, the manager or owner of the store had a chart, where he charted all the salespeople's progress. Mine was just off the chart because I had sales experience plus an electronics background.

When someone would come through and wanted to build a hobby project, they'd be buying various components. I'd be like, "Oh, what are you building?" And I'd talk to them about it, and then I'd give them suggestions, and I could upsell all kinds of parts, help them on their project. It got to the point where people wouldn't come in unless I was there. So the owner was really pushing to get me in there more days a week. When I first went in, I only wanted to do two or three days a week, because I was going to be traveling and trying to start my career in electronics. At one point, he threatened me with, "If you don't start coming in these days, then I'm going to have to let you go."

And I said, "All right, I quit."

He said, "Whoa, wait, wait, wait." But it was too late and I just quit on the spot.

Osborn: That backfired on him.

Ellsworth: I have a bit of an attitude that way.

Osborn: At least you didn't hit him with a book!

Ellsworth: I know. Good thing it wasn't in my hands. I might have. My little bit of temper gets me in trouble from time to time. So I kept going to Silicon Valley.

I ended up getting my first real big break at an electronics show. I met the president of the company. I met him then rode the Greyhound bus back up to Portland, and like a week later, I had to come back for the interview. So I was on a Greyhound again. At this point, I had done a dozen interviews with them—all "no." Most of the interviews ended with the HR people rejecting me, very early in the day when they found out I didn't have a college education. So this interview was going exactly the same way, and they dismissed me early in the morning, and I was walking down the stairs, out of the office building, and I ran into the president of the company coming back up. He was like, "Hey, how's it going? Where are you going?"

And I said, "Well, they said I was done." He said, "Really? Have you talked to any engineers yet?" I said, "No."

He said, "Well, come with me." And he marched me right into their lab, introduced me to all the engineers, gave me my first break, and I did a really good job for them.

From that came other recommendations and other jobs, and that's how my career started. I just worked extremely hard to prove myself, and then I just got the next job off that, continuing on and on.

Meanwhile, I was continuing all my hobby stuff because I saw that as a way I could prove my skill. In my spare time, I'd be making Commodore 64 emulators on FPGAs and various little widgets. I started talking about this online. At this point, having an online presence was a pretty new thing to me. I talked about some of these weird artsy/emulator projects online.

Then this toy company contacted me out of the blue in 2003, I think. They wanted to make a Commodore 64 joystick toy. It was a joystick that had a full Commodore 64 in it and could play old retro videogames. They saw that I had been working in this area.

We eventually struck a deal to build this chip. I would build a chip to emulate the Commodore 64. I had never done a full custom chip before. With a lot of conviction and fear, I went forward and them, "No problem. I can make this." So we all worked day and night. We were scattered all over the world, working on IRC Chat. I was making FPGA boards and sending the boards off for them to test with. They would make test programs, and they were porting Commodore 64 games to make them work on my hardware.

Some of the biggest problems were that all of these old Commodore 64 games were on floppy disks. They had to be converted to work on flash memory. Right up until the wire, it was just a few weeks before production, we were still trying to make all this stuff work. I had sent the chips off. It was extremely scary. I was uncertain. I didn't have a chance to really test them very well in simulation, because it took so long on these old computers to simulate even one frame of video.

Software guys continued to work. All the chips went off to China. They got bonded onto circuit boards. And I got a phone call from the toy guys that they didn't work. Oh my God! I was terrified. This was hundreds of thousands of dollars' worth of chips that the toy company had bought. They were dead. So they were like, "You're going to China, now!"

They had booked me a flight the next day. Actually, it had crossed my mind at some point to run to Mexico and just hide from them because these guys were really intense New Yorkers. "You're destroying us," they said. But I went to China. I got there, looked at what the factory had done to all the reference circuit boards I had sent over. They had decided they wanted to cost-reduce them themselves and had changed my design. I opened up the toy and I was like, "What is this?" They had thrown away all the decoupling capacitors that were for the chip. They said, "Well, the sample board that you sent over with the FPGA on it didn't need any of those." That's because it was a four-layer board! And they put it on a two-layer board, with no decoupling capacitors. All these design sins.

We started working through that, and there were some other problems on the chips. I guess my hacking background helped me come up with, on the spot, an elegant way to reset the chips, with just a couple pennies' worth of parts.

Osborn: So the final product was a Commodore 64 toy that was in the controller, all-in-one?

Ellsworth: Yes. You put batteries in the bottom, you plugged it into your TV, and then it had thirty built-in videogames. But we decided, the whole team, the software and hardware team, unbeknownst to the game company, we decided that we were going to make it hackable, and we were going to give back to the community. I put extra connections on the circuit board and on the chip, so you could hook disk drives and keyboards and various things— you could open up the joystick and hook up peripherals to it and use it as a real Commodore 64, to have access to everything.

The software guys added a bunch of secret videogames, too. One of them was Cliff Diver, where you jump off the top of a cliff and do backflips, and you're supposed to time it just perfectly so don't you crash into the rocks below. They also added a bunch of pictures of them drinking beer with this famous programmer, Jim Butterfield.

So I was in China. We were doing the first production run, and I drop into the secret mode, and one of the toy execs was over there, overseeing the manufacturing. And he saw this, and he said, "What is that?"

And I said, "Oh, we added a few things." And they flipped out. They're like, "You can't do that! Oh my God. Show me everything you put in there." So we had instructions in there of how to take the toy apart, which freaked them out. We had pictures of the guys drinking beer. They were worried it was going to change the rating of the toy, because this was at the time when there was some scandal about videogames. There was a sex scene in some videogame, and they were worried that whoever does this rating system would come down on them and they wouldn't be able to sell it.

They forbid us from talking about it. They were like, "Hopefully, no one will find out about it." And I thought, "Well, I have nothing to lose," so I went back and one of my web hacker friends helped me make a blog post that was backdated. It was supposedly a blog post, a blog site from a Chinese factory worker, so we made a broken-English blog post, with fake teardowns of other products. Then we did a teardown of our toy and put all of the instructions on there. Just a couple of days before the toy hit the market, we leaked that and let the world know that it was hackable.

It went to QVC first, the television home shopping network. It ended up selling out in a couple of weeks, it sold ridiculously well—hundreds of thousands of units sold immediately. QVC actually called the toy company and asked them, "Why are forty percent of these toys going to foreign countries and we're not even pitching them in these countries?" It was because we'd put all this love into the toy and people really wanted that. At first, the toy company was threatening to sue me when they found out about the blog, but then when it immediately sold out, they had a change of heart. The next revision of the toy, the next production run, they had us remove some of the edgier stuff. Then they, in the paper instructions in the box, talked about how to get into the secret menus, which I was really offended that they did that.

Osborn: It's no longer a secret.

Ellsworth: Apparently, the software guys have told me that there are a couple more secrets still in the toy that people haven't found yet, so that's exciting. They haven't found them all.

Osborn: That can be a challenge to readers of this book, to figure out what they are. I know you have worked on a number of projects since then. One that is very interesting to me is the home chip lab. I've seen some of your videos on it. In engineering, there always seems to be a layer below where you are working that is magic. If you are a programmer, maybe it's the machine code that is generated for you. For an electrical engineer, in most cases, I would guess it's how the components are manufactured. So to me, making your own transistor still sounds like a bit of black magic.

Ellsworth: I felt exactly as you did. Maybe I should take a step back and frame why there are all these videos online, and then I can get back to the home chip lab, because I think this is important.

After that toy, the joystick, there was all this press around it, and then ultimately I became—at least in nerdy circles—a minor celebrity. People wanted to get to know me. This is around 2004, 2005. It freaked me out, all these Internet people wanting to get to know me. So I pulled back and isolated myself from the Internet.

The toy really jumpstarted my career. I had no problem getting jobs at that point. I was doing tons of work. Five or so years go by, I start going in for various contract or job interviews, and I started hearing the interviewers say things like, "I googled you." I'm like, "That's interesting. What are they seeing when they google me?" So I googled myself. I was appalled at how wrong things were. People had met me at various events and I told them a story or two, and then they go and put it on their blog and get it wrong.

One of the problems is that they were emphasizing that there was just this one toy. It just seemed like I was a one-trick pony, and it was starting to affect my ability to get jobs. I had taken a job at this company called NewTek that made video-streaming equipment. At this time, streaming video over the Internet was pioneering. I was working on this piece of hardware, which was this thing that you would hook a bunch of cameras up to it and it would stream live video. Now, with Google hangouts and Skype and all these things, it's very common and everyone's familiar with it. But I decided, "Maybe I need to learn about this space, and maybe I can take control of my online persona."

So I started, with a couple friends—we started doing this weekend show where we would get together and invent things. We would just do our normal weekend hacking. On Sunday, we would turn on one of these streaming boxes and broadcast it live to the Internet and show, "This is how we did it." So I started making videos that way. Actually, that's a big, long story that—eventually, it evolved into cameras all over my workshop and the Internet being able to control the cameras and a text-to-speech setup. I'd be working on a project and I'd say, "What's the pinout of a 74LS04 chip?" And a hundred people's fingers online would just be punching up, "Here's the pinout." It became this very interesting and collaborative thing.

Osborn: I'm just picturing YouTube comments dribbling through your speakers.

Ellsworth: It was all live, though in my workshop, but it grew. A bunch of makers would set up their video cameras and there were all these live feeds. It actually outlived me doing it. There are still people on this, called GeekStreams, that stream their workshops twenty-four hours a day, hang out and work together, collaborate on projects—that's what it turned into.

It started off with just Sundays where we'd turn on the cameras for one hour and show our crazy inventions. They were silly things that we'd do for fun, but people really enjoying watching it. They were like, "Well, can you turn on your camera Saturday and let us see you guys working then?" So we started doing that.

We had a projector with all of the text and they were trying to get our attention all the time to tell us that we were doing something wrong or they wanted to help. One of the guys wrote the text-to-speech thing, and then they could talk to us. People were always frustrated because the cameras were pointing in the wrong part of the workshop. So we got some pan-tilt-zoom cameras, and one of the guys wrote a piece of software that would move the cameras around. Then it got to the point where it was just so complicated that I didn't want to manage turning on and off all of these computers. So I thought, "Fine, I'll just leave it on all the time and you guys can just be here during the week if I'm working on hobby projects or even clients' projects." It became this community of people that were very protective of me and the other people in the community, too. The YouTube commenters, the really bad comments, those people would come through every once in a while and say some rude thing, but the community had the ability to kick them out and ban them. Instantly, they would filter out the bad people.

So I did the live video streaming, and then I started putting them on YouTube, and I realized that I got a lot more views that way and could do them on my own timeframe. I could edit out when I slipped up and said the wrong thing. So I started doing YouTube videos. This was in 2008, 2009, something like that. People started loving all these nerdy videos that I posted. Pretty much any hobby project that I do these days, I videotape it and I put it up there, for good or bad. Sometimes bad things come out of my sharing this stuff.

Now, back to your question about the chip lab. That was something that, like you, I was very, very fascinated with what was under the hood, just like when I was a kid. I don't like not understanding why things work the way they do.

I started researching the semiconductor process, because I wanted to make my own chip someday, actually physically push the wafer in. It got to the point where I thought I wouldn't be able to do it myself. I thought, "This is really, really complicated." Which was actually a big mistake. I decided to enroll in this Adventist College in Walla Walla to use their semiconductor fabs. They have this little, tiny semiconductor fab. I actually derailed my career a little bit to be at this college.

It was no problem that they're Adventist or anything, but it was very interesting having come from my background and being rough around the edges being with a very conservative bunch of people who were very sweet and kind. I'm all rough around the edges and swearing, getting in trouble.

I don't know. This may not be appropriate for the book, but this is a funny story so I'll tell you anyway. They wanted me to go to chapel. I had no interest in going to chapel. It was once a week. I just skipped out. I thought, "What's the harm?" I didn't know they were actually monitoring who went. So when it came time at the end of the first semester to enroll for the second semester, where the actual chip lab stuff would start, they were like, "You can't enroll because you didn't go to any of the chapels."

"Uh-oh."

Then they said, "There are two ways you can get around this. One is if you check out the audiocassettes of each of the chapels and then do a one-page book report on each of them. Or you can pay." I don't remember what the dollar value was. It was something like five dollars a chapel. I'm like, "Done. Five dollars a chapel? No problem."

So after all that they ended up canceling the chip foundry class, so I wasted all this time and derailed my career for nothing. But I still had this passion for it. So for about four years, I did intensive research on how to do a chip lab at home. It actually took me about four years to make my first working device. Probably the first year was pure researching. And after the second year, I got some equipment and started experimenting. Nothing was working. That went on.

I had this Mason jar next to my diffusion furnace where I has been putting the silicon wafers in and trying to experiment. It was just filling up with little pieces of silicon that I had tried to make even a diode on. So I'm like, "Well, I need to go find a mentor," and I started asking around. A friend of mine put me in contact with this guy named Peter who mentored me in the semiconductor process. He was an old chip foundry guy from the sixties and seventies. So he started giving me some hints. I was so frustrated. I couldn't get anything to work. Finally, he says, "Okay, e-mail me exactly what you're doing."

I'm wrote, "I'm doing this step, that step, etched the oxide off, and then put my contacts on."

And his response back was, "LOL. You're such a newbie. You can't etch the oxide off a PN junction."

And it's one of these things that nowhere in a book are you actually going to find this, it's all buried—that little piece of wisdom is buried in surface-state equations and stuff like that—you just don't see it written in a paragraph: "Don't etch the oxide off a PN junction." So once he taught me that trick, I got my first device to work.

I expanded from there. I made a CMOS device, proved I could do that, made some MOSFETs, made some solar cells. It was a whole lot of fun. I made some videos around that and posted them online. They've been very popular. People are fascinated. People have been inspired to do it on their own devices. Again, it's lived beyond my experiments. There are people out there working out lithography steps to actually make really high-resolution chip at home, which is very exciting. I feel honored that maybe I was part of what inspired them to do that.

Osborn: I'm looking forward to some eight-bit computers that people are building in their garages from household chemicals.

Ellsworth: Exactly. Someday I hope to get back into doing that, but right now, I'm kind of focused on something else.

Osborn: Let's talk about that something else. You started a company called CastAR after leaving Valve, right?

Ellsworth: The company's called Technical Illusions. Our product we're working on is called CastAR. Valve Software, which is a videogame company, contacted me almost two years ago. They wanted to get into the hardware space. They wanted to take control of their destiny. They're kind of under the whims of the PC industry, or even Microsoft or any of the companies that influence hardware. So they pestered me over and over again to come do a hardware R&D department for them. So eventually, I said, "Okay, I'll do some contract work for you. I just don't know how committed you guys are to really doing hardware." I came up, I started working with them—started helping them recruit and build this hardware lab. They pretty much took me to a floor of their building and said, "If you need this whole floor, it's yours." So we started building up this hardware lab, recruited some really good makers, like Ben Krasnow, Jeff Keyzer, Alan Yates, some of the best makers out there.

We started to put this hardware lab together. Really slow going. We really struggled to be able to recruit people into the company for many reasons. A lot of electrical and mechanical engineers had the same concerns I did about Valve not sticking with it. They're also really sensitive about their culture. They have this flat culture, where there's supposedly no management in the company, although in reality, it ends up being more like a high school, where there are popular people who take power and unpopular people who are troublemakers. Well, I ended up being in the troublemaker camp because I was complaining about not being able to recruit all the time, that they didn't have a methodology to make hardware and stuff. Eventually, I rocked the boat so much that they fired me.

Initially, they tasked us with researching input and output devices for gaming, anything that could enhance a gaming experience. We looked at everything: virtual reality, augmented reality, motion controllers. At first, I wasn't too keen on the idea of augmented reality, but as we started researching it, I started to see very interesting applications and game play experiences you could do with it, and I got very excited. Then there was a bit of a split off in the development. Some people were doing virtual reality, and some of us went off and did augmented reality. My focus over the last year was AR.

Then I rocked the boat and I got fired. On my way out the door, I went to Gabe Newell, the founder of the company, and said, "I can't believe you're doing this. You're just going to throw away all this technology," because he pretty much fired everybody that was working on my project. He was like, "Fine, it's yours." Actually, it wasn't that easy as him handing it over. It took a lot of negotiations, but we actually got all the tech out, all the prototypes, and we started a company, Rick Johnson and I, one of the other folks who got laid off at the same time.

So that's what we're working on. These are augmented-reality glasses. When you're looking through them, we can project holographic-looking images. So if you can imagine *Star Wars* chess—little characters standing on the table. We can project graphics or characters that are at the surface of, say, a table, in the surface of a table, or above the surface of a table. We developed all the input devices for that, which is a magic wand where you can interact with these characters with this wand. So you just poke the wand into the space where the virtual characters are, touch them with it, and click the buttons, command them to do things or interact with them in the virtual space with that. We made a figurine tracker that lets us put real figurines, like miniatures for D&D—we can put those out there and render graphics around them. So you can imagine D&D-like games where you set up your terrain with all these figurines and props. And we know those props are on the table, so now the virtual graphics and characters can interact with these real-world objects.

We developed the glasses which work in a very interesting way. Instead of doing the more complicated way of overlaid graphics—most people are projecting directly into your eyes, so they have special, big, heavy glass optics that do that, which makes the glasses expensive and very heavy and causes eye strain—we're projecting off the top of the glasses with two micro projectors to this special surface. And this surface is what's called a retro-reflector, and the retro-reflector is a special surface that bounces the light that you project from your glasses directly back at you. So no one else in the room can see what you're projecting.

Each person sitting around the table is wearing these lightweight glasses and can be projecting their own images. So if you have a 3D character standing on the table, I can be looking at the front side of the character and you can walk around the back side of the character and look at the back. The other part of our magic is the world tracker that we made. We have this really super-high-speed tracker that tracks the position of the world. As you walk around the table, it knows where you're looking so it can render the graphics for each viewer correctly. In developing this, we were very sensitive about cost, and we—since we're talking about makers, a lot of skills that I learned in the process of doing hacky, maker things got applied to this product.

We knew that we had to be very cost-sensitive, so we didn't start off using two hundred–dollar cameras. We started with two-dollar image sensors that you would find in every cellphone, which normally wouldn't be capable of doing this kind of tracking, but we worked really hard and found some optical tricks and various things to make sure that we could use those really inexpensive sensors. Same thing with the projectors. Normally, projectors are very expensive, so we found a way to cost-reduce these down by using novel materials in them.

The way we knew how to do this stuff is because we were always exploring and looking at things and understanding how they work. By taking everything apart and experimenting at home, it gives you a new perspective. When you look at a problem, you're like, "Oh, I saw a solution for our problem here because …" And it's in some totally different area. Someone solved a similar problem. I don't know if that makes sense, but you can start correlating across much broader fields by just being exposed to it all.

Osborn: So just for the readers' sakes, can you briefly explain the difference between virtual reality and augmented reality?

Ellsworth: Probably the main difference is that virtual reality completely cuts you off from the real world, you don't see anything in the real world. Everything is one hundred percent synthetic. Augmented reality does the opposite: instead of trying to replace everything, it only replaces or adds small amounts of graphics to the world. For instance, the little characters for a chess game are added to the world, the rest of the world is still there. The advantage is that you don't have as many issues with getting dizzy or sick, which is one of the big downfalls that kind of steered me away from virtual reality: simulator sickness, since you have no correlation to the real world to your inner ear. People lose track of which direction is up, and that manifests as feeling sick or dizzy.

Osborn: You've worked on a lot of other projects. I saw that you worked a little bit with Ben Heck on the pinball machine, and I saw something about the TSA scanner clone. Are there any other projects like that that would be interesting to talk about, a good story?

Ellsworth: The TSA clone is interesting. I was very upset about the TSA scanners, and that was more of a political statement, which actually turned into an interesting piece of tech. So as the story was breaking about these body scanners going into the airport, I started looking at it as how could I actually recreate that piece of hardware and make a statement about it? So I started looking at, "They're working at millimeter-wave. What if I work with centimeter-wave resolution? Would that work?" I did some simple experiments. You can actually see some of these experiments progressing up until my big video of "This is how I made my own TSA scanner," as I was learning. So I learned a lot about microwave transmission and reception and how to measure distance and depth with it.

The fallout from that was interesting. It got people thinking about the subject, but also as I mentioned earlier, sometimes there's good and bad that come out of this stuff. So by making a strong statement about these body scanners, I opened myself up to being attacked by people that were pro-body scanners in a very mean way. It was interesting, kind of watching the dialog go back and forth between various groups. Much like when I was doing the live video streaming, my YouTube followers are very defensive of me. Kind of like knights in shining armor, they will come out and defend me. It's interesting. Every time I do something that's kind of edgy, I can see a spike, positive or negative, in people joining or leaving my social network, which is interesting. It's almost always a positive, even if I drive people away by making a strong statement. More people recoil back and find it interesting and join up.

Another one along those lines that was just kind of a statement: There was a thing in Portland, Oregon, where I used to live, where they were adding these big PA speakers outside the public transit buses, where, as the bus would turn, it would start announcing to the pedestrians in the crosswalk that the bus was turning. The reason they had done this is that several people had been killed over the last year or two because the bus drivers weren't paying attention and ran people over. So I cloned their device, which was costing the taxpayers $20,000 apiece, or some huge amount of money, and showed how it could be done for ten dollars–worth of parts and then kind of discussed how it was not really going to help and it's going to cause noise pollution. I had actually lived on a bus line, so it was frustrating for me actually hearing the buses—to have voices made it even more annoying. I made little animation out of cardboard cutouts. Boy, that upset a lot of people when I posted that.

Osborn: It sounds like you've done lots of interesting things, whether it's just to learn a new thing or to prove a point. Are there some projects other people are working on that you're interested in or that you are excited about? Not your own project, but something somebody else is working on that you just think is cool technology?

Ellsworth: One of my co-workers, Ben Krasnow, made a body scanner than actually used x-rays, which was very brave of him and very cool. I like the folks online that are doing hybrid rocket engines. That's something I've always dreamed about doing. I made solid rocket motors when I was a kid. You know, doing this new startup, I've been kind of offline and out of touch. It's been taking my time lately. There's stuff I want to do, and it's queued up. There's stuff that's half-filmed that I haven't posted yet.

Osborn: When I was talking to Sylvia Todd, she mentioned all the cool stuff that you did. I asked her if there's some stuff she'd like to learn. I think that she sees you as a role model.

Ellsworth: I'm honored. That really makes me feel good because not only does it help my persona online to make these videos, it also—a lot of mentors have helped me over the years. I feel like I'm giving back, because if it wasn't for the mentors, there's just no way I could have done most of what I've done. Or at least I couldn't have done it as fast as I did. Unfortunately, a lot of my mentors don't get as much credit as they should. Mentoring is kind of a win–win situation for a lot of these folks. For instance, the machinist that I was talking about: He was a machinist for twenty or thirty years, worked mostly by himself in his one-man machine shop. People generally don't take an interest in it. So by me taking a strong interest in it, he gets to pass his knowledge off, and I'm very eager about it and happy, so he feels good.

So likewise, when folks like Sylvia really like my videos and projects, it makes me feel really good. When I had my computer stores, I was into mentoring. I used to go into junior highs and high schools and take old computers, take them apart and reassemble them. Then we'd have a big celebration at the end of the three-, four-week program. We'd plug them in and see if they'd catch fire. Sometimes they did! It was really fun back then hearing these kids prog-ress as they moved onto college, getting e-mails from them saying, "Thank you for doing that. If it wasn't for you coming into my high school and showing me how to take apart a computer, I would never have gotten into the sciences."

Osborn: I was making notes about mentors because you talked about the guys who helped you out with the ham radios, and the cars, and when you were doing the home chip lab. The guy who helped you out at the hardware store and gave you advice. I was wondering how does somebody go out and find these mentors? Also, today, with the resources available on the Internet, it sounds like some of these things you'd be able to learn, having the resources, but the chip lab thing, like you said, some of this stuff, there's no manual for. You really need to find a mentor.

Ellsworth: Exactly.

Osborn: So how do you do that? Is there any advice you have for finding great mentors?

Ellsworth: Sure, sure. You have to be very brave. I'm not naturally a very brave person, so I have to work at it. For instance, the machine shop: I just had to muster up the courage and walk in the door and very genuinely explain my situation and try to get their attention long enough to say, "I'm a high school student. I want to build a race car. I know nothing about machining. I really want to learn about this. Can I exchange work for your teaching me how to do this?"

I suppose finding the people and then trying to figure out how you can come up with a win–win situation. Some people will be completely happy with just telling you the information because it makes them feel warm and fuzzy. And sometimes you may actually have to work to make it worth their while. But you can't necessarily replace hands-on experience with virtual. There is a lot of this stuff online, but, for instance, one of the things I learned from the ham radio operators is that your finger is an excellent debug tool. And that's some-thing you probably won't pick up online, unless you're actually there working with someone building a circuit in front of you and they're touching circuits for some reason. Why are they touching a circuit? And then they'll explain to you, "Oh, well, it will inject noise or add stray capacitance to the circuit," and you can make observations about how it's misbehaving or behaving better because of that. But certainly online mentoring is a lot easier to come by.

There was absolutely nothing when I was a kid. I had to call chip vendors and lie to them and say that I was a secretary for a chip company and they should send me samples and databooks. Nowadays, you can go online and find almost any piece of information you want, or at least a high level understanding of it, which is fun.

Osborn: And you get a lot of chip samples for free now. TI has a great sample program.

Ellsworth: Just getting information is awesome. Back in the eighties, it was all about even getting the databook. If you got a databook with circuit examples in the back, that was awesome. Or you somehow got your hands—one of my most valuable books as a kid was a twenty-year-old copy of the *AARL Handbook for Amateur Radio Operators* because it had practical circuits in it. Now you can get tons of practical circuits for free.

Osborn: Is there a good online resource for design patterns for circuits, something like that?

Ellsworth: It varies. It depends on what you're doing. I haven't really found a single place to go to. You have to take everything with a grain of salt and be brave and build some of this stuff yourself. I'm very thankful that in my professional career I've gotten to work with older engineers, what they used to call "gray hairs," because they taught me to work with techniques that probably aren't even taught in school these days. There are some test equipment and techniques that I used, like a grid dip—you couldn't go to a school and ask anyone what a grid dip meter is. There are so few people in the world that know how to use those anymore. But it's a super valuable and useful tool to use on all kinds of things, but it's just been replaced by thirty thousand–dollar oscilloscopes. There's knowledge out there from the old-timers that's going to help you in your career or with projects as you go forward because so much focus is always on the new tech, and there's a lot of valuable stuff to do if you use old tech.

For instance, on the CastAR stuff that we're working on—while I was at Valve, we were talking about doing the figurine tracker, and some of my colleagues were like, "You're never going to be able to do this technique you're doing cheap enough." I ended up going back and using some parts that are probably thirty years old that no one even thinks about using anymore. I was able to do the same thing, just using a different technique, for a dollar or two. If I didn't have had exposure to that, I would never know to even consider going back and using those legacy parts.

Osborn: There is a lot of hidden knowledge, I guess, still in people. It seems like electrical engineering in the US, at least, went through this phase where it just wasn't sexy and people didn't do it, didn't talk about it, so the people who have a lot of this deep knowledge are people who are older. There's seems to be this gap between them and us now—electrical engineering seems to be this sexy thing again.

Ellsworth: It would certainly help if the maker community—with all of the Arduinos, the various little, easy-to-do, entry-level projects—is piquing people's interest.

Osborn: Stuff like the Adafruit line is very awesome.

Ellsworth: Exactly. I often worry that the old-timers are going to retire and die and this information is going to be lost, because—a lot of these techniques, like the whole thing about the oxide layer—there are probably 100 people in the world that know that because there's only that many people that are the process engineers that worked on that piece of the semiprocessor puzzle. It's just handed down. Maybe it doesn't get handed down at some point and a new technique comes along.

Osborn: That type of thing has happened throughout history.

Ellsworth: Oh yeah. I've often said—I don't have enough energy to do this myself yet—I always thought it would be nice to just grab a recorder and go to these old-timers and plop it down in front of them and just have them tell stories: "Tell us the nitty-gritty little stories about what you did and how you solved problems in engineering," and get those recorded because it's pretty exciting. All this media right now—we're recording audio today. It's not very searchable, but speech recognition is going to become more and more searchable in the future. If we could at least capture that information now and someday down the road it will become searchable. Video will become more searchable, too.

Osborn: If I had one question for them, it would be, "Tell me about abusing some components to do things that they were not designed to do, and what did you use it for?" Those are always the best kind of stories.

Ellsworth: I abuse parts all the time, like using parts out of spec or using parts that were designed for something else to do a different task. It's the way you go from an impossible project to making something possible. For the TSA scanner, I took a satellite dish receiver and cut a bunch of stuff inside it and abused it and turned it into a transmitter and receiver simultaneously. Something you wouldn't really off the top of your head think that you could do, but thanks to the local old-timer mentors teaching me about local oscillators and mixers and how all that stuff works. I pulled from that knowledge, "Oh yeah, since I've got this oscillator here, why not make it a transmitter and mix it down?"

Osborn: A simple example is that you can use an LED if you detect light, too.

Ellsworth: Have you interviewed Forrest Mims?

Osborn: No, I haven't.

Ellsworth: Talk about mentors. He wrote the books that were in Radio Shack and influenced many of us that are in the electronics industry. That was one of his techniques, abusing LEDs to measure color and light.

Osborn: I've interviewed a few people who said that's how they learned electronics, with old Forrest Mims books.

Ellsworth: A couple of years ago, with a friend online, we were talking on Twitter about this 555 timer, which is this really old chip, just a great chip. I started this debate, "Is it even relevant these days, because microcontrollers can probably do the same thing?" So we decided to do a contest, and we really started promoting the contest a lot. People started joining in.

Osborn: I remember this contest.

Ellsworth: Oh, cool. Companies started donating stuff, and it was this grass-roots thing. Blew me away: we got something like three hundred–plus entries. It was really hard to narrow it down to the top winners because there were so many creative things people did with this chip that would be difficult to create with microcontrollers. So we proved our point that they are still valid today—and abused them in many ways in the process. Some guy turned one into an amplifier by driving it in a very funny way, which you would never think to do. Those are the kinds of people I would want to be stranded with on a desert island.

Osborn: That's all the questions I have. I had a whole list of questions here, and you kept rolling through them, so I just shut up and let you drive, but thanks for all of the amazing stories.

Sylvia Todd

Maker

Sylvia's Super Awesome Maker Show!

Sylvia Todd is the host of Sylvia's Super Awesome Maker Show (sylviashow.com), where she shares a variety of fun and exciting projects for people of all ages. What started out as a fun weekend project with her father, James Todd, turned into a hit Internet web show for makers of all ages. Sylvia's show encompasses everything from Silly Putty to circuit boards, and includes step-by-step instructions, fun scientific facts, and important safety tips. Sylvia's fun personality and serious maker skills captured the attention and sponsorship of MAKE, and landed her appearances on numerous TV and web shows.

Steven Osborn: Hey Sylvia and James. Nice to have the chance to finally meet you. I'm going to start off by asking you something that I've been told to never ask a girl, but I think it's pretty relevant to our readers. How old are you Sylvia?

Sylvia Todd: Well, I'm eleven right now, but I'll be twelve in like ten days.

Steven: You're eleven, going to be twelve. I know you've been to the San Mateo Maker Faire. Have you guys been to the New York Maker Faire?

Sylvia: Yes, and the one in Kansas City.

Steven: You have the *Super Awesome Mini Maker Show*, and it has half a million subscribers on YouTube and hundreds of thousands of views, which is quite an accomplishment, regardless of age. Tell me a bit about your show and what kinds of things someone would expect to see there.

Sylvia: So my videos can be either crafty or they can be about electronics. I've done episodes on Arduino. And I did one where I mixed Silly Putty using Borax, which is just really cool. I make a lot of stuff. My newest episode was a Lilypad[1] heartbeat pendant, where I made a pendant using a pulse sensor, and we made it blink when your heart beat. It was really cool.

In the show, we're showing people how to make something—easy weekend projects—for kids and adults to do. It shows a little bit of the science behind it. So when we were making the "Crazy Putty" episode, we were teaching about poly—what is it called?

James Todd: All about chains.

Sylvia: Polymer chains, yes, polymer chains. And in the latest episode, we talked to them about heartbeats and what blood is for.

James: And about photoplethysmography.

Steven: So I saw a picture of you, Sylvia, recently at a science fair with President Obama. Can you tell me what that was about and what you were doing there?

Sylvia: So Maker Media and Cognizant invited me to go to the White House science fair. They invited Joey Hudy[2] last year.

James: Someone nominated Sylvia. And then the White House contacted us. The White House didn't actually tell us who nominated us or even that there was a nomination process. Make and Cognizant had to tell us after the fact.

Sylvia: And it was pretty hectic, because the White House science fair was overlapping with my school science fair, so we practically had to make two science fair projects.

James: There was no practically about it. We did it!

Sylvia: Yeah, we did both science fair projects. We used the WaterColorBot[3] for the White House science fair. The WaterColorBot is a watercolor-painting robot.

So we have the WaterColorBot on the desk. I've been working with Evil Mad Scientists Laboratories[4] with it since January. We're going to hopefully make it into a kit very, very soon.[5] It's basically a tool for kids and adults to get into making robotics things and programming.

---

[1]http://lilypadarduino.org
[2]http://lookwhatjoeysmaking.blogspot.com
[3]http://watercolorbot.com
[4]www.evilmadscientist.com
[5]Funded successfully on Kickstarter:www.kickstarter.com/projects/1894919479/super-awesome-sylvias-watercolorbot-0

Steven: Cool. I have a Shapeoko[6] CNC machine, the one Inventables sells, on my desk. But I hadn't thought to make it paint in watercolor.

Sylvia: Nice.

Steven: So you got to meet President Obama and show him the WaterColorBot?

Sylvia: We were in the same room as Joey Hudy was last year. It was like the robotics room. He [the president] went around the entire room. I was the last person to see the president. He went around the entire room and asked everybody almost the same questions: "What's your name? Where are you from? What's your project?" He didn't really make such a big deal about the WaterColorBot when he came over, but I think he liked it. The exciting part was that he shook my hand at the beginning and at the end, so he shook my hand twice. Everybody else did it once. So I was really excited and super nervous at the same time. It was just a mix of a whole bunch of feelings.

James: And he got to use it.

Sylvia: And he got to use it! Oh yeah, we had an iPad app where you can draw something on the iPad and it will print it on the WaterColorBot. He wrote, "Go STEM," which stands for "Science, Technology, Engineering, and Mathematics."

Steven: The bot will paint in real time when you draw on the iPad?

James: Yeah, the neat thing about the way we're doing this is that it doesn't matter where the input is coming from. I'm actually the one writing the software for the non-real-time version. We're calling it RoboPaint. So the non-real-time version will paint whatever picture you happen to have, and the real-time version will simply allow you to draw as an input. So you can import a picture from somewhere and WaterColorBot will paint it. We've done Catbug from *Bravest Warriors* and then there's the *Mona Lisa*.

Steven: That's better than I could do with my fingers, I'm sure.

James: Oh definitely, definitely. And the neat thing is that it's really just an XY output device, so you have an input, whatever that happens to be, and we can output to it. So we're thinking about doing LOGO programming or something like that, so the paintbrush would be the turtle and you'd have it go paint on real paper or something.

Steven: I loved LOGO programming in school. I have a few posters back I made back then of just abstract, mathematical squiggles that repeated. I turned them into posters, so that was pretty cool.

Sylvia: Nice.

---

[6]www.shapeoko.com

Steven: Have you met any other famous people or celebrities through the show?

James: She did an interview with LeVar Burton and Bill Nye the Science Guy.

Sylvia: Oh yeah. We were outside and it was lunchtime during the White House science fair, and Bill Nye and LeVar Burton and this other lady were interviewing a couple of kids, and I was one of the kids that they wanted to interview. I was surrounded by both of them and I was so excited to meet them for the first time. It was really cool.

James: Admittedly, she would not know who Bill Nye the Science Guy was since the show hasn't been running on TV and we don't even have TV anymore, but I downloaded *all* the episodes of *Bill Nye, the Science Guy* and I put them on our media server, so all the kids had access. They would watch entire seasons in a day, just eat it up. It's really good TV. I think TV shows like that do a really great job of clearing up complex science things.

Steven: Did I just make this up, or did I see you with Adam Savage[7] recently?

Sylvia: Yes. At the Maker Faires, Adam Savage comes and he does a talk and he does autographs and pictures afterward. We always go and get in a line. I'm usually the first in line and I always get up there and I take a picture. We've done this photo in a photo in a photo for each year, so we hold up the photo of previous photos—what's that called?

Steven: Photos of photos? Meta.

Sylvia: We did that with Ben Heck and Jeri Ellsworth. So we had four recursions, one, two, three, four years. Maybe five. I forget. We have been doing this for a long time. One time I even got to interview Adam Savage. It was kind of weird. They wanted me to go over there and ask him some questions, and I was really nervous, but I did it and I was so excited. I'm always excited to meet him.

Steven: Adam is a cool guy. I love watching *MythBusters*.

James: He's crazy. He's a super geek and he's not scared of letting that flag fly. He's so *good* at doing this stuff because that was his job for years, making crazy movie props.

Steven: I saw an excellent video recently with Adam talking about the failures in his career. The moral of the story was really to not be afraid to ask for help. Don't be afraid to say, "I don't know what I'm doing."

Sylvia, what would you say is your favorite project you've worked on or video you've done? What would stand out in your mind as a favorite?

Sylvia: Hmm, that's a tough one.

---

[7]Co-host of the Discovery Channel's *MythBusters* television series.

James: It's a common question. It's always hard for her to dredge up something. It's usually different every time.

Sylvia: It's almost all of my projects. I've really liked all of them. The WaterColorBot I really liked. I really liked making it. A lot of my shows I really liked doing. The part of my shows that I like doing is the making part. Putting together a project.

I did get a medal from RoboGames. When I made the WaterColorBot. I got a silver medal. I lost by one point. I almost got the gold. I kind of wanted the silver though because it looked really cool.

Steven: It sounds like your favorite project is really just doing what you do, making things, and doing videos. I guess doing what you love to do is a constant, continuous thing, not necessarily a one-time project, which is pretty awesome.

Sylvia: Yeah, that fits.

James: It's always on to the next thing. When you do an episodic, nonserial show, you get a chance to do new stuff all the time. We have a giant box of kits that we're always pulling from to do the next interesting thing, and we're always trying to come up with something cool for it every time. We actually came up with the idea for the beating heart, the Lilypad heartbeat pendant, in a day. We were going through the kits, "What can we do with this? What can we do with that?"

Sylvia: We found a board lying around that looked like a tree.

James: It was an example board, but you couldn't actually solder on it.

Sylvia: But you could stick teeny-tiny, like really small LEDs inside and wire them together.

James: And then we said, "Okay, where's the science aspect of it? What kind of cool stuff can we talk about?"

Sylvia: We can talk about a heart!

James: Maybe not everyone knows how that works.

Steven: Have you two seen openmaterials.org? I bet you would like it. There's some cool stuff on there. It's has stuff like open-source superglue or some putty made out of some sort of silicone. There are some cool projects on there. It is an interesting site to learn about materials.

James: I have it up on the second monitor here. You've completely distracted her now.

Sylvia: That's so cool! Green-tea leather?

James: Oh dear. What have I done? End of interview. We're done!

Steven: I'm sorry.

Sylvia: It's fine.

Steven: So that's a good example of projects other people are working on that are pretty cool. Can you think of anything that you've seen other people are working on that excites you or you'd like to see more about?

Sylvia: Hmmm.

James: What did we see at Maker Faire?

Sylvia: A lot. There was so much. The titles escape me. Oh yeah, Google Glass! Oh and Jeri Ellsworth's 3D gaming glasses. She had these glasses that you would put on, and one of the demonstrations is that there is this tower of blocks. And when you put the glasses on and it looks like you are knocking over the blocks. They look like they are right in front of you. It was so cool.

James: And it takes into account how far away you are from it, so you can simply have the glasses on and walk around and see things in your environment and move your head around. It's *totally* groundbreaking.[8]

Sylvia: There's a little zombie game that Jeri and her team made. You could see the maze and how the zombies were moving around you and how you were moving around everyone else.

James: It was actually a physical place and you could look around in it. It is a sort of augmented reality. It was actually projecting out into the world. When Jeri worked at Valve,[9] we had her sneak us in there, and we walked around and saw Valve. It was really crazy fun.

Sylvia: It was crazy.

James: She showed it to us in its early stage. It was this crazy, top-secret, hush-hush stuff. Now that she and a couple of other people have defected from Valve, I have a feeling maybe Valve thought it was the wrong direction for their company or something like that.

Steven: Those are good examples of other people building cool stuff. So what's something that you really want to learn how to do? Maybe something you haven't had time to do, but you want to learn in the near future?

Sylvia: I know: programming and welding.

Steven: Welding?

Sylvia: I haven't done welding. One year at Maker Faire, my dad and his friend made a pedal car and did pedal car racing. I've done some virtual welding before. I actually haven't done real welding. I do want to do it. I really want to learn it.

---

[8]See the Jeri Ellsworth interview (Chapter 15) for more on augmented reality glasses.
[9]www.valvesoftware.com

James: We would have had her do more welding. It's just that—

Sylvia: We only had two weeks to do it.

James: No, no. The real problem was that we were welding galvanized pipe. You're not supposed to weld that because it lets off these horrible fumes that give you cancer or something awful.

Steven: That stuff will make you nauseous pretty fast.

Sylvia: But programming also. I've done a little bit of programming and learned some of that, but I do want to make my own web site or make my own game. There's a lot of stuff I really like.

James: She's completely designed her game. I think there's a napkin edition to it somewhere, because I said, "With this Raspberry Pi, you can program your own game." And she said, "I know exactly what I'm going to do."

Steven: Are you using Scratch[10] for that or haven't really decided yet?

James: I think we're thinking about JavaScript because it will run everywhere.

Steven: You are probably aware of this, but the JavaScript stuff on Khan Academy is amazing for learning.

James: The JavaScript stuff is neat. They worked out a way to make editing live so as you're typing, you can see the how it affects the outcome of your program. We should do that later.

Sylvia: Oh, Khan Academy. My friend Julie does that on her own.

Steven: It's dangerous. You start playing and solving math problems, and then you get badges and points for it. Pretty soon, I'm so tired I can't really think, but I'm solving trivial math problems like how to tell time, just for the points.

Sylvia: I've got some energy points and badges, but I haven't been able to go on it that much.

Steven: I just have one more question. I still ask myself this question sometimes: What do you want to be when you grow up? What do you want to do?

Sylvia: When I was younger, like when I was four or five, I wanted to be a chef, but now I really want to be an aerospace engineer or an astronaut. I get really excited about space camp.

James: After her trip to the White House, and probably after the *ABC World News* thing,[11] somebody got her a full scholarship to Space Camp in Alabama.

---

[10]Interactive programming environment (http://scratch.mit.edu).
[11]http://abcnews.go.com/blogs/technology/2013/05/11-year-old-web-series-starinspiring-girls-in-the-name-of-science/

Sylvia: I'm so excited. I can't stop thinking about that.

Steven: I talked to Eric Stackpole from OpenROV. He started a CubeSat club and built satellites as a hobby. Then he got hired by NASA and worked for NASA for a while. Now he builds these open-source ROVs and goes to places like Antarctica and drills holes in the ice and drives around in his underwater robot.

James: That is so awesome.

Steven: He's really passionate about what he's doing.

Is it just the two of you working on the show?

James: The show is just done by me and Sylvia. We don't really have anyone else helping her out.

Sylvia: Well, there's mom. We do family things sometimes. When we're doing our puppets, I sometimes get my sister to help or my brother. Sometimes when we're doing crafty things, like sewing, my mom helps just to get it done.

James: The start-up I was working at in San Francisco sold. They completely ran out of money. So my full-time job now is just being dad and some side jobs. Hopefully, something will come along. I'm thinking that maybe we should just start Sylvia Corp.

Sylvia: Sylvia Corp!

James: She'll be CEO. I'll be CTO.

Sylvia: What's the difference?

James: So CEO is the chief executive officer. You make the decisions. You're the head of the group. And then CTO is chief technology officer. I get to operate the cameras and do very fun stuff—like the web site, which I already do anyway.

Steven: The important thing is you'd still be his boss, Sylvia.

James: You're the boss man.

Sylvia: Boss!

James: The only episode for Season 3 will be the Lilypad heartbeat pendant. The next episode is going to be Season 4, episode one, because the seasons are actually based off the Maker Faire. We've just been so completely busy running around. We haven't been able to make any other episodes in that time. Plus, you might have noticed, we don't actually post the production time post on the episode listing. You can see it on the video. But it's not on the web site. Kind of a secret thing we did.

Steven: Well Sylvia, James, it was super awesome talking to the two of you. I can't wait to see some Season 4 episodes.

Sylvia: Bye!

Dave Jones

Host

EEVBlog

Dave Jones is an electronics design engineer in Sydney, Australia, with over twenty years of experience. He hosts the Electronics Engineering Video Blog, also known as the EEVBlog, (eevblog.com) which is a favorite among professional engineers and electronics hobbyist alike. Dave's in-depth equipment reviews, crazy antics, and lack of political correctness provide an endless stream of entertainment for his growing fan base.

Steven Osborn: Hey Dave, tell me how you got started in electrical engineering and making things.

Dave Jones: I'm not sure how well I fit into the maker category, because I'm a traditional electronics hobbyist, which is just a small subset of the new maker community. Electronics hobbyists have been around for more than half a century, way before the term "maker" even came around. Really, I tinker with electronics things more than I "make" finished stuff.

Osborn: Electronics as a hobby has gained a lot of following recently. A lot of people are getting into it now because of the maker movement, though.

Jones: Yes, it's certainly made a huge comeback, which is great. So if you're asking for interesting stories about stuff I've made, then you're not going to really get too many. "I made my own test equipment." means little to most people. One interesting thing of mine that did actually make it into *Make* magazine was the world's first DIY scientific calculator watch. I built that from scratch for a design contest—no, I didn't win. That generated quite a lot of excitement and I sold many hundreds of kits for that. The challenge was to do it using all off-the-shelf components, using the PCB and screen itself as the housing. I think it turned out quite well, if a little non-robust.

Osborn: I think you have a unique perspective. I try to interview people from all different backgrounds. I didn't want a monolithic story. The maker movement is extremely broad, so I'm interviewing people with a lot of different backgrounds.

Jones: Of course, I've got the video blog. That's something that came out of nothing. And it's been my full-time business for two years now.

Osborn: This is the EEVBlog.

Jones: Yes, and there's The Amp Hour radio show also, but that's not really my full-time business. That's just another side hobby.

Osborn: So when did you start the EEVBlog?

Jones: Just over four and a half years ago.

Osborn: And you've been doing it full-time for just a couple years now?

Jones: Yes. It took about two years from the day I started until it became my full-time job. That's how I make my living. The interesting part is I seem to break all the rules when it comes to online video. The video I just edited before this interview runs for an hour and twenty-five minutes. It's a review of a piece of test equipment. Who else in the business does that? It's insane. Everybody tells me I'm doing it wrong. Everybody's attention span is seven minutes, tops. If you go over that, you'll never be a success. You'll be a complete failure.

I make a full-time living from doing long videos. I think my average video is at least thirty minutes. You go to all these seminars and you buy all these books about how to be an online superstar and a success, and they all tell you the same basic rules. You have the seven-minute attention span limit, absolute max—preferably three to five. Below that for certain kinds of material. Then you've got to have a certain type of intro, which draws people in to watch the rest of the video. Then you've got to have an outro and you've got to do all this jazz. Google and YouTube will tell you that. All the marketing books, all the seminars—they all tell you that. I don't do any one of them, yet here I am. This is my full-time business and it doesn't look like it's slowing down. I'm continuing to grow.

Osborn: A five-minute review of a really technical piece of equipment is not going to be satisfying, and people who watch these videos are going to want an in-depth review of the equipment. I think it really caters to what your audience wants. Plus, it's really entertaining listening to you carrying on, and cussing and whaling about something for an hour.

Jones: Yeah, exactly. Well, that's why people watch me. I learned pretty early on that the reason people watch me is not so much to learn stuff. I don't just do how-tos. For some reason, they find me entertaining, whether they find my comments entertaining or they find my delivery entertaining. It's essentially infotainment. I think more than half of my audience watches for the entertainment value. It's just something that they enjoy watching—not that by watching a video, they're going to get an hour's worth of learning out of it. They'll learn little snippets here and there, sort of pick up the odd thing, but it's more for entertainment. It's nerd entertainment.

Osborn: I would agree with that.

Jones: There's a market for that.

Osborn: I watch your videos myself, and I've watched a lot of your reviews when I go to buy a piece of equipment. I start watching it because I want to learn about this equipment, but I would never stay with it for an hour and a half if it were boring. I've learned a lot more—like some colorful Australian phrases.

Jones: Excellent. I'm glad it's spreading. So I learned pretty quick that that's what a lot of people like, so I gave up on trying to follow the rules and just keep doing what I want to be doing and make my videos as long as I actually waffled on for—that's how long the video actually turned out to be. I don't put much effort into making them less, because—well, the other thing I've learned is that people ask, "Why don't you just produce a five-minute summary of the product review?" or something like that. In reality it actually takes two to five times longer to produce a polished five-minute video as it does a one-hour video. Some of the top YouTubers can take all week to produce a single polished 5 minute video. People don't understand that aspect until you've actually been there and done it.

Osborn: To produce a one-hour video, you rant for an hour. To produce a five-minute video, you rant for an hour and then spend three hours editing it down to five minutes.

Jones: And go, "Ohhh, I spent too long explaining that. I could get that down to a minute instead of two minutes," so you decide to reshoot it. You're always going back and reshooting things if you do that. It takes a hell of a long time to produce a good five-minute video. That's why I just don't bother.

Osborn: Why did you start EEVBlog in the first place? What inspired you to roll it out?

Jones: I've always been into sharing my knowledge of engineering and electronics. I was first published in the electronics magazines when I was a teenager because I grew up with those electronics magazines. This was before the information revolution and the Internet came along, when the only way you got your information was via the monthly magazine you bought at the local newsagent. There was no other way to get information. Really, there was no Internet as we know it. A lot of young people can't comprehend that these days.

I've published a dozen different construction projects in the electronics magazines. When the World Wide Web first hit the mainstream, I set up my own web site to publish my electronics information and stuff like that in the mid-nineties. I shared all my information, and found an online audience. I found that my web site would get quickly indexed, so you search for "build your own oscilloscope." and I'd be number one. I'd get all this e-mail from people wanting more information or help on their own project.

Even back in the magazine days, it was fascinating because my name and address were published along with the construction article. I'd get letters from people, "Can you explain this?" Then I'd spend an hour or two handwriting a reply, and I'd lick an envelope and a stamp and send it back to them, snail mail. I just loved sharing information and helping people, even if it was one person at a time, and the information wasn't public. Then that moved from the magazine snail mail world to online when the Internet came along. My information could now go instantly to a world wide audience.

Osborn: That was really early to be on the Internet.

Jones: Well, it really started back in the bulletin board days in the 1980's, when you had a 300-baud modem and you had to dial up yourself. I'd be logging in there and chatting with people and helping them out, all sorts of stuff, way, way back before the internet/web as we take for granted today. So I've always had that history of just sharing my knowledge of electronics and my enthusiasm for electronics. That's one of the key reasons a lot of people watch me, for my enthusiastic approach and that sort of stuff. I was pretty popular on the Internet, even though I hadn't done my video blog, nothing else. It was just a web page, had all my projects. I found I was still very popular. A lot of people would find me.

Before the video blog, I actually had the idea for what now is the Internet radio show, *The Amp Hour*, so I had that idea first actually because I had a studio microphone for another project which I did, an online fitness program. I needed a studio mic and bought one. And when I had that, I thought, "What else can I do with this studio mic? Oh, I know, I can do a podcast, an audio podcast-type radio show and share my knowledge of electronics that way." But I thought, "No one is going to listen to me just waffle on for an hour." I thought that was a stupid idea. So I canned it. And then I started hearing about these video blogs that were becoming all the rage. This was in 2009. Video blogs had been around before that, but you really started to read about people in the paper, how they're making a living on YouTube.

So I thought, "I wonder if I could do a video blog. There's a way to use my studio mic and, well, I need a camera I guess. Maybe I can a video blog-type thing about electronics." So I looked around, and nobody seemed to be doing one. There were lots of WordPress blogs and text blogs about electronics, but no real electronics video "show" as such. So I thought, "Well, okay, I wonder why? Maybe there's no interest, or nobody's thought of it, but hey. I'll give it a go. Why not? I'm not afraid to make a fool out of myself."

So I thought that would be a great idea, but I had no thought whatsoever of making a living from it or making money from it, no concept of that. It was just fun. I wanted to share the information. I thought, "Oh yeah, it will last a couple of episodes maybe. The novelty will wear off and I'll move on to something else."

Anyway, I found an old webcam I had, 320x200, and by then it was five years old, and it was so crusty. I set it on a box in front of me, and I had my studio mic, and I went, "Right, press record and say something." I started to—there was no script, so that's how this whole off-the-cuff no-script thing started, which is the basis of my blog. There are no scripts whatsoever. I just waffled on for ten minutes. Back then, YouTube had that ten-minute limit, if you remember that. So I had to fit in within the ten minutes.

Sure enough, my first video was like nine minutes and fifty-five seconds or something. It just fitted within that. And I had a mix of stuff in there, all just off-the-cuff. I just made it all up. But I hated the final result. I thought it was awful. Oh my goodness, I played it back. The video quality was awful. My delivery was awful because this was the first time I had been in front of a camera, and I went, "Do I have to act? Or do I have to speak slowly and clearly and articulate things like this?" I wasn't sure how to deliver, so I did this wooden delivery. Horrible video quality, and I hated it.

But there's one thing that I knew from all my experience in doing stuff: if you think about it for too long, if you try and perfect it, it will never happen. You just do it, put it up there, put your content out there, and don't worry about it. Don't try to polish it, nothing like that. I went, "Bugger it, I'll just upload it. It's embarrassing. I'm going to make a fool out of myself, but what the hell?" So I uploaded it to my personal YouTube channel and I went to the electronics forum that I was on at the time. It was one of those old school Usenet forms. So I went on to my electronics group on there, and I said, "I've started a video blog. Here's my first episode. Tell me what you think. I think it's embarrassing, but what the hell?" Within the first day, I had fifty people watch it. I thought, "Wow! Fantastic! Fifty people watching me." I had fifty people asking me, "When's the next episode?" I had nothing but positive feedback. I thought it sucked, but people loved it.

Osborn: These days if you get fifty. It's like, "Man, what happened? Nobody paid attention. Nobody cared."

Jones: I thought I'd get a couple of people to view it, but within that one twenty-four-hour period, fifty views and people asking for the next episode. Well, that's it. That's the story. I just thought, "This is great." I'm used to just putting things out on the Web, like my content out there, and I might hear back a year later when somebody stumbles across it as part of a search and they have a question, and I thought that was great. But here I was producing content that people followed, and people were waiting for me to produce new content. And as soon as I uploaded it, they watched it and then gave me immediate feedback and comment, and that felt really good. It felt like it was worthwhile producing that content, even if just fifty people saw it. I thought that was a win. I was stoked. The novelty didn't wear off, and I just kept on producing material, and people kept on watching, and it kept on growing and growing and growing. Two years later, it was my full-time business.

Osborn: That's great.

Jones: That's the story of how it started. It was just something for fun, just another medium that I wanted to share my knowledge in. It's very common in the electronics hobbyist community, back in the magazine days, and now that same philosophy seems to find itself in the hacker maker movement, in the open-source hardware movement. People just love to publish all this knowledge and information and just give it away. It's fantastic. But it's not new. People think the hacker maker movement is a new movement, but it's not. Essentially, the same thing's been going on for almost a hundred years, way back, even before that. The electronics magazine I was published in started as a weekly magazine called *Wireless Weekly*, back in 1921 or thereabouts. People would—you could just get your project, your idea, your article published in there, and you shared information with all of those readers. The same reasons people did it back then are the same reasons people do it now. They just love to share knowledge. It's great.

Osborn: You had the Home Brew Computer Club the Apple guys were part of. I think part of it is just that hardware has become sexy again. There was a period of time people who were passionate about it still did it, but it's become of more trendy I think. It's got a lot of attention.

Jones: If you asked me ten years ago, maybe fifteen years ago, "Has the electronics hobbyist movement died?" And I'd say, "It's pretty darn close to it." It was in its death throes. It really was. All the old electronics magazines were folding. And online, nobody cared about it. All the kids cared about these days was playing video games and using their iPod or whatever consumer gadget. And then this hacker/maker movement started up again. As you said, it became trendy to hack something, take something apart, see how it works, modify it. It's amazing. It has revived the whole electronics movement with it, right there up on the shoulders of the hacker maker movement now. It's fantastic.

Osborn: There seem to be a lot of people like me who are engineers, programmers who have been doing programming for maybe ten years, or even longer, and started to get into it just because they're able to understand at a lower level, play with the hardware.

Jones: And it's fun, because you get to control a robot or you get to flash some lights. There's that—rather than just writing a line of code and something appears on a screen that started with the early home computer movement back in the late seventies to mid eighties. Hardware has that tangible aspect to it. You can get a bit more satisfaction than just software. Not that you can't get that same satisfaction out of writing good code and software and stuff like that. I'm sure you can. But hardware has its own unique feel to it as well.

Osborn: I think the satisfaction is not as immediate as writing code. A lot of time you have to spend an hour, say soldering something together. But part of why I think it's so satisfying is that you've got that time invested and worked through it.

Jones: And you're working with your hands. You're physically building something. I think there's something innate in our nature, or innate in the nature of curious people, who have a natural feel for wanting to do this stuff. Physically holding and playing with something has a more tangible aspect to it than just writing some code and seeing something appear on a screen.

Osborn: What are some of the most popular blog episodes? Can you give me some examples of just one or two episodes that are just for some reason really popular?

Jones: If I blow something up, that gets views. That's a cheap way. There are so many other channels out there that just blow stuff up, and they get hundreds of times more views than I do. If I was just after the views, then I'd be blowing more stuff up. But my most popular video is currently a soldering tutorial.

Osborn: I've seen that guy who blows up things with high voltage.

Jones: Andy is his name, he's Photonicinduction on YouTube.[1] He does high-voltage and blows up stuff.

Osborn: He's just a bat-shit crazy bloke right? Blows up all kinds of stuff in entertaining ways?

Jones: Well, yeah, same with me, except he works on high-voltage stuff. I'm bat-shit crazy too, but I work on more electronics test equipment stuff.

---

[1] www.youtube.com/user/Photonvids

He actually quit at one stage, he threw in the towel. Now, in the blogging electronics industry, if you get so fed up with maintaining a blog audience, it's called "doing a photonic induction." He had ten million views, fifty thousand subscribers. He was going great guns. And all of a sudden, he just shut down his channel, removed all his videos, and said, "Bugger it, I'm not doing any of this anymore. I can't take it." and just wiped out his entire audience and all of his views overnight. Now he's come back though. I don't know if he's regretting that decision, but he's come back and set up a new channel from scratch, and he's going into the whole thing again. But he got fed up with all the negative comments and people saying what he does is dangerous and all that stuff, and he didn't want anyone to get hurt. He thought if he keeps putting up these videos, people will get hurt. They'll try to replicate the experiments, which are dangerous.

Osborn: Yeah, they're dangerous.

Jones: So, yeah, that's called "doing a photonic induction" now, where you get so fed up. And I can understand the pressure he's under getting all the negative comments and things like that, and some people just can't handle it. You really need a thick skin to do the kinds of stuff that we do to a large audience.

Osborn: YouTube comments are all just garbage.

Jones: Yes, so hateful, a lot of vitriolic garbage.

Osborn: People create YouTube commenter accounts to feel better about their terrible lives, I think.

Jones: I know. I think so. And it's a real problem. It doesn't matter how good your material is, it doesn't matter what your intentions are, you put material out there and once you get that critical mass of enough viewers, you will get the haters. It's inevitable. You will get the people who just want to comment to put you down and say you're doing it wrong and blah, blah, blah. Sure, if you get one person who says that, it's not a big deal. But if you start getting hundreds or thousands of people—if you've got a million subscribers, as some of the big channels do, they will get thousands of hateful, vitriolic comments every day. It really does take a tough mental stance to ignore that.

Osborn: Do you think it's worth it to leave the comments open or does it hurt to just turn them off?

Jones: I was just talking about this to another guy the other day who's from The Geek Group, another YouTube channel,[2] and they do exactly that. They actually have to approve all comments. I mentioned in a reply to him on my forum that it's almost tantamount to channel suicide if you do that. If you shut

---

[2] www.youtube.com/user/thegeekgroup

off comments or you monitor or you have to approve every comment before they go up, it can hurt your success.

I don't know any really successful channels that block comments like that. There probably are, but it's the exception. Because by blocking off comments it does several things. The fewer comments you have on your videos, the lower your videos get ranked in the search engine, in the YouTube Google search engine. So the less snowballing effect you're going to get on the success of your channel if you get fewer comments and fewer thumbs-up and thumbs-down and stuff. Just that general interaction, that plays a big part in your channel's search results ranking. So right there, you're just cutting your throat really if you want your channel to be a success.

Osborn: It's a little ironic that hateful spewage helps raise your views.

Jones: Yes. It does help raise your video views because it's a snowballing effect on YouTube: once one video gets ranked, then another one, and it all ties into some huge complex algorithm.

Osborn: And the more hateful the comments are, the more people want to laugh at it and post more comments.

Jones: Yeah, that's the ironic nature of it. The more vitriolic comments you get, the greater the response and the more successful you are. It's a double-edged sword, of course. Sadly, it's effectively impossible to be a big success to a large audience and not get this sort of abuse or discouragement.

Osborn: It sounds like the recipe for getting a lot of views is blowing stuff up.

Jones: There are quite a few things that are popular. Blowing stuff up is one. Keeping to those rules I was talking about before about the attention-span limits. Those really do help. I'm limiting the success of my channel by having hour-long videos. But, hey, it's my niche. I'm already number one. I can't afford to spend more time to make shorter and more polished videos. And then if I do get them down, I'll have all of my existing audience complain, "Oh no, you're doing five-minute videos now instead. of fifty. What's going on? I subscribe because your videos are fifty minutes, not because they're five. I love the detail." So, you know, you can't please everyone. There is an audience out there for short 5 min electronics videos, but that's not what I go after.

Osborn: Besides videos where you blow stuff up, what tends to get a lot of views?

Jones: Surprisingly, I do a segment called mailbag, where I just open my mail.[3]

Osborn: Yeah, I actually have a question to ask you about that.

---

[3]One example is at www.eevblog.com/2013/02/15/eevblog-425-mailbag/.

Jones: I tried it and thought, "No way anybody's going to like this," but I thought I'd just do it for a bit of fun, and it's one of my most popular segments. People kept pestering me. "When's the mailbag? When's the mailbag? When's the next one? When's the next one?" And I'm not sure of the exact reason why it's popular. It's a bit like the opening of presents at Christmas. People have commented that they love it because there's always something interesting in there that they would never have found otherwise. It's that sort of random nature of—I open it up and I have no idea, and I'll start ranting about anything people send in. So I'll have twenty thousand people sit there for an hour watching me open my mail. It's incredible. It's just amazing.

Osborn: So people mail you random devices and then you take them apart?

Jones: Then I take them apart or just talk about the stuff they send me.

Osborn: What's the strangest thing you've gotten in the mail?

Jones: Oh, I got some women's lingerie. I'm not sure what they wanted me to do with it, but there it came, from an anonymous sender. I'm sure I'll continue to get weirder stuff. I guess a lot of people love to say, "Hey, Dave read my letter." A lot of people just send a thank-you letter or a postcard, and I'll read out their postcard on the video. People seem to like that. I was incredibly surprised by the success of that segment. It's just amazing. It shows you there's a niche audience for just entertainment, like opening your mail. And I guess it shows that once you're a successful channel, people are watching because of you, because of the personality. I don't think somebody else can come along and open that same stuff and get the same number of viewers, because people don't have that connection with that person. So it's a strange world.

Osborn: Besides the lingerie, can you give me an example of something you're received in the mail and took apart on the show?

Jones: I can tell you something that I got a lot of complaints over. Most people love my mailbag shows, but there was one mailbag segment where I got so many thumbs-down and so many hater comments for it. I had my son, Sagan, on there. He's only two years old. I let him open a couple of the packages. I thought, "Hey, that would be fun. Everyone likes Sagan." I've had him on a few videos before. Then some guy in Australia sent me a whole bunch of old computer equipment. It was a secondhand video card, but apparently, it was a top-of-the-line, really kickass video card, and then, of course, Sagan pulled it out and tossed it onto the bench. And then he started poking it with a screwdriver and stuff. I didn't let him damage it, but then I got all these computer nerds write, "Sacrilege! How dare you let your child poke at that! I would kill to have that video card! And here you are, letting your child play with it."

And apparently, I didn't recognize the value of this card he told me he was sending me. I thought, "Great, an old high-end video card. I might be able to use it for my video rendering." But I had no idea it had a cult following, this video card. I got so much hate mail over that. It was unbelievable. It was an innocent thing like that. If it touches a nerve with people you really have to be careful. But I had no idea that that gear was so valuable to people. And he sent old, secondhand computer fans, and they had dust all over them, and they looked pretty crusty, and I had no idea they were the best silent fans in the business. All these computer nerds, they love their silent fans and their high-end video cards and their other stuff. I just insulted every one of them. Oops.

Osborn: Were they the brown computer fan, the Noctua ones?

Jones: Yes, the brown Noctua. And apparently I didn't bow down in front of them and show then due reverence, so all hell broke loose.

Osborn: I expected you to say you took apart some Apple product and didn't give it proper blessing.

Jones: Yes, something like that. There are so many passionate people, and I can understand people like this. I have passion, and that's what I put into my videos. I have that same enthusiasm. They just have enthusiasm for different things, and I certainly understand why they got so upset. A lot of people have a lot of passion for a lot of different stuff. And that's what makes, well, I think my channel popular. Nobody does a channel like this as a pure business reason: "I'm going to go and make video blogs and I'm going to make a lot of money." Nobody does that. I don't know a single person who does that, who's been a successful video blogger because they thought it was a great business venture or something like that. It just doesn't happen.

Osborn: Do you still do some electrical engineering consulting, or do you just focus on the blog nowadays?

Jones: I'm one hundred percent focused on the blog now, have been for about a year and a half. When I first started it full-time, I actually lost my job. The company packed up and moved to China. I got made redundant or retrenched, as we call it here. I don't know what you guys call it in the States, but anyway, I was laid off. I was quite happy about it actually, I really didn't want to be at the company any longer. The first thing I did was I go home and tell the wife that I was made redundant. I was happily smiling. She said, "Right. Go out and look for another job."

Our first baby was due in three or four weeks and here I was, I just lost my engineering job, and of course she's away from work and will be for the next year because of our kid. And she said, "Go look for a job."

And I said, "I've got several months' pay from the company. I've got at least several months. Can you give me several months to work on the blog?"

"No! Go look for a job."

So I said, "Ok, I'll do some consulting work." I had a friend who got me some consulting work I did from home, so that paid the bills for a little while. But as it turns out, at the same time that I was doing that, a couple of months after I was retrenched, the forum sponsor came along and I got more advertising. It just seemed to all happen at once. And then, bam, I was making enough money so the wife was happy and didn't want to make me go back and get a real job again. It turns out I was struggling to find enough time to do consulting, keep up the blog, and having a family life as well. So once I was making just enough money to make the wife happy from the video blogging work, I dropped the consulting work and I haven't done it since.

Osborn: So you've got four hundred ninety-ish episodes now, something like that?

Jones: Yeah, almost five hundred.

Osborn: How many are you doing a week now?

Jones: I calculated it the other day, and ever since I started, I've done three on average, but, of course, some weeks are more productive than others. I've got two regular segments now. There are two regular weekly segments, so I need to keep those up plus all the odd stuff in between that, so yeah, that averages out to about three a week.

Osborn: Besides the "Monday Mailbag" episodes, do you have any other themed episodes that you do?

Jones: I've got "Teardown Tuesday." I've been doing that for a long time now, so every Tuesday I do a teardown of something. Mailbag Monday is supposed to be every week on a Monday, but it's not. I do it maybe once every month or twice a month. And I've got a new segment, "Fundamentals Friday," so I teach fundamental theory in something, a fundamental principle or a fundamental circuit building block or something like that. I have that every Friday, or try to.

And that's the thing. I've found that you really have to have those regular segments to keep the blog going. It forces you to get off your ass and actually do something. You're like, "Holy crap! It's two or three pm on a Tuesday, and I haven't done my "Teardown Tuesday" video yet. Oh no! I'm going to get hammered with hate mail, so I'd better hurry up and get off my ass and actually produce a video." It forces you to do it. Otherwise, you can get quite lazy. Well, I can. I won't speak for other content producers. I can get quite lazy and always find an excuse not to do something. So having that regular content there forces you into a pattern. It's like a work pattern, going to work every day, five days a week. It gets you into that pattern, doing something. And I've found that very helpful.

Osborn: Are there some new technologies coming out or tools or things you're excited about, that you're looking forward to doing on the show?

Jones: There are, but unfortunately, I don't have time to experiment with them. There's an infinite amount of new technology I would love to play with. But I don't have the time unfortunately. If it's a new chip—for example, Microchip came out with this new hand gesture technology. It senses where your hands are in this field, so you can interact in 3D space, you can know where people's hands are. To get a demo kit for that and experiment with that and understand it and play with it, I could spend a week full-time doing that—easily. And then, well, I don't get any of my regular videos done. I don't have time to work on any of my own projects. I don't have time to see my family. I don't have time just to relax.

So, unfortunately, I'd love to do that, and you'd think I would. A lot of people have that expectation of me, that I should be able to do videos on new technology like that, but it just takes so much time and effort that, really, I can't say, "Right, I'm not going to do another video for the next two weeks, and then I'm going to experiment with this technology and then I'm going to produce one video at the end of it." Then I'll have half my audience complain, "Where's my "Teardown Tuesday"? Where's my "Fundamentals Friday"? Where's my "Mailbag Monday"? Where's my other stuff? I didn't sign up for this one video." There's that constant pressure of having to produce content that pleases everyone. And it's tough. I'd love to.

No one appreciates whether it takes you an hour to shoot a single video, or two weeks, it's just one video to them.

Osborn: If you figure out how to make everyone happy let me know. Then you'll have something for sure.

Jones: I could actually bottle that and sell it, exactly.

Osborn: You'll certainly have no money problems.

Do you have any advice for aspiring electrical engineers? I've watched some of your "Fundamentals Friday" videos. To be completely honest the last one was a bit over my head. Do you think you need an EE degree to really be effective in this field? Or do you know people who have successfully made a career out of it learning on their own?

Jones: No, you don't. Some of the best people I know are self-taught. I'm effectively self-taught. I've been doing electronics since I was five years old. Before I ever studied it formally I was already published in the industry. I've had my own lab, my own workshop since I was eight. I've found in the industry, the best kind are the ones that have that passion from the hobbyist background and also the formal education side of things. You can certainly be a very effective and successful electronics engineer without any formal study. But obviously, that helps.

Effectively, almost everything you learn in engineering is self-taught. If you think you can spend four years at university and you come out being a proficient engineer with knowledge of everything, you're crazy. You just learn the fundamentals. You learn how to think. But there's so much in electronics. There's so much technology out there. You can't possibly learn it all. I learn something new every day, and I've been doing electronics for more than thirty years. And there's not a day that goes by where I don't learn something new that I didn't know before. It's just infinite.

Osborn: So do you have an advice for people who want to learn electronics?

Jones: The biggest thing in electronics or in probably almost any field is you have to fail in order to learn. I always say to people, "I hope the next project you build doesn't work. I sincerely hope it doesn't work." Because if it does, you haven't learned nearly as much. If it works on its first go, you followed some instructions, you build up this kit and it works, okay, you've learned how to build a kit. But if it doesn't work, then you've got to put your thinking cap on and go, well, why doesn't it work? You've got to go back and actually measure everything from scratch, figure out, track down where the problem is, understand how this part of the system interacts with this one over here. That's where the real learning happens. When you have to troubleshoot and fix problems.

It's probably like code. You probably understand that you learn a lot when your program doesn't compile the first go and you go, "Whoa. That error message. I've never seen that before. What does it mean?" You've got to look up that error message and understand what caused that and why. It's a similar thing in engineering as well.

Osborn: In fact, in software engineering, a lot of times it's so rare that you write code for half an hour and it works the first time that on multiple occasions, I've heard somebody go, "Holy cow. It works."

Jones: Exactly.

Osborn: You almost expect it to fail the first time. And these are people who have ten years of experience writing code.

Jones: And that's the thing that formal education won't teach you. It won't teach you the practical aspect of doing stuff like that. Well, a lot of education won't. There are some places that will be better than others. But generally, not. That stuff you have to learn on your own. When shit hits the fan, when things go wrong, you've got to understand why things went wrong and how to fix it. That is the big takeaway. If there is one thing that people can do to learn engineering, electronics engineering, is to (a) build stuff and (b) troubleshoot. That's it. That will turn you into a great electronics engineer. And you've got to have enthusiasm. Enthusiasm is number one. If you don't have enthusiasm and passion for what you do, what's the point?

Osborn: Yeah, do something else.

Jones: That's the thing I found when I went to study electronics, because I had been doing it since I was a young kid and I had so much passion. That's all I ever wanted to do. And then I went to study it full-time and I found that 99% of people here sitting around me in this course don't give a shit. I'm like, "Why are you here? What do you mean you don't read the electronics magazines when you go home? Why not?" They were just doing the course because their friends were doing it or because they thought they might get a stable job or because their parents wanted them to do something, anything. "I'll do engineering, that's pretty popular. I'll get the degree and then go and get a good job in sales or something." That really gets me down. I don't understand that. From somebody who has so much passion, that doesn't make sense to me.

Osborn: I think it's pretty rare to graduate high school and know what you want to do in the world. People have no idea, and so they just draw something out of a hat.

Jones: I totally agree. That's right. And I found the percentage was massive. It was 95 percent or more. There were very few other people I ran into during my formal study that really seemed to care, that really had a passion for it. That doesn't mean that they can't become good engineers. I know a lot are who have absolutely no interest in electronics or engineering outside of work. And they're still very good career engineers. But as I said before, I've found the best people in the industry are the ones who started from that hobbyist background.

Osborn: That's good advice. I'll remember it the next time my project doesn't work. It's because Dave wished it not to.

Jones: That's it. That could be a caption in the book: "I hope your project doesn't work." It can be one of those pop-out things.

Osborn: With absolutely no context.

Jones: With absolutely no context, exactly. Dave says: "I hope you fail."

Osborn: I think you have some good perspective on what it takes to run a successful YouTube blog or video blog. The maker space is so wide open. Nowadays, it's everything from knitting to woodworking, a lot of different perspectives. I think a lot of different people are interested in doing just what you're doing, where you start a blog and talk about what they're building and doing. I think that's some good content for some people.

Jones: Excellent. I just hope they don't start to expect that it will lead to success for them. I think if you do that, you're just going to fail. You have to start it, as I said, because you enjoy it and you want to give that information. If you become a success, that's great. Even today, I've still got no plan. I had no plan at the beginning, and I still have no plan, even though this is my full-time business. I just continue to make videos because I enjoy it, and maybe that's to my detriment. I could probably be making a lot more money and probably have a lot more success by thinking like a business and being smart about the content and what people want and all that stuff. But no, I just keep doing it in the format that I like because I enjoy it.

Osborn: And like you said earlier, if you had worried yourself to death about how it was going to work, you probably would have never done it because ...

Jones: Exactly, exactly.

Osborn: ... you'd try to get it perfect and you can't.

Jones: Oh yeah. There's no point perfecting your material. Just put it out there. It most certainly becomes diminishing returns at some point. Publish and be damned. There's another quote: "Publish and be damned" because you're never going to please everyone. You're going to have people who say you're wrong, haters or whatever, regardless of what you do or how much you try and make it right. It's an unfortunate fact.

Osborn: Well, thanks Dave. As always it was fun and entertaining.

Jones: Oh, no trouble.

Bre Pettis

CEO

MakerBot

Bre Pettis is CEO and a cofounder of MakerBot Industries (makerbot.com), a company that designs and sells 3D printers. Before starting MakerBot, Bre was a schoolteacher, artist, video blogger, and puppeteer. He helped start a maker space called NYC Resistor in Brooklyn and is well known for the popular video podcasts that he produced for MAKE magazine.

Steven Osborn: Before we get too much into MakerBot, I want to learn about you and what you were doing before MakerBot. Can you tell me a little bit about your background?

Bre Pettis: So I had an early experience as a kid visiting my uncle Joe. He would wake up at four o'clock in the morning and go out in his pickup truck before the trash man came and pick up all the good trash. He would then fix up the things he found and sell them on the weekends at flea markets.

During one of my visits with him, when I was maybe six or seven, we picked up a couple bicycles and merged them into one bicycle and fixed it up and painted it black. That was *my* bike. He did it in such a way that even though he probably did a lot of the work, he really explained it to me and I got to do it as well, so at the end, I felt that I had made a bike from scratch and that it was *my* bike and that I could fix it. And I just got hooked on that feeling. It was really powerful. That was a strong moment for me as a kid, where I said, "I can fix things, and then they're mine." I think everybody should have that feeling, and a lot of people never get that feeling in their life. We've got to fix that.

Going forward, from there, I was really into guitars and amps and being loud throughout high school. I went to college at the Evergreen State College, which is a pretty special place. Then when I was done with that, I ended up landing a gig at Jim Henson's Creature Shop, working on film sets and doing stuff with animatronics. I got to work with these amazing people who did some fun and interesting things. We pushed rubber gorilla technology farther than it had ever gone before. That was really fun. Then I burnt out on the film industry and came home to Seattle.

To make ends meet at that time, I started doing these puppetry workshops for kids, teaching them how to make puppets. I enjoyed working with kids enough that I went back to school and got my teacher's certificate and was a teacher for seven years. Because I was that puppet guy, I ended up landing a really sweet art job right away. So mostly I taught art for seven years and empowered kids to make stuff. My goal with that was to give them as many different ways to express themselves as they could, because most of the rest of school these days is embarrassing for our culture. It's mostly just rote testing and book learning. I was the class where they got to learn how to sew a button, as well as work with ceramics, and drawing, and painting, and sculpture, and all that kind of stuff.

I started making videos for that, and then I'd put them on the Internet. I was fairly early—I was probably number thirteen in video blogging—and ended up becoming friends with this whole group of people, like Steve Garfield[1] and just the whole crew. We were doing pre-YouTube video blogging. I'm still friends with folks at Blip.tv and YouTube, people who started YouTube, and all of these people who were doing video blogging in 2004, 2005. There just weren't that many people, so we all knew each other.

I ended up leaving teaching to make videos for *MAKE*.[2] I kind of shifted to the bigger classroom of the Internet. Every week, I would have to make something, and a video about it, and a ten-page PDF tutorial. I would publish these things every Friday at noon. Every Friday, I would have to have a project that I had made, documented, and shared in one week. I was doing a five-minute video a week. I was writing all the music for it, I was making the stuff. Usually, I would do it twice. I would make it once to learn how to make it and then I would make it again to actually shoot the video.

To make it interesting, I was taking on crazier and crazier projects. At one point, I worked with a group in Seattle called Hackerbot Labs,[3] and we made a robot that takes your picture and draws you. This was before Arduino. It was really a challenging time. Things are so much easier these days, with the modular tool sets and the amount of code that's out there that you can use,

---

[1]One of the Internet's first video bloggers (www.stevegarfield.com).
[2]http://archive.makezine.com/pub/au/Bre_Pettis
[3]www.hackerbotlabs.com

and projects like Arduino and Raspberry Pi that are out there that let you kind of plug and play. It wasn't like that back in the day.

Then I moved to New York and started a hacker space here called NYC Resistor.[4] I really wanted to create this community that could make anything. And what do you do when you can make anything? You make a machine that can make anything. Zach Smith, Adam Mayer and I started MakerBot to create a 3D printer for everyone. The next thing you know, I'm still here cranking them out, creating wonderful products that make people happy and empowering creative explorers to do wonderful things.

Osborn: I've heard good things about NYC Resistor. It seems like a great community of folks. Can you walk me through the history of MakerBot then, how you got started? You touched on it a little bit there. Can you talk about the progression of the machines when you started building the hardware?

Pettis: I got involved in 2007, when I first met Zach. I worked with him on early RepRap prototypes and then ended up putting together my own kit of parts to build a RepRap. I went to Austria for a month and put together—it's really pre-RepRap, or what we called in the day a RepStrap or a McWire bot, probably one of the least best ways to make a 3D printer, out of plumbing material. That almost worked.

Then I came back from Austria and was making stuff for the RepRap community and selling it essentially at cost. Zach at that time was not an electrical engineer. He was just getting started in making circuits, so the traces were too thin. They were always literally letting out the magic smoke. But in 2009, Zach, Adam, and I started MakerBot because we saw people working on RepRaps, but very few of them worked. There were maybe twenty people who put together a machine, and very few of them actually worked with any semblance of repeatability. Everybody's machine was different, because we were all digging motors out of old disk drives. Every machine was unique.

So we started MakerBot so that we could have a 3D printer that everybody could own, so if somebody solved a problem, they would solve it for everybody else, too. This way we weren't all wasting effort solving the same problems. We originally thought we might just make RepRaps. We could make 3D printers that would just make more 3D printers. If you knew someone with a RepRap, they could print you the parts to make one for yourself.

At that time, Zach went to a workshop in Portugal, I think, and while he was gone I was like, "This sucks. We've got a laser cutter. We're just going to make a laser-cut machine." So by the time he got back, we had a really rough 3D printer prototype that had been laser cut, and Zach had done a workshop

---

[4]www.nycresistor.com

where he had spent a week trying to make a machine work and it wouldn't work and he was fed up with it.

At that point, very early on, within the first month, we made a commitment to using the laser cutter we had at NYC Resistor. What that allowed us to do was prototype ultrafast. We could make machines that didn't require tooling, which can be really expensive. And we could iterate as we learned. In many ways, we shipped our first prototype. Well, we didn't ship our first prototype. When we launched the Cupcake, it was really a good 3D printer, and they're still out there and they still work, but there was still lots of room for improvement. We weren't engineers, but we iterated and designed a 3D printer in less than three months and it worked, and so we shipped it. We made twenty of them. We thought that would be enough for a couple of months and while we were selling them, we could make more. Instead, we sold all of them. They sold basically instantly. So we immediately had the problem of too much demand, not enough capacity.

We started out in Resistor and then quickly we moved over to Jake's. Jake Lodwick had an office, and he let us have a corner of it. After a few months, we had pretty much taken over his whole office. So we moved into the place at 87 Third Avenue in Brooklyn, what we call the Bot Cave, and started making more, trying to keep up.

In 2010, we launched the MakerBot Thing-O-Matic, which had an automatic build platform, which worked but required frequent replacement. Like a conveyer belt, it required replacement belts pretty regularly because it had to put that belt under a lot of tension. Most people didn't use that function even though it was really cool.

In January 2012, we came out with the MakerBot Replicator, and then in September of 2012, we came out with the MakerBot Replicator 2. One of the things we do really well is we iterate quickly and fast, and get things done.

Osborn: Did the early versions of all these machines use some Arduino-based hardware?

Pettis: Technically, the hardware could be considered an Arduino. We have the same chip on there, but because an Arduino doesn't actually have a lot of room, it ceased being an Arduino and became a MakerBot. We built it on Arduino architecture but pretty quickly scaled out of that and had to customize it.

Osborn: So you still have an Atmel microcontroller, but that's about all you have in common at this point.

Pettis: That's right.

Osborn: There are a couple of different types of filament technology out there, PLA and ABS. Can you talk about the differences in the two and why you chose PLA for the Replicator 2?

Pettis: The MakerBot Replicator 2 is set up for MakerBot PLA. The MakerBot Replicator 2X is set up for MakerBot ABS. That's because people still just love ABS, even though I think PLA is a more elegant solution. PLA is just a beautiful material. It has very low shrinkage, high-dimensional tolerance, and it's a renewable bio plastic, so it's guilt-free making. We really like it, and it makes beautiful models.

Osborn: I don't know for sure, but it seems like there's a lot less smell when you extrude PLA. Is that correct?

Pettis: You know my guess is that they probably have the same amount of smell. It's just that PLA smells so much better because it's made out of corn.

Osborn: Like corn instead of melting plastic?

Pettis: Yeah.

Osborn: In addition to the MakerBots, you guys built this great community site called Thingiverse.[5] I think anybody that owns a 3D printer has probably been to Thingiverse. I remember seeing a blog post that mentioned there are over one hundred thousand things on Thingiverse now.

Pettis: Yes, we surely have seen an uptick recently. I think it's more than one hundred twenty thousand now.

Osborn: Wow. Can you tell me what Thingiverse is and what people go there for? What is its purpose?

Pettis: We actually started Thingiverse before we started MakerBot. It was a Saturday afternoon project for me and Zach. We wanted a place where we could share digital designs. We were making things on the laser cutter and we were misplacing them on our hard drives. I was literally uploading the 3D design files to my DreamHost account, and that wasn't going to scale. So at the time, Zach was working at Zinio, a place where people share video files. We sat down on a Saturday, and after about an hour, we were like, "This is pretty interesting. Let's keep going with this."

We decided on the name, Universe of Things, Thingiverse. We liked that. We just kept going. We were sort of the early power users, along with a couple of other community members. We made Thingiverse in 2008. By the time 2009 rolled around, it was starting to pick up some traction. I think in the beginning, if we could get one thing a week uploaded, that was awesome. And then pretty quickly that turned into one thing a day. Now hundreds of things a day are shared and uploaded to the Thingiverse. Thousands of things a day, maybe tens of thousands are downloaded. People really use it. It's a great place for designers to share their work and really shine and be a superstar.

---

[5]www.thingiverse.com

Osborn: There's a bit of—I don't know if you'd say controversy or concern in the community about people applying DRM to designs and selling their designs. I don't think we really understand what that's going to mean to the community and what impact it is going to have on society. I don't know if you have any opinion on that. If I 3D-scan this object, should I have the right to print my own copy?

Pettis: It's an exciting frontier. For us, we really work hard to set up the site so it would have great features for attribution. When you make something, we encourage you to upload an image of it so that the person who designed it can see your manifestation of that digital design. It gives you this feeling of the dad watching your design go out into the world and do wonderful things.

We are about to launch the MakerBot Digitizer, which is a desktop 3D scanner. I think we're at probably the same place that the audio industry was when it launched—when the tape recorder came out, or the VHS machine. It's a little bit different because it's things. It's not music and it's not video. All of those things fall under copyright. Things actually fall under patent law, so for us, there's a whole frontier out there to explore. Our goal is to create a wonderful place for people to share things that they want to share and really shine a spotlight on them and allow them to shine. While I'm excited to see how things go in the legal world, we really don't know yet—nobody has brought it up in the courts, so it really hasn't worked its way through the system. Everything is conjecture at this point. Our goal is to create a wonderful place for people to share the things they want to share—to point a spotlight at them and allow them to shine.

Osborn: I think the most controversial 3D project was Defense Distributed. It is this really shoddy 3D printed weapon, but has got a lot of attention because 3D printing is an exciting topic right now.

Pettis: I would say there are many things that are way more interesting. Have you seen the Robohand project?

Osborn: No, but that leads me to my next question, which is interesting things your customers or people are printing with MakerBot.

Pettis: I think we made MakerBot with the intention that people are going to use them for wonderful and positive uses, really explore the creative frontier. The Robohand project is a project by two people. One is in South Africa and one is in Seattle. They use MakerBot as a 3D fax machine. They designed a prosthetic called the Robohand for kids. Kids don't usually get prosthetics because they cost ten grand each and they grow out of them like sneakers. But when you have a MakerBot, you can make them.

So these guys made a model. They shared it on Thingiverse. There have been a few derivatives. Now you can make a hand for a kid who has amniotic band syndrome, which is where you're born without fingers or a thumb. This gives kids a robohand. They get to go to school and it's like they're Iron Man or something. They've got a robotic hand. It cost about $5 in materials. When you grow out of it, it's not a big deal. You scale it up and you reprint it. This really changes the game when you think about how prosthetics work, specifically for kids. It opens the door for all sorts of other ways of thinking about how 3D printing can change any industry.

Osborn: There are definitely some interesting medical use cases for 3D printing. I saw where they printed a woman's entire lower jawbone.

One thing you guys did recently that I thought was pretty interesting was open a retail space for 3D printers in New York. I was wondering what led you to do that, and how's the response been?

Pettis: My goal with that was to have a space where people could see, and touch, and feel, and hear, and smell 3D printing. In some ways, it's sort of a community center. People who come to New York and are into 3D printing, it's on their tourist list. We see people come from all around the world to just really experience 3D printing. A lot of them walk out with MakerBots as well. We sell 3D printers there, and we sell projects designed to be printed on the MakerBot. For us, that's just a great place where people can experience what a 3D printer is, because for most people it's still science fiction.

Osborn: Besides the Robohand, can you give me some other cool projects that people are building with the MakerBot?

Pettis: We just had a birdhouse challenge where we got lots of people in the community making birdhouses. It's on Thingiverse. Thingiverse is a great place to find things.

Osborn: I saw that recently.

Pettis: People are making rockets, making their own games, making a necklace or tie rack. There's just an amazing amount of things on Thingiverse for pretty much anything that you're interested in.

One of our users is Kacie Hultgren. She's at Pretty Small Things.[6] She's a Broadway set designer. She used to use cardboard and glue and X-Acto knives to design things. Now she just makes things digitally and prints out this amazing model—making set furniture on her MakerBot, and then she has a whole side business where she sells dollhouse furniture. Super cool. There's a whole bunch of folks using Minecraft as a modeling tool. That's super cool, they just build things in Minecraft, then print it. They're using MakerBot in the Natural History Museum to scan dinosaur bones. Then the art museum scans precious works of art that nobody can ever touch, so they can make copies of it that people can touch.

---

[6]http://pretty-small-things.myshopify.com

Osborn: My favorite project I think I found on Thingiverse is OpenRC.[7]

Pettis: Yeah, the RC car.

Osborn: I have some wheels that I've printed. I glued the tires on recently. So, how many people are out there making things right now with a MakerBot?

Pettis: I think we're around thirty thousand. I don't have the exact number, but I think we're around there.

Osborn: That's a lot of people. That's a big community.

Pettis: We're still at the beginning. We've got a lot of work to do to make people feel comfortable with 3D printing.

Osborn: It seems like MakerBot has become the go-to printer for 3D printing. I read that Ford bought a MakerBot for all of their design engineers to have on their desks. A company like Ford could purchase any 3D printer on the market. I was wondering what makes the MakerBot stand out amongst what seems to be an endless number of competitors right now? There are a lot of people building 3D printers. I think a lot of them got a lot of cues from you. There are a lot of them out there, cut out with a laser. What makes the MakerBot the favorite for a company like Ford, as well as makers building things in their garage?

Pettis: I think it's a couple things. The first thing is that we're on our fourth-generation machine, so we've worked out a lot of bugs. We're ambitious. It's a very large build plate. It's a very large build volume, and that means you can do a lot of things. On the Replicator 2, it's six by eleven by six inches, so it's just a really nice, large build plate.

I think the other thing you can look at is the software. We've come a long way with MakerWare. When we started, we created a very basic command-line tool. Now it's a really nice tool with a beautiful GUI. It's just a pleasure to use a MakerBot. We have a huge support team. I think we have forty or fifty people right now in our support department, whose job it is to support people in doing amazing things with their MakerBot.

So all of those things add up. We're a company that's in it for the long haul. We're not just going to do a Kickstarter, make something and deliver it, and disappear into the world. We're going deep.

I think besides that, it just looks good. You can have it in any color as long as it's black. We made it into something that not only looks good on the outside, but we set up the lighting on the inside so that the objects you make look beautiful, too. It's a special machine, the MakerBot Replicator 2. It strikes a chord with people—it's a professional-quality machine, but still affordable enough that it's like the equivalent of a nice laptop.

---

[7]www.thingiverse.com/thing:42198

Osborn: Tell me a little bit about the recent Stratasys acquisition.

Pettis: That's pretty exciting. We've been at this nearly five years. MakerBot is nearly five years old, so we've been doing this for a while. When you're growing fast, you have a couple options for scaling up quickly. We chose to take venture capital, and that means we were dedicated to really building a large, sustainable company that would do really wonderful things in the world for a long time. We were actually out raising our next round, and in the middle of that Stratasys came knocking at our door and said, "Would you be interested in talking to our president?" And we started talking about it and basically, they're just really cool people. They're just as big 3D-printing geeks as we are.

Before the acquisition we had to work around a lot of patents in this space. That's one thing I think a lot of people jumping into that space don't realize that there's—even if the original patent is expired, there's another five hundred patents in this space that you have to work around. We've made a point to be very respectful of IP as we go forward. Actually, we've worked around a lot of Stratasys patents, and when you do that, you don't necessarily get the best solution. You get a solution. I'm super excited to have access to the Stratasys IP.

Plus, these folks have been doing 3D printing for twenty-five years and there's a lot we get to learn from them in terms of expertise in being able to just put the pedal to the metal on what we're doing. They have the same mission: We want to grow the worldwide adoption of 3D printing, so that more 3D printers can be out there. More people can be empowered to make the things that they need in life.

Osborn: The last question I have is what's next for MakerBot? You mentioned the 3D digitizing scanner. What else do you have going on?

Pettis: Well, the next big thing for us is the Digitizer. We announced it at South by Southwest, and we showed a prototype there to give people a glimpse into the future. Since then, we've actually developed it and we're getting ready to ship this fall just an amazingly beautiful product. What I can say about it now is that it looks like a spaceship.

Osborn: Cool.

Pettis: It just changes the whole game. CAD is hard. We're creating a tool that allows people to be creative without having to go deep into the CAD world.

Osborn: Do you have any words of wisdom for people getting started in 3D printing?

Pettis: I would kind of circle back to where I started and just say that it's just an amazing time to be a creative person in the world. There's so much infrastructure and support for people who have ideas to bring them to fruition and explore the market, whether you need investment or whether you go on Kickstarter, whatever it is you do, whatever it is you want to do, there's so much more support now than there was back in 2004, 2005. So in many ways, if you have an idea, there are fewer excuses for not executing that idea and nurturing that idea and bringing it to life. I would sort of wrap this up by encouraging people to really explore their ideas, explore the frontier of what's possible, and live it up.

Osborn: If you don't have a 3D printer, there's probably a place like NYC Resistor or TechShop in your area, so you probably have access to those machines if you really need it.

Pettis: I think that's a really good place to wrap it up. I think that's a good message.

Eric Migicovsky

CEO

Pebble Technology

Eric Migicovsky is an engineer and entrepreneur who received his bachelor's in engineering from the University of Waterloo in 2009. While in school, Eric began building smartwatches. That led to the development of his first product, the InPulse. After struggling to find hardware-savvy investors, Eric launched his new watch, the Pebble (getpebble.com) on the Kickstarter crowd-funding platform where it became the most successful crowdfunded project in Kickstarter's history. The success Eric achieved with Pebble has sparked an interest in hardware start-ups by investors and entrepreneurs, and is helping to pave the way for new, innovative consumer products.

Steven Osborn: I'd like to just start by having you tell me a little bit about yourself, your background, your education, and what got you interested in making physical products. What is your background prior to Pebble?

Eric Migicovsky: I started working on Pebble five years ago. I was finishing my engineering degree at the University of Waterloo and was on exchange in the Netherlands. The idea for Pebble came while I was studying industrial design. Everyone in Holland bikes everywhere, so I started biking with my smartphone.

Dutch people have an innate ability to text and bike at the same time. I didn't have that skill yet, and I didn't want to drop my phone into the canal. I started thinking about how cool it would be to have a watch or a device on my bike that would talk to my smartphone and retrieve information. A watch was perfect because it's something people wear every day. I started sketching it out, designing it. I soldered together the first circuit boards myself in my dorm.

I actually published a YouTube video[1] of my first prototype online. But even before that, I always knew I would be an engineer of some sort.

Osborn: Just from birth you knew that you wanted to build things?

Migicovsky: Yes, I was a builder from the start. Playing with LEGOs, building tree forts, building robots, playing with electronics, burning myself while soldering and welding. I always knew I would be building things. Looking back, you probably could have predicted that I would have gone into starting a hardware company, because not only did I like building things but I also liked running businesses. I was always selling something I had a newspaper route from a pretty young age.

In high school, I opened a store, called the Black Market, and sold snacks and drinks from my locker. I undercut the vending machines and the actual store in my high school. It was fun. I ran it for a couple of months before we got shut down. It was my first little foray into providing a service and doing something that people wanted.

Osborn: So your motivation was this want or need, or the novelty of having this display on your wrist that didn't require you to get your phone out while you were riding your bike? Is that how most of your users use it or are there some interesting use cases you hadn't really thought about?

Migicovsky: The original idea was for notifications. That was the bread and butter, the basic feature set. Our first smartwatch model, which was InPulse, worked exclusively with BlackBerry smartphones. I was just finishing up school in Waterloo, Ontario, which is home to Research in Motion. It was kind of a natural thing to work with BlackBerry at that time.

We started shipping the very first version of InPulse in the fall of 2010, and it was still very much hacked together. We were using metalwork that we had gotten from a local CNC milling shop that had read about us in the newspaper and then e-mailed asking if they could help build the casing for the watch. And they did.

Then we got the circuit boards made in China at a small factory that one of our friends introduced us to. We were assembling the watches piece by piece—including the straps and the glass—in our garage and sending them to our first customers.

The best part about that whole experience is that we were shipping the product to customers early and seeing what people thought of having a smartwatch. At the beginning, all the watch did was show notifications for your phone. It showed e-mail, SMS, caller ID. Naturally, the number-one feature request was, "Could it tell the time as well?" The very first version of the

---

[1]www.youtube.com/watch?v=qVZDx86FtOo

firmware couldn't, so we decided to add time-telling onto the watch. We had a process of releasing new firmware once every week. We would think of new features that we wanted to add, write them into the operating system, and then send that operating system out to these early beta users.

There were about one hundred people who tried out the watch, writing us long e-mails practically every day about their experiences. It was pretty awesome. We got instantaneous feedback from people after we developed new features.

Osborn: So you were shipping them to customers at the point, but you were at the scale where you were still building them in your garage?

Migicovsky: Yes.

Osborn: I think a lot of people make a prototype and then want to launch it on Kickstarter, and then the next day expect to sell a million of these things. Or I guess the worst thing that can happen is they sell a million of them and then they have to figure out how to make them.

Migicovsky: Well, keep in mind this is five years ago. Hardware start-ups were not unpopular, but they were still not the coolest thing in the world at that time. So we were fighting to get money. I borrowed money from my parents, and I borrowed some money from the government. We got some loans. We were back in Waterloo, Ontario, and this is outside the Silicon Valley environment. We didn't have that much cash, so we did what we could with the small amount of money we had. Instead of trying to raise money, which we thought impossible for us, we just started selling the InPulse watch.

We explained to people that it was an early-stage product and probably had a lot of bugs, but we would do our damndest to fix them. The early users had a lot of requests, and one of the most popular requests was for people to write applications for the watch. We had thought about it, but we never knew that it was such an important feature.

In January of 2011, we launched an SDK[2] for the InPulse watch. It was extremely rudimentary, but people started creating beautiful, stylized watch faces. It caught our attention that there was this uncapped number of people who were interested in hacking on the watch and building something, converting it into something that no one would have expected.

We ran with that idea when we were architecting Pebble, the next generation of the watch. App development became one of the core experiences that we delivered with Pebble. We added Android support and iOS support, but I think the most important feature that we added was the ability for third-party developers to write apps on top of Pebble.

---

[2]Software development kit.

We launched the Pebble in January 2013 and then announced the beta SDK in April 2013. In the months after the SDK launch, we saw a huge number of apps that came out very quickly. We've seen sports and fitness apps that help people track their activities, and provide a display on their watch while they're exercising. Then there are apps that enable people to control things, like remote controls for lights in their house. There's an app to control a Nest thermostat from a Pebble. I think someone controlled their microwave from their watch. It's pretty incredible to see people connect Pebble to things around the world. Then there's a category of apps that download information from the web to display on the watch. Just last night I downloaded an app that shows you the latest ocean tide, so if you're a surfer, you can know exactly when it's time to head out to the beach.

In most cases, people are not building these apps for other people to use. They are building a product that solves a problem for them in their everyday life. It's awesome to see what people create. And now we're starting to work with more corporate partners who are building apps that connect their products to Pebble.

Osborn: Can you tell me about some challenges you've had along the way, whether it be manufacturing or engineering? It sounds like you had some trouble initially just trying to raise some funds, but were there any other challenges—manufacturing or engineering? Something that didn't go as expected?

Migicovsky: Back when we were still making InPulse in the garage, we ran into a whole bunch of challenges. Four years ago, we were worrying about a problem with the straps on watches popping out, and we had to come up with a solution. Now, we're flying back and forth to China to check on production, and we're talking about moving tens or hundreds of thousands of parts around the world to different manufacturers. Solving problems is on a much different scale now. It really puts things into perspective.

Osborn: I think it was a good thing you had that experience, that learning experience, before you made it into the thousands.

Migicovsky: One of the most important lessons we learned with InPulse is that right from the get-go, we knew that over-the-air updates—the ability for the watch to upgrade itself over Bluetooth without having to plug it in by USB—would be extremely important. So we built that into the bootloader of the InPulse, and it later became part of Pebble as well. For this we had to test extremely thoroughly because we knew that if it broke at any point, all of the watches in the field would be unable to be upgraded. When you're building software that needs that work one hundred percent of the time in the field, there's a lot of work and a certain amount of finger crossing that goes into it. So the first time that we did a firmware update was a bit exciting.

Osborn: Tell me a bit about how you guys launched on Kickstarter—what the Kickstarter experience was like. How did you make the decision to do

Kickstarter? You guys are still the most successful Kickstarter campaign, but I think you're also a really early hardware device on Kickstarter. Like you said, it's kind of gotten to the point where hardware start-ups are a sexy thing to do now, but you started well before that.

Migicovsky: We decided to go on Kickstarter mainly because we were unable to raise money from standard, more typical investment sources. We joined a program called Y Combinator, which is an incubator in Silicon Valley. That was our first connection to the Valley.

In Canada, we were initially trying to raise money from angel or seed investors, and it was nearly impossible. The only funding sources that I found in Canada were my parents and the government. We were unable to convince any private investors. It was tough because as a hardware company, we had to physically make things.

We finally got the chance to go down to Silicon Valley to join the Y Combinator program in early 2011.[3] We thought it would be a massive change in our ability to raise money. Silicon Valley and is where people dream big and they believe in random, crazy, and potentially difficult ideas.

After going through three months of Y Combinator, we went into the demo day and tried again to raise money. I talked to tens, if not hundreds of investors and was only able to raise money from a couple of people. It was tough. I thought it would be a little bit easier in the Valley to get money. It turned out it wasn't.

Osborn: The economy was still pretty bad around 2009. It was pretty tough to raise money at that point in, even in the Valley.

Migicovsky: Maybe, but I think there was also the idea that hardware companies were harder to do and needed more money. And, there was not much evidence that hardware companies would be able to go big at that point in time. We were able to raise money from about five or six angels. For that, I'm extraordinarily grateful. But unfortunately, we weren't able to raise enough money to grow the company significantly.

We had a small amount of money, so we said, "We have a product that's on the market. Let's invest in the product, buy some more components to manufacture into these the InPulse watches, and turn around and sell them at a profit." It was rough because we had enough money to do this, but it was not enough money to do it well or fast, and so it took us twice as long as we expected to get the units manufactured.

By the time we were manufacturing the watches, the market was in a severe depression cycle, and we weren't selling them as fast as we thought. At that

---

[3]http://ycombinator.com

point we had locked up a lot of our money into the parts costs, and it very nearly killed the company. Luckily, we had started working on Pebble, which was the next-generation watch.

So at the beginning of 2012, we went out to VCs and investors again and said, "We've sold $200,000 worth of our first product, and we've designed the next product with full iOS support and full Android support. It's much more beautiful, and it solves the problem of landing third-party apps. What do you think?" We were greeted with the same message that we were greeted with the year before: Hardware companies are difficult. We were unable to raise money at that time as well.

The solution was Kickstarter. Some of my friends had launched projects on Kickstarter, so I reached out to a few of the entrepreneurs behind other major projects that were out there, like the guys who were behind the Twine project.[4] I talked to them about when it makes sense to go on Kickstarter, and we put together our Kickstarter video and page. We launched it in April 2013.

Osborn: You guys ended up raising close to $10 million on Kickstarter then?

Migicovsky: It was just over $10 million.

Osborn: What do you think the key successes were? Was there some need there that the investors didn't see? Do you think there's something that you guys did that people can replicate, or was your success just timing and the market fit? What do you think?

Migicovsky: I think it was a combination of things. One was the fact that we had been working on smartwatches for about four years, and we were making something that our users wanted. We had customers who were telling us, "This is what's useful. This is what actually works." We also had made a lot of mistakes on the earlier product. With Pebble, we had the right combination of features, and more importantly, we were able to explain to people how useful the product was.

On the Kickstarter page, we talked about the consumer use cases. We explained how you could see who's calling on your watch, how you could control your music from your watch, and how you could customize the display on Pebble so you could change the look and feel of the watch.

Osborn: What advice would you have for somebody who has a hardware product that they want to bring to Kickstarter? It seems that Kickstarter is changing attitudes toward hardware products. I don't know how it's affecting people.

---

[4] http://supermechanical.com

Migicovsky: I think there's a very good platform right now that a lot of people are using. It's a forum for crowd funding called Selfstarter[5] that was started by the Lockitron guys. It's pretty cool, and I recommend that. But generally, the way you start working on a product for Kickstarter, for anything really, is the same. You have to make something that people want and give it to them. It's really important to get feedback from people before going out and trying to make it big. It's about making something that people want. And the corollary to that is figuring out how to explain your product so that people actually understand the value and want it. Accomplishing those two things, will help drive the company or the product forward on any platform that you choose.

Osborn: So what's next for Pebble or the next iteration? Are you rolling out new software, new hardware? What are you working on now?

Migicovsky: Our biggest goal is software. The hardware is out there. We've shipped over one hundred thousand Pebbles. Our job as a company right now is delivering on software, pushing out updates, adding cool new features to the watch, and enabling developers to write more awesome apps for Pebble.

Osborn: That's pretty cool. I'm really interested to see what sort of applications people come up with for it. Thanks for your time, Eric.

---

[5]http://selfstarter.us

Ian Lesnet

Slashdot Troll
Dangerous Prototypes

Ian Lesnet is an entrepreneur and electrical engineer who has lived and worked in cities all over the world. Ian has written about his open-hardware electronics projects on many popular electronics blogs, including DIY Live and Hack a Day. He is the owner and creator of Dangerous Prototypes (dangerousprototypes.com), an electronics blog with a focus on DIY electronic projects and tools. Ian's most popular creation, the Bus Pirate, is the equivalent of an open-source electronics Swiss-army knife. The Bus Pirate is a go-to tool for beginners and experienced hardware hackers to communicate with and debug electronics components.

Steven Osborn: Ian, tell me a little bit about yourself and how you got started in electronics.

Ian Lesnet: I was doing a PhD in urban planning and regional development, and I wanted to use wireless sensor networks to measure things in cities. So I got a grant to buy some Smart Dust wireless sensor equipment, from a company spun out of [University of California] Berkeley that came up with the technology. I simulated everything, and everything looked good to go, but then once it was on the ground, once I was using the equipment, it was just flaky. It didn't work, and I was just very unhappy. I couldn't get it to work at all. So from there, I thought, "I spent all this time messing around with this equipment. Then maybe I should just design it myself at this point." Through that process of learning how to use that Smart Dust equipment, I learned how to build my own. In building my own, I acquired a lot of electronics skills. From there, I tinkered with things, but I never really had a purpose for any of it.

I built tools to help me build the wireless sensor networks, tools to debug them, tools to help fix problems. I just learned a lot about microcontrollers and electronics hands-on. Then I started putting my things on the Internet.

I posted first at Instructables,[1] which is a do-it-yourself site. From there, I was hired to write for an AOL blog called DIY Life. They were trying to get back some of the mojo they lost when Hack a Day[2] was split off from AOL by Weblogs Incorporated. I wrote there for a while, and there was some big crisis, a budget crunch at AOL, and they cut three blogs, one of them was DIY Life.

Osborn: About what timeframe was that?

Lesnet: That would be maybe five years ago. From there, I don't know if I wrote to Hack a Day or if Hack a Day wrote to me, I moved to Hack a Day, which is probably the best-known do-it-yourself, hacking, tinkering, gadget blog. I wrote there for about a year. I wrote feature articles about the designs I had come up with, about tools, about toys I was making.

I published a design I had worked on for years, to help me learn about electronics and to debug problems, called the Bus Pirate. It's a little tool that lets you type into a computer and it converts what you type into the right signals to talk to a microchip, and then it gets the reply from the chip and shows it on the computer screen. So it helps you learn how a chip works without actually writing any code. It eliminates the process of writing some code, compiling it, uploading it to your microcontroller, and running the software. Usually that doesn't work the first time around, so then you have to figure out what exactly went wrong, and you're pretty much blind. You don't know whether it's your chip. If it's your connection to your chip. If it's your microcontroller. If you've got some software problem. Who knows?

So the Bus Pirate is a known, working implementation of the common protocols that chips use to speak to each other. It was just a toy I made for myself, a tool to debug some problems and get to know protocols better. But it became very popular on Hack a Day.

Eventually, I got a letter from a company here in Shenzhen China, Seeed Studio, which Eric Pan was just starting. He's like, "Hey, people have been asking if we'll make this. Do you want to do a small manufacturing run of the Bus Pirate? We'll do as little as twenty."

I told him, "No, no, no. If you make twenty, you'll be stuck with nineteen, because nobody wants this thing."

We talked about it for a while. He was like, "Don't worry about it. We'll do a preorder for twenty, and we'll see how it goes."

[1] www.instructables.com
[2] http://hackaday.com

So as a fundraiser for the Hack a Day blog, we did a presale for a week or two, selling an early manufactured version of the Bus Pirate. In that time, we sold a thousand of them, presale. This was before Kickstarter and Indiegogo. There was no crowdsourced funding concept out there. We just took preorders from people with the promise to deliver it as quickly as we could.

From there, I thought, "Wow, there might actually be something to this." I started my own site so that I could sell my own designs. I couldn't do that while I was an author at Hack a Day because the editorial guidelines prohibited it. So I started my own site, Dangerous Prototypes, with the goal to post one new open-source hardware prototype every month, giving away all of the source code. All of the documentation is open license. All of our hardware designs are open. You can readapt them and reuse them in your own projects however you want. We do about a project a month on average, though sometimes in manufacturing things, you have holdups in the process. So we don't actually do one every month, but we do more than twelve a year, and we've been doing that for about four years now.

Osborn: I found out about Dangerous Prototypes because I bought a Bus Pirate on SparkFun and ended up on your site to read through the documentation. You said your inspiration to make the Bus Pirate was just learning the protocols that it speaks?

Lesnet: I needed to learn the protocols, but also I would be working with a new chip, I'd have no idea how it worked, and I'd be stuck in that cycle of writing code, compiling it, burning it to a microcontroller, and then checking to see if it runs. Does the LED light come on or not? Does it work or not? And then, what's wrong? Instead, I wanted a way to be able to sit down with the datasheet and then send the commands to the chip. Once I could do that, it sped up my ability to write software for new chips and figure things out.

Osborn: What other types of hardware products do you have on Dangerous Prototypes now, besides the Bus Pirate?

Lesnet: The Bus Pirate is by far our biggest thing. We have manufactured tons of them. Bunches of people sell clones or imitations, a clone being the exact same board made and sold, and the imitations being people's own adaptations of it. That's our biggest thing so far. But we try to do tools.

Our goal is to make tools that help people make electronics. I say, "I want to make open-source tools to help people make more and better open source." So we have a logic analyzer that we developed in conjunction with the Gadget Factory, another open-hardware shop. We have an Infrared Toy, it's an infrared receiver/transmitter that helps you learn about infrared remote controls and also control things, record signals, replay them, and that sort of stuff.

We sell debugging tools. The Bus Blaster is a JTAG debugger. JTAG is a protocol used for programming CPLDs[3] and ARM chips like you find in cellphones. There's a lot of open source software for working with these chips, but there wasn't a manufactured open hardware debugger to go with it. So I saw the software out there and thought, "Well, I can make some open-source hardware to go with this open-source software."

We make development boards, a lot of development boards to help people learn about a chip and to take chips that are difficult to solder and put them on a breakout board so you can just wire into them.

The most popular things, and my favorite projects, are stuff I needed myself. That's always been our most popular stuff. I'm in my workshop. I need something, so I have a passion to make it. I knock it out and then, wow, other people find it useful too. And because we manufacture in such small batches we can try out a design with very little risk. It used to be we'd do twenty, but now make maybe one hundred of the initial batch. In these quantities can throw things at the wall and see what sticks, and that's something a bigger company can't do.

Companies making thousands and tens of thousands have to do market research. They have to know what's going to sell. Otherwise, they can't sell it and they're stuck with widgets rotting in a warehouse in China. But if we make one hundred, it's likely we can move that many.

That's something that I really enjoy about running a small open hardware business: that we don't have to worry about the big stuff. We can just make a small batch and see what sticks. The most popular stuff has always been the stuff that I make because I have a need in my workshop. I have something I want to accomplish, something I want to get done, and then sometimes other people find it useful too, and then it becomes a project that we sale.

Osborn: In a lot of large hardware companies your whole focus would be, "How do you get the parts cost down, because we can't absorb an extra fifty cents?" or something.

Lesnet: Yes, absolutely. We are able to iterate because we do small batches, too. So we'll put one out, and if it costs way too much to manufacture the first batch, fine. We'll take less profit just to see if it sells, and then if it sells and it's worth continuing to manufacture it, then we'll work on getting the cost down. We'll say, "Where can we tweak it to get the cost down? What changes can we make?"

A lot of these designs are supported by the community, and a lot of our improvements come from the community, so getting it out there where the community can tell us what we should have done and point out really stupid

---

[3]Complex programmable logic device.

design decisions, that's really the most important thing for us, getting stuff out there as soon as we can and as quickly as we can. This way we can get it in the hands of people who are way smarter than me. They contribute so much to getting costs down, to improving designs and making things better.

Osborn: Sounds like you are applying what some people call agile development practices in the software world. Hardware tends to move slow, but what you're doing is not typical for the hardware industry, and it's really cool to see.

Lesnet: It does take longer to build hardware because you have to have boards made, you have to solder things to the boards, you have to write firmware and test it.

That's why I'm in Shenzhen now, because here I can take care of those things so fast. I live a five-minute walk from Huaqiangbei, the huge electronics parts markets and wholesale markets, so now when I need an extra header, when I'm missing something, when I need a chip, I ride my bike down there. I can pick things up right in the market, and that makes things so much faster. There are people who sit along the street with a sign, "Can solder BGA[4]", meaning "I can solder chips without any legs on them and I can do it right here." So if I need a board made, I take the most difficult parts down the street and give it to some kid with a soldering station and they'll put it together real quick and at a very good price.

That helps me iterate my designs even faster than before because until now, I'm the only person that soldered things for Dangerous Prototypes. We're a very small company. Everybody works from home. We don't have a central place with parts and stuff. It has been me in my lab soldering every board, every design that we've made, by hand. And now that I'm in China I have access to resources that I've never have had before, and I'm able to have people help a bit, which is quite nice.

Osborn: So you were in Amsterdam before China, correct?

Lesnet: Yes.

Osborn: I don't know about the hardware scene in Amsterdam, but in the US, even in Silicon Valley, there are not many hardware companies. And there isn't a decent electronics market.

Lesnet: I've been to big electronics wholesale markets all over the world. In the third year of Dangerous Prototypes, maybe the second year, I went to my first Maker Faire, the Bay Area Maker Faire, with Seeed Studio, the group that manufactures and sells all of our hardware for us. It was my first Maker Faire.

---

[4]A *ball grid array* is a microchip without legs. It cannot be soldered using a hand-soldering iron.

I had never been to one, and to be honest, I was a really shy geek. I wanted *nothing* to do with it. I liked the fact that nobody knew what I looked like. Nobody knew my voice. I did not want to meet people. But Seeed was going, and they convinced me to go and join them at their booth. I had a really, really good time. They thought I was an old, retired engineer. They had no idea I was a twenty-something kid. That's how secretive I had been about my identity. But meeting the community was amazing. People are so nice, tossing ideas back and forth, seeing other people's work. It was just amazing.

From there I was totally hooked. I immediately set out to go to every Maker Faire and hacker space I could find. Over the next two years, I went to New York Maker Faire and the Open Hardware Summit. I went to the Singapore Maker Faire, the Tokyo Maker Faire. I went to Seoul, South Korea, to see their hacker space and the big parts markets. Along the way, I realized that there are big electronics wholesale markets all over the world. It's not just in Shenzhen, China. You can find them anywhere manufacturing was a big industry. In Tokyo, you have Akihabara, which was a big market when Japan was a big manufacturing powerhouse.

Then you can go to Seoul, South Korea. There's a neighborhood called Cheonggyecheon with a ton of wholesale distributors with little offices that sell components and microchips. Korea of course is also a big manufacturing hub. But nowhere is bigger than China.

Huaqiangbei, a neighborhood in Shenzhen, China, is probably the world's largest electronics wholesale market. It's certainly the largest one I've seen. It's a collection of maybe twenty to thirty buildings, each three to five floors with nothing but little stands the size of a desk selling electronic parts, tools, and supplies. Each stand has a glass top and inside are samples of products they sell. You'll find buttons, LEDs, connectors, microchips, circuit boards, everything related to electronics.

Each stand represents a manufacturer that's either someplace in Shenzhen or somewhere further north, usually in Dongguan or Guangzhou. Both around an hour north by high-speed rail. All these little stands represent manufacturers in the market. They don't just sell the parts they have. If you need something custom, you can say, "Hey, I need a header that's got a pin this exact length. It's exactly this long." They can make that stuff for you. You have access to all these resources in the region and the prices are amazingly low.

If I need some headers they'll sell me a bag of a thousand for what it would cost to get fifty or one hundred from Mouser or Digi-Key or somewhere in the US. The access to those resources is amazing, and they're in Shenzhen because this is where all the manufacturing happens. They're not there for tourists and designers like me. They're here because there's manufacturing going on all over this region, and when the manufacturer needs a header or when they need parts, they send a kid out to Huaqiangbei to finds a good price, and then the supplier ships over what they need. What was the question you were asking?

Osborn: Really, just describe the hardware environment in China versus in other cities.

Lesnet: I started coming here about a year ago. I started coming here for a little over a week each month, to hang out with my manufacturer, to learn more about the parts markets, to get hands-on experience with all the stuff. Electronics designers aren't just engineers doing math equations. You're working with parts. There's an artistic side to it. There's stuff that you need to hold in your hand to understand how it fits in your design. Touching a part that exceeds anything you get from looking at a catalog or a datasheet or surfing a web site. So actually being able to play with the parts—and I do mean play, to touch them, to hold them, to play around with them, to see what's available— that is a very empowering experience. There's a lot of value in that.

I had been coming for about a year to do that, and then three months or four months ago, I came for a three-week trip and threw away my return ticket. I've just been on an extended business trip since then, hanging out here, working in the market, and building things. I've been in cities with big electronics markets like Tokyo and Seoul, and the difference between what I see here and anywhere else is that this place is built to do business. This place is built to get things done.

Thirty years ago, there was no Shenzhen. It was a little fishing village just across the border from Hong Kong. Now it's a city of ten to twenty million people, depending on how you count it. And this has all grown up around the Special Economic Zone that China designated for manufacturing. It's a very, very special place. There's nowhere else in China like this. It's built to do business.

Osborn: So Shenzhen became the city that it is by design?

Lesnet: Yes, that was by design. It really is. It's such a special place. It has a vibe unlike anywhere else in China. It's not just, "Get the business done." Everyone here is so young. It's like London during the industrial revolution or New York in the 1800s. People are coming from all over China to make their fortune here. Not just to make a fortune starting a business, but to make money to send back to their families. Everyone is in their twenties. Even the people who own companies are barely thirty. The guy I work with, Eric—I think he's twenty-eight, twenty-nine. He runs this amazing open hardware manufacturing company.

Going out in Shenzhen is an amazing experience. I never went to clubs. I never went out to bars. I never did that stuff when I was in Amsterdam or when I lived in Hawaii or when I lived in the middle of the US. But here in Shenzhen you go out because the people who sell you parts invite you. What are you going to do? You go out with them. People are very nice and very friendly, and it's very easy to meet people and have a good time. That's been my experience here.

Along my street, at midnight a street barbeque pops up. All the street food vendors come out at midnight. It's not technically legal. The city doesn't allow it, but after midnight the police turn a blind eye to the whole thing. You can buy noodles, you can buy tofu, you can grill little bits of meat sitting around a little table.

Then there's a game called Shaizi, which is Liar's Dice in English. Everybody has a cup with five dice in it. You shake the cup and look at your dice, and everyone places bets on the combined value of the group I learned to play this game as soon as I came to China. That's how I made all of my contacts in the electronics markets. Sitting with the kids who work at the distributors' stand, and drinking beer, playing this dice game and grilling meat. I have half a dozen contacts who call themselves my little brother. When I need a part, I go to that stand, I show them a picture, run off and get it for me. Usually at a better price than I could ever get negotiating on my own.

Osborn: So you're in your twenties, and all these people call themselves your little brother?

Lesnet: Well, I am in my thirties now.

Osborn: So you're an old man by Shenzhen standards?

Lesnet: I really am. I really, really am by Shenzhen standards. If I went to the market, it would take me years of buying things from people, building relationships, buying large quantities, ensuring them that I am someone they can make money from and have a long-term relationship with. It would take me years of doing that to build the relationships I make from eating street food and playing Shaizi with kids on the street. I say "kids." They're not kids. They're in their mid-twenties, too, but they're younger than me.

I still consider myself a tourist. But I can sneak in and I can tap this resource and use it to build more and better open source hardware. Really, that's my goal, to build more and better open source hardware and expand that open-source ecosystem. By being here, I have access to resources so I can turn things around so much faster. It's just amazing. I imagine it's not permanent.

Lots of people tell me that most of the big hardware manufacturers just order things now off the Internet. They have relationships with people they find on the Internet instead of in the market. They don't go to the market so much. The market is more for small manufacturers, and it's becoming outdated. There's no doubt that eventually all of this is going to move somewhere else. Someday Huaqiangbei could be Akihabara. It will be a has-been. It will be where people used to go to source things. But right now, right now I think it's at its prime. Maybe people are right. Maybe it's declining, but when I walk down there right now, there are thousands of people pushing carts full of boxes of parts everywhere. I don't know anywhere else in the world like that right now.

Osborn: That's pretty incredible. I order just about anything on Amazon Prime, or Mouser and Digi-Key right now.

Lesnet: I think, unfortunately the lax environmental regulations have allowed this to grow here as opposed to other places. I don't have a strong opinion on that, but that's certainly one of the factors that have allowed this to grow. The PCB manufacturers can do things cheaper and easier here than they can in the United States abiding by US environmental laws.

Certainly, the access to this stuff, though, is going to benefit the Chinese. The kids that are growing up in Shenzhen have access to equipment and materials and supplies that no one else in the world does. So I think that you are going to see more and more really amazing Chinese engineers just because they have access to it. People going to the Shenzhen universities, they can roll down to Huaqiangbei and pick up a soldering iron when they need to. They don't have to delay three days for shipping. They don't have to deal with whatever crappy option Radio Shack has in stock.

Osborn: Or wait for weeks to get a PCB made. Is there anything else besides the availability of parts that makes the environment in China unique?

Lesnet: One of the things that I think is so amazing about Huaqiangbei that I don't hear anyone talk about is that the whole cycle of electronics life happens here. You can get the little tiny components that you use to build stuff—resistors, capacitors, connectors, and chips. You can get the PCBs made. You can find people to assemble them. Then you move up. You can find enclosures and people to design enclosures. Then you move up. You can buy assembled things and tools, the tools to make stuff, the soldering irons, pick-and-place machines, ball grid array rework stations. You can move up. You can find computers and all sorts of consumer electronics. There's a huge consumer electronics market. It's not just parts in Huaqiangbei. There are computers and televisions and radios and DVD players.

Then you move up another level, and you find stuff to repair things. There are three buildings that sell nothing but little, tiny components for cellphones, like replacement cameras, replacement screens, all of that kind of stuff. Then there are people there who can fix a phone. Then you move up another, there are two buildings, literally just across the street from me that sell used cellphones and broken cellphones. People can take those over to the market, to the cellphone repair place and have them fixed, but generally, what happens is people buy them by the kilo.

Then on my sidewalk at night, they break down the phones and pick out the recyclable components that go in big mailbags, then into the back of a truck for recycling. So you can buy parts, you can build things, buy the completed stuff, get replacement parts and have things repaired. Used and broken stuff is sold and broken down for recycling. It all happens within this ten-block neighborhood. It's the whole cycle of electronics going on right here. I think that's amazing. Everything happens here.

Osborn: One thing I saw on your site—Dangerous Prototypes—that was really interesting was a pick-and-place machine that you got for just a few thousand dollars. That seems like a potential game-changer for people building electronics in small batches.

Lesnet: They even sell those at the Huaqiangbei market now. You can do cash and carry on that. You can walk down the street and buy a tabletop pick-and-place machine here.

When I came in January, I was like, "I'm going to buy a bunch of tools. I'm going to take them home, I'm going to learn how to use these tools." I don't manufacture my own projects, so I don't have a lot of familiarity with manufacturing tools, but I thought knowing the tools and knowing how they work would make me a better designer. There are shippers at what I call "shipper row" or "shipper alley," just garages of people with boxes and tape. You can take your stuff, and they'll put it in a box, tape it up and send it anywhere in the world, by FedEx or air freight or boat. I went down there, I compared prices, and I found somebody who would FedEx a twenty-kilo box to Europe, airfreight, in three days or four days. It was like $3 US a kilo, at twenty kilos. So I bought reflow ovens, I bought hot plates, I bought a pick-and-place machine, I bought all the tools of the trade, and took them down to shipper row. They stuffed them in boxes for me, they taped them all up. The sound of tape is deafening. It's nonstop, just tape and tape. Everything gets completely wrapped in yellow packing tape.

Osborn: I wish there was a way to capture some of these sounds in the book.

Lesnet: I'm making the "sounds of Huaqiangbei" record. I don't know how you can capture it in a book, but I can give you an MP3. There's that sound, and there's also—they do this tax receipt thing. It's called a *fapiao* and it's a tax receipt from the government. There's a little scratch part on it, and you scratch it off and it tells you if you won a prize. The goal is to get people to pay their taxes by giving them a prize for issuing a receipt.

Osborn: A lottery ticket on your receipts?

Lesnet: Yeah, but there are dozens of people at every subway station and all throughout Huaqiangbei that sell false tax receipts. So you buy something, you don't pay your tax, and then you buy a fapiao, and then you either turn it into the government or you turn it into your boss. So you buy a fapiao that says you paid one hundred Yuan and you only paid thirty Yuan for it, and then your boss gives you one hundred Yuan, so you make seventy on the deal. But the people that sell them stand at the subway exit, and it's deafening.

They say, "Fapiao, fapiao, fapiao." And altogether, it just turns into, "Meow, meow, meow!" Like a herd of cats. I think it's the sound one of those Chinese luck cats with the swinging arm would make.[5]

Osborn: The sounds of China soundtrack. I love it.

Lesnet: So shipper row. I sent all this stuff back and got to know how to use it. It's not the greatest quality, but if you're tinkering with electronics it's more than good enough. The pick-and-place machine is an incredible tool. It's an example of Chinese ingenuity. They were not concerned with building the perfect pick-and-place machine. I think they were concerned with making an inexpensive device for small-run manufacturers. That was their design goal, and they did it. It's not perfect.

You have to have cheap labor to use that machine in a manufacturing process because it doesn't have a vision system, it can't see where it's actually putting the parts on the board, and that's an absolute requirement. If your machine can't see where it's putting the parts and adjust to little problems, then it's just based on math. No PCB is perfect. No calibration of the machine is ever going to be exact enough to place thousands of parts on hundreds of boards. So it doesn't put things in the right spot. It kind of puts them wherever. A lot of that is corrected during the reflow process. When you heat up the board to melt the solder paste, the surface tension of the solder will right the parts. That will take care of a lot of it, but still, thirty to seventy percent of the parts have to be manually tweaked a little bit before it goes into the reflow. Then afterward you still have ten to twenty percent of the parts need to be reflowed with hot air.

If you have more labor than you have capital, then that's totally fine. This machine would help a small manufacturer churn out boards, and all they have to do is hire somebody to sit there and tweak them, and that's going to be way cheaper than spending $30,000 on a proper pick-and-place machine. But since I did some videos about this machine and did some blog posts, I get one or two requests a day from people saying, "Can you help me buy one? I want to use it in a small-run manufacturing facility."

Osborn: A couple requests a week is quite bit of interest. Do you recommend this pick-and-place to people to bootstrapping their manufacturing process?

Lesnet: I discourage people overall from trying to do a garage manufacturing line because running a pick-and-place machine is a whole industry unto itself. Being an engineer and running a pick-and-place machine are two different jobs. What you end up doing is getting into the pick-and-place business if you buy one. Suddenly, you spend six months learning how to use the machine, how to

---

[5]http://en.wikipedia.org/wiki/Maneki-neko

calibrate it, how to care for it, how to get usable results out of it. Then you're not designing hardware anymore. You're running a pick-and-place machine.

I know a lot of people who have bought machines and spent six months getting them up and running and then still have to use a contract manufacturer because the yield is so poor. And those are good machines, with vision, not a two thousand–dollar or three thousand–dollar toy. So I really discourage people from going the garage-manufacturing route until they have extremely high-mix, low-volume stuff, like SparkFun or Adafruit. They can't send out a hundred or two hundred different designs. They have to have a pick-and-place machine. Once you're at that stage, you do that. It becomes obvious.

If you think about Adafruit, Limor bought her first pick and place two years ago, three years ago maybe. She was well established and selling a lot of stuff by the time they ever considered getting a pick and place machine. So I discourage people from doing it period, because I think it's a whole separate job. Once you reach the point where you need it, you'll know. It will be very obvious. With the little machine, it's especially important not to count on it for manufacturing. It's fun.

For me, it's very good because I make all my own prototypes and I can set up the machine with one click of a button, and it can put down all the capacitors, resistors and passive components that I need. I'm not placing those by hand anymore. The machine can do that. I have to straighten a bunch of them. That's fine. It's still easier than placing every resistor by hand, but that's because I do one-offs. I don't mind adjusting.

I think if you're trying to do it with volume, you're going to end up doing that a lot, and especially if you're in the US or Canada, then labor costs are so high it's not worth paying someone to sit there and straighten resistors. It's probably better to buy a used machine and get some training on it, something with a camera system that can see where it's putting parts and properly place them on the board. I think a lot of people are trying to use the cheap pick and place in small-volume manufacturing. I don't think it's the world's best idea. It would not be what I would spend my time on.

Osborn: It would be interesting to see somebody build an open-source vision system for it. I'm not sure how difficult that would be, but I could see someone hacking the Raspberry Pi with the new camera to work as a vision system.

Lesnet: That would be amazing. What really I would like to see is somebody open up the machine, figure out what's inside of it, and then we can rewrite the software for it. Or just getting rid of all the internals and making a controller board for it that can be run from the PC. Because once you have it connected to a PC, then you're not messing around with embedded programming, and you can toss on a camera, no problem. It's beyond my abilities. It's beyond what I would want to do. That's a labor of love, right? You'd spend six months to a year designing a board and software for a little machine when you could just go out and buy a quality used pick and place for seven, eight, nine thousand dollars. I'd define that as a labor of love. If you love it, go for it. If you have the passion for it, go for it. But I think trying to skimp and save money by doing that is a false economy.

Osborn: I'm glad I get to hear your thoughts on it that. When I first saw it my thought was, "I have to have this. It's a shiny new toy." But I also knew that I was probably going to spend more time figuring out how it works than actually building things with it.

Lesnet: That's why I got it. My thought wasn't, "I want to build things." My thought was, "Maybe it will speed up my prototyping," but I think it costs $3,500 including shipping, something like that. I couldn't take a university course that would teach me about pick-and-place machines for that much money. I couldn't go to a community college and take a course on that for that much money, and I wouldn't have a machine to keep at the. My thought was, "I'll get a crash course on pick and place. I'll have some hands-on experience with it, with one that's in my own shop. If it's useful, great."

But the goal was really just to learn about it. If you want to learn about a pick and place machine, it's a good learning tool. It's better than buying some behemoth used thing, getting it dragged back to your place, and having it sit in your garage. It is a nice size for learning about pick-and-place machines.

Osborn: I'm interested in what projects are you working on now, now that you're in Shenzhen?

Lesnet: I tell people I'm here making wine. What I love about coming to markets, and that's all markets in the world. Huaqiangbei is obviously the biggest—is the hands-on part, the playing, the touching, knowing a part before you use it in your design. I find that so valuable. What I wanted to do was come here and put that in a box and share it with other people. One of the big projects we're doing here is to make part kits with one of everything, so we have a connector kit with pre-crimped wires and all sizes of a certain connector type, from one by one up through twenty by one. You can just stick the pre-crimped wires into the connector and make a custom cable.

Right now you either have to buy a cable of the right size, or you have to hunt through datasheets and web sites to find the right connector. Then where do I get the little connectors to crimp onto the wires? Do I have the right crimping tool? How do I use the crimping tool?

Here, I can get that all for you, put it in a box, give you a complete set of parts. Be it connectors or buttons or LEDs or whatever, you can have a complete set of parts on your shelf. Then when you're working on a project, you don't have to do all this hunting and searching through parts catalogs because you've got everything there. I feel like I'm going out to the vineyard, I'm plucking the choicest grapes off the vines, and I'm making wine. I'm trying to distill the best of Huaqiangbei, but not just any part. I touch all the parts. I feel all the parts. I say, "This connector is a good connector. It's quality material. It doesn't look like it's going to break. I'm very happy with it. This will be in my connector set."

Osborn: That sounds a little bit like what Inventables did early on, what Zach Kaplan at Inventables did for industrial designers.

Lesnet: That's sort of a vision we have. I'm working with a company in the UK called Oomlout on this project. Another goal in this is to eliminate that last-minute Mouser order, when you're working on a project and you've got the two by five connector, but you don't have the two by six, and what you really need is the two by six and you can't finish your board because you don't have the right connector. But instead of ordering ten from Mouser or whatever and waiting two days for it to show up, you have a connector box with every connector, at least every popular and common connector, and a complete set of all the sizes. And then you just pull out the right envelope, you open it up, you pop it in, and you're good to go.

This is another example where I needed this for myself. This was not made for other people. I was so sick of making that last-minute Mouser order, making the minimum order to get free shipping, and then spending too much. Instead, I have a nice box with every one of them on my shelf. When I'm designing a board now and I need a part, I go to my shelf and I pull it out. It's neatly organized and it's easy to reorder stuff.

Osborn: What I find myself doing is, when I want a certain type of connector or I'm not sure exactly what would work best for my design, I'll buy one or two of maybe twelve different connectors, and then pay for two-day shipping, which is expensive. I get it and look at each of them to decide which one works best for my design and then I make the order for the part I end up using. Then it's another three days. At this point, I've spent more than a week basically trying to make a selection for one part.

Lesnet: That is exactly it. That is exactly the problem we are trying to solve. I was facing the same dilemma. I needed hex standoffs, and I didn't know which hex standoff I needed. So I literally went on Mouser, and I ordered, I think, ten or twelve of every size they had. It cost me like three or four hundred dollars, just for ten or twelve of each, to get a complete set. I was floored. Instead, we have a box now, with both nylon and stainless steel hex standoffs, one of every size, and we can sell it for twenty bucks. It eliminates the problem you just described.

Everything is open source, as always. We have open-source datasheets, open-source renderings of all the parts, open-source mechanical drawings, all the footprints in both Eagle and KiCAD. You don't have to design your own footprints. We have the equivalent part numbers from every vendor we can find, so that way, if you design with something out of the box and then you want to order a thousand for your small production run, your Kickstarter, whatever, then you have the Mouser part number, the Digi-Key part number, the manufacturers' equivalent part numbers if you go directly to the manufacturer. It's going to make it easier for me, and hopefully other people like it too.

We're trying to change our focus because we don't sell anything. We don't have our own shop. We don't handle products. Seeed Studio sells things. They're our main retailer. They take the money and ship things for us. We have a lot of distributors around the world, too, that sell things for us, but we don't sell anything ourselves. We never have what I call the sweet bundle of wires money.

As I understand, a lot of the open hardware retailers make their money by selling stuff like wire bundles. They buy it for five cents and sell on for five dollars. SparkFun does it, Adafruit does it, and Seeed does it. Oomlout does it in the UK, and Watterott in Germany. They're making their money selling bags of LEDs, wires, the simple high markup stuff as I understand it.

Osborn: Even large retailers like Best Buy do that sort of thing. They sell you an LCD TV cheap and then they convince you to buy a forty-dollar HDMI cable.

Lesnet: Exactly. And there's no development overhead in that stuff. They don't have to write firmware. Then they don't have to support it. There's very little support for a bag of LEDs, whereas I spend four or five hours a day in my forum answering questions and helping people with stuff and taking community feedback and integrating it into projects. There's none of that when you sell a bundle of wires.

Our goal is to get into the sweet, sweet bundle of wire business. We can't do it, because we don't have our own shop. We can't sell a Dangerous Prototypes–branded bundle of wires because Seeed already sells that, and we can't compete with them in their own shop. So these boxes are our way of doing the bundle of wires. We're added value to it because we're providing a lot of information and making it convenient, but we're also able to sell things that don't require a whole bunch of development and support.

We're also trying to expand what we get out of our current products that are very popular. The open-source hardware market is flooded now. It's just flooded. There are so many Kickstarters and great projects out there. When I started, there were just a handful of people doing this. Right now, there's just so much stuff, it's hard to keep up. So we're trying to get more value out of our existing stuff, instead of just trying to make new stuff and depending on that.

So we're trying to do a Bus Pirate educational kit. We're trying to put together a set of chips and a nice illustrated booklet, a nice breadboard with overlays that show you how to wire up the chip to the Bus Pirate. We're trying to sell this as an educational experience, something that teaches you about electronics, about high-level electronics, about how you communicate with the chips. How do you store information on a chip and get it back? What do the commands look like? So we're trying to take our projects like that and build an educational experience around it. So that's where we're trying to go with this, to expand our market a little bit in that way that doesn't require as much user support and development time.

Osborn: I think everybody wants you to continue to make these great cool monthly projects, and you've got to be able to support that somehow. You've got to be able to make enough money to do that in the long term, and it sounds like a good way to do that.

Lesnet: Until now, I have not run this as a business. It's just been a hobby. It's been something that's fun, and it's always taken care of itself. But if I'm going to live in China and I'm going to be serious about it, then I actually need to think of it as a business just a little bit. I'm trying not to think about it very hard as a business. I'm afraid that if I do that, then the fun drains out and then what's the point? The fun is where the creativity comes from. So I've been trying not to think of it too much as a business, but being mindful of the business side. It's time to be mindful of the business side.

Osborn: I think the kit product you've described adds a lot of value. The last question I have, I like to ask people is what projects are you excited or some things you've seen that get you excited which are outside Dangerous Prototypes?

Lesnet: Well, we have a very active community, and there's a guy in our forum, Mats Engstrom. He's not part of our company. He's a star community member. He's been doing a project a week for—oh man—a couple months now, and posts them in the forum. He started off just doing simple things, tools and boards and little helpful things. Now they've gained enough popularity that he's selling a few of them on Tindie. He's manufacturing them at home and selling them off. I don't know the volume, but he wanted me to get him, I believe, a thousand or five thousand quality-control stickers in Huaqiangbei and bring them to him at the Singapore Maker Faire later this month. He must be doing quite well at it, and I'm excited about his posts because he really keeps it up. He also posts the failures, which I like. Not everything works. I like to post my failures, too, because maybe somebody finds some use out of it and the files live on. Mats always shows the projects that don't work, too. I love that.

Let's see. I'm not a 3D printer guy. I think it's very cool, but I'm not into 3D printers. I'm really into pick-and-place machines. When I see people doing a DIY pick-and-place project, I think that's very cool, because it's not as complicated as a 3D printer, because you just have to put parts in about the right place, and you can use a vision system to do it. A 3D printer has to be very, very precise and get the goo at the right place. A pick and place doesn't have to be as stable, it doesn't have to be as precise, it doesn't have to be as calibrated. You can just make up for it with a vision system. There are open-source vision systems out there. I don't know if they're specifically for pick and place, but the software is there.

Osborn: I have a Shapeoko CNC mill on my desk. It's basically a three hundred–dollar CNC platform. I've always thought it would be really interesting to see somebody turn that into that platform and then add, like I said, a Raspberry Pi and a thirty-dollar camera. Now you have, for under four hundred bucks, a really good starting platform for that sort of thing. I think that would be a really cool project.

Lesnet: It would be so cool to see an open-source pick and place for a low cost because it's going to help out in places like India. There is a lot of open hardware going on in India and there are a lot of open hardware people there. They need to manufacture small amounts of open hardware locally to reduce costs and eliminate stiff import tariffs. A simple platform to do that helps hobbyists, but it also helps students. We did a tour of markets in India. The students have inexpensive clones of Arduino and stuff there. They have access to very inexpensive parts, but they don't have access to the manufacturing capabilities.

I'm also very fond of just about everything that bunnie Huang does, but specifically, he is building an open-source laptop, and it's not a little hobby board. This is major, professional-level stuff. Bunnie and Sean have the experience. bunnie's here all the time in Shenzhen, so he's got the connections to get it done.

His business partner, Sean Bonner, is a programming genius. He brought up the board in an evening or something. I wouldn't even know where to start getting the software to start, getting Linux running on my own homemade laptop. That is an amazing project. That's way beyond all of my little gadgets. I can make something that might help them debug that, but I wouldn't even know where to start on that. That board fascinates me.

Osborn: That wraps up my questions. I love your insight on manufacturing in China and learning about the history behind the Bus Pirate. One piece of front matter I have left is I don't have a title for you. Should it be "founder," "blogger," "CEO"?

Lesnet: Really, I prefer "Slashdot troll." That's usually what I tell people. I don't think of myself as a CEO, nor as a blogger. I just like to play with electronics, and I'm lucky enough to be here doing it.

Osborn: What about "founder"?

Lesnet: Well, that's okay. That sounds very technical, though. There are so many founders. So many people contributed to the Bus Pirate, and it wouldn't be here without the hundreds of people that contributed to it. So I can't say I'm really the founder of that either. I don't feel like I am. I feel like it's a group project.

Osborn: Well, if nothing else, people will want to read this to find out about your title. Thank you.

Lesnet: Oh, no. Thank you. Thank you so much for including me. It's my pleasure. I have no problem sitting here and talking about myself for an hour. That's easy to do. It was fun.

Massimo Banzi

Cofounder
Arduino

Massimo Banzi is cofounder of Arduino, an organization dedicated to providing open-hardware tools that can be incorporated in the classroom, used in interactive design projects, or used as building blocks for many maker projects.

Massimo spent four years at the Interaction Design Institute Ivrea as an associate professor. He has taught workshops and has been a guest speaker at institutions all over the world. In addition, he started the first maker space in Italy, FabLab Torino.

If you would like to learn more about the Arduino development platform and how to use it, there are a lot of resources online (http://arduino.cc). Also, Massimo wrote Getting Started with Arduino (O'Reilly Media, 2011), which will get you on your way.

Steven Osborn: Hey, Massimo. What made you interested in being a maker and working with hardware?

Massimo Banzi: Well, I guess the whole thing started because as a kid, I liked to take everything apart. So that was the starting point. After that, I studied electrical engineering in high school, but I was doing electronics before I even started studying electrical engineering formally.

Then I even went to college to study electronics, or electrical engineering, but I never really finished because it was a bit too boring. There was a lot of theory, but there was zero—zero—practical information, so I didn't really like it because we were not doing anything apart from doing theoretical exercises.

I worked in a few companies doing software development and hardware development. Then I did web development for many years. After being a software architect, working in the UK and Italy, I worked briefly for a venture capital fund, and after that I decided that was not what I wanted to do. So after that, I wanted to change what I did. I bumped into this design school that had opened in Ivrea, Italy, in 2000. A friend of mine happened to visit and they mentioned that they needed somebody who could teach the students interested in design about electronics. So there were a number of requirements. I had a personal interest in design. I had followed the world of design by myself, and I worked on a lot of projects, but on hardware and software, so I thought, "Okay, I'll try out." I applied and they gave me a two-week contract, which became three months and then became four years or so. My job was to teach designers about technology and electronics, in particular. So that's where I started to look at the problem of making tools that were simple for everyday people.

Osborn: What university was this at?

Banzi: Sorry, it's a design school, but it doesn't exist anymore. It used to be called The Interaction Design Institute Ivrea.

Osborn: So while you were doing that, you got interested in building tools for students?

Banzi: Well, it was a graduate school that basically was a master's degree program in interactional design. It focused on this idea that you can actually design the way people interact with artifacts, objects. But the interesting part about interaction design is that it is interested in how people interact with technology and how we can make that conversation simpler or more natural. So obviously, the overall topic of the school was about the relationship between people and modern technology. And by extension, people working with hardware fell under the generic scope of the school.

Many professional software development tools tend to be designed mostly by engineers, so there's not a lot of work that gets done by providing proper user interface design on a lot of these tools, so you can see that some tools are extremely complicated to use for beginners. The problem is really how do you create tools that encourage absolute beginners to take on complicated tasks, like learning how to program a microcontroller and stuff like that?

Osborn: I know where this is going, but before we get there, I want to you to tell me a little bit about FabLab Torino. Did you start that? What is your relationship with FabLab?

Banzi: Well, when I started working on Arduino, there wasn't a proper maker movement. Then later on, the maker movement developed and Arduino became one of the cornerstones of that movement, so we started to look at the maker movement in general and all the different aspects, not just physical computing, which is what Arduino is about, but we also looked at the making and manufacturing—all of that.

So what happened is that back in 2011, it was the one hundred fiftieth anniversary of the creation of Italy as a nation. They organized a lot of exhibitions about the past, and they organized one exhibition in Torino about the future of Italy. It was the only one that really was about the future. So they asked me to think of something that had to do with work. So I said, "I'm not going to make an exhibition where you have a glass box with some stuff in there that represents work. You want to be there to represent the future of work."

So we said, "There is this concept called fab lab.[1] We should really have a fab lab that operates there." Luckily, at Arduino we already had some collaborators who were working with us already in Torino. We had the people on the ground that could put this together, so we made a proposal and we got some—they gave us the budget to create the fab lab inside the exhibition, to create a community, to hire a few people to manage it. And we had it successfully running between March and November 2011.

Then after that, we had this community. We had the right situation, but none of the political entities in Torino showed interest whatsoever in bringing this project forward. So Arduino decided to singlehandedly finance the creation of a fab lab/maker space/Arduino office, all combined together. And we found this co-working space in Torino. They gave us a space for free. We were able to start in February 2012. We officially opened the doors to the first fab lab/maker space in Italy.

Osborn: Awesome. That's cool that you guys took initiative and got it done regardless of the conditions.

Banzi: The problem is that Italy is not exactly an innovative country, so people are getting all worked up about maker space/maker stuff now. They've started to get interested in fab labs right now, so everybody wants to have a fab lab, but it's because we have one that works, which demonstrates that the moment you create the place and you create the conditions, people start to gather around these spaces, and they start to create projects, they start to have ideas. Lots of stuff happens, so it's a pity to throw all this stuff away, and that's why we created it.

And it was good for Arduino, honestly, as well, because we get a lot of creative energy, we get to see people using our stuff and work with them. And when you need to hire, the best way to do it is to look inside the community, inside the maker space and say, "Okay, what about working with us?" And you basically

---

[1] A fab lab is a collaborative workshop for digital fabrication.

pull people out of the community. So it's a great way to have a connection with your real users, and you have them right in your office and you can look at them all day.

Osborn: So getting back to Arduino, I think most people know what an Arduino is by now. We talked a little bit about your inspiration. You were working at a university. Can you walk me through a little bit more of the creation process, for instance, and why you made some of the decisions you made? Why AVR[2] or Wiring?[3]

Banzi: So when we started teaching, we picked up the tools that everybody was using, which was the BASIC stamp. The problem was that the BASIC stamp was very expensive to buy in Italy because it was imported by a small company, so they charged a lot of money, and you ended up spending almost $100 for a BASIC stamp that cost a maximum of $50 US. So clearly, there was this huge gap, and also, if you look at it, you say, "Wow, this thing is expensive and it runs only on Windows and it runs this BASIC language, which is different from the language that we teach students learning how to program." So there was this gap where you teach students for a month how to program in a language and the month after, you say, "Okay, forget about everything. Now we're going to move to another language." And this is very confusing for people who have zero background in programming, so we clearly needed something that could be used at different levels.

I did spend quite a lot of time experimenting with PIC chips, did a lot of tests with PIC chips, and I produced a platform that is the grandfather of Arduino, called Programma 2003, which was like a PIC-based board using a weird language called Jal,[4] which is a BASIC/Pascal language-type thing. The issue became that it was hard to find a C compiler that would run on the PIC that was open source and that could run on all the platforms, because one of the big issues for me is that most of my students were running on Mac. There were very few tools running on Mac, so we had to figure out something that would be quick and easy to use and run on Mac, which had a USB port, because most of these tools have the problem that they tend to run on Windows and have serial ports, so back then, it was tricky. Some of the requirements for a tool like this started to slowly form in my mind, as I worked with students.

We started to use this tool called Processing to teach students how to program. So we thought, "We should try to figure out ways to run this thing on

---

[2]A popular line of microcontrollers by Atmel. Most Arduinos and Arduino compatible boards use Atmel AVR chips.
[3]A port of the Processing language for microcontrollers (http://wiring.org.co/).
[4]http://jal.sourceforge.net

a microcontroller." So there were a number of experiments based on what I learned from the Programma 2003. Then one of my mentors, who is a professor at Stanford named Bill Verplank, told me, "You should really look at AVR chips. We use them at Stanford. They are cheap. They have a free open-source C compiler that works very well, and using some tricks, you should be able to make it look like Processing, but it's actually C."

So I remember there was a conversation that I had with Bill Verplank and Casey Reas, who's the inventor of the Processing language, in a bar in Ivrea. The three of us were chatting about where to take this technology next. And Bill suggested AVR and using the C language, and Casey was there, so we talked about it. Then we decided it would be a good idea to get a student to do a thesis on it. One of the students, Hernando Barragan, offered to work on a thesis based on physical computing. So a lot of the things that we discussed ended up in his thesis, and he implemented the first version of the API that we use on Arduino, as the Wiring project.[5]

As we were developing the thesis, I was more interested in making something using a much simpler chip that could use through-hole parts so you could put it on a breadboard and you could manufacture it yourself. I really wanted something that you could build yourself, while Hernando chose a processor that was much more powerful but required assembly by a machine because it was very hard to solder by hand. So there was a diverging philosophy. Then I guess, Hernando is a designer by background, I'm obviously more of a geek, as I am very familiar with the open-source software. I used Linux for a long time, so for me, it was very obvious to make everything I did open source, while he was much more attached to his baby, and he didn't really want to open it up too much. At some point, we tried to work together a few times, but then I needed to be able to teach with this tool going forward. I didn't want to have all this research done and the school—I mean, Ivrea—paid to get all the boards made. There were a number of resources that got purchased to actually make this thing happen. We decided that we needed an open-source version of whatever was done in Wiring so that we could move forward.

That's when I met my friend David Cuartielles, who came over to Ivrea as a visiting researcher. By sitting in his apartment at night talking about the fact that he was also teaching physical computing to students, we came up with a bunch of requirements for things we wanted in a product and the reimplementation of Wiring became the Arduino. At the beginning, it was called Wiring-lite because it was essentially an idea to make Wiring lighter, and simpler, and open source.

---

[5]http://wiring.org.co

Osborn: How much do you think making Arduino open-source contributed to its success? Why do you think the Arduino has done so well even though there are all these other platforms out there? I guess if you look at all these platforms now, a lot of them are in response to the Arduino. I would say the TI Launchpad was TI's response to Arduino. Were there many other platforms when you started? It sounds like BASIC, the PIC chips, were out there. Was that really the only competition at the time?

Banzi: There were a bunch of products based on the BASIC language, because there was this idea that BASIC language was the language for beginners. And I guess it was back in the tradition of the home computers in the eighties. BASIC was the language of beginners back then. But then we wanted something more powerful. We had all this work done on Processing that we didn't want to throw away. Students were learning it and so we wanted to extend that experience. Also, as I said, there were not many products with USB directly on the board, which was a big issue. We tried multiple USB-to-serial converters, and they were all crap. There was only one model that worked really well, but it was very hard to get in Italy.

I remember the moment when I decided that it was going to be USB-native. That was when I asked the IT people inside the institute—they used to be the people who also did the purchasing—to buy twenty-five of this specific model of converter that I knew worked on a Mac, and they ended up buying whatever they found that was cheap. So I got really, really furious because this thing didn't work properly. A few months later, some very nice guy made an open-source driver for this thing that worked on a Mac, but the installation process was hell and it was crashing all the time. So I said, "That's it. Whatever we make is going to have native USB using a chip that just works."

Osborn: So then students didn't have to fuss with finding a serial converter.

Banzi: Yes. I remember I was seriously, seriously pissed off. I was shouting at this IT guy on the phone, because he was trying to make it look like I basically okayed switching to this stupid thing because he was simply too lazy to find the right model. So I said, "Okay, that's it. I don't want to deal with this anymore. I want USB directly onboard." So there were a number of things that happened as a result of looking at current products and their limitations.

So both David Cuartielles and I had a long history in open source. We were long-time Linux users, so we wanted something that would be open source, that people could build upon, that people could adopt this platform without feeling that maybe we will decide to become pizza makers and if we abandon the platform, then it will be a disaster. No, no, we wanted to be able to say, it's open source. You can continue using it without a problem. But also the idea of making it open-source hardware was so that you would allow people to build upon our work. We thought it would be cool to just try to see if we could apply the same concept to Arduino. We didn't really have a lot of knowledge about open-source hardware. I sort of vaguely read this project called the OpenEEG,[6] where they said, "We are also open sourcing the hardware." It was the only public reference I had back then in 2004, when I started thinking about open-source hardware. So when we released the first Arduino in the beginning of 2005, we decided to make it open source as well.

This ended up being actually quite good, because at the beginning of 2005, we got news that the institute was going to shut down. An Italian telecom operator owned the institute. So we were worried that one day lawyers would show up and say, "Okay, now all of the stuff that you did at the school is property of Telecom and you have to stop working on it." So the fact that we made everything open source happened to be a good idea, because a lawyer told me, "Now everything you did is open source. It's online. What can they do? They cannot come and say this is not open source anymore, because you released it." So in a way it protected us later on from a potential shutdown of the project related to the shutdown of the institute.

Also making the board something that was a simple, double-sided PCB that you could manufacture easily helped. We even had a version that was single-sided so you could etch it in your kitchen sink. I remember at the beginning, we got some pictures of users in some countries where there were no official Arduino sold. They started to etch their own boards and drill them by hand, because you could create the whole platform from scratch with the instructions you had online. That was one of the ideas for me, since we were not really interested in setting up a proper, classically structured company. We just wanted to make this thing available, so we wanted people to be able to reproduce whatever we were doing, wherever they were, by themselves. I had a feeling that this could work.

The first summer, in 2005, when a Swiss student showed up in Ivrea to visit, I gave him a couple of blank Arduino boards, and I gave him pointers to all the documentation, and he went back home to Basel. I thought, "Okay, I'm not going to hear about this guy anymore." A couple of months later, he writes to me and says, "We built the Arduinos you gave us and we are now using them. We like them. Where can we get more? Can you come and teach Arduino here?" So that was a big "aha" moment because this guy disappeared, and two months later, he had it built and working. So that, for me, was quite cool.

Osborn: You talked a bit about people making Arduinos in their kitchen, etching their own boards. Now there are literally hundreds of Arduino clones. Part of making it open source was enabling that, but I've also seen the Hall of Shame[7] you have on your blog. Is that specifically for people who are trying to use the Arduino trademark on their clone?

---

[6]http://openeeg.sourceforge.net/doc/
[7]www.massimobanzi.com/category/hall-of-shame/

Banzi: Yes. I just published an article on our blog, which tries to clarify once and for all the official position, where if you take the Arduino files and you make your own board and you call it Steveino, that's great. I'm happy. That's fantastic. I love it. If you take the files as they are, and you just manufacture the boards and you call them again Steveino, and it's just a one-to-one copy, I'm okay with that. I'm not happy because you're not adding anything to the ecosystem. You're not giving anything back to the community apart from maybe charging less money than we do. But that's part of open source and I'm okay with that.

The problem is when people download the files and then they basically buy an original board, and then they use ways to reproduce the graphics, and they sell it to people in a way that creates the illusion that this is an official Arduino product. The problem with that is people buy it, it doesn't work, they think, "Oh, Arduino is crap." Or they think they're buying an official Arduino. Some people are actually thinking they're supporting the Arduino Project because they're buying this thing.

So for me, since we're doing everything open source, there is no reason to copy the branding. The only way you copy the branding is to trick people into buying your product thinking that they are buying the original product. I can understand that somebody says, "Well, a Louis Vuitton bag is $1,000, so I'm going to buy a copy for $50 from Canal Street and who cares?" Some people think that the people at Louis Vuitton are superrich, so who cares?

Well, an Arduino costs $29, but the cost of the board helps support the development. It also provides, for example, the fact that if your board is defective, it will be replaced, no questions asked. Obviously, there's a whole set of procedures we have signed with all the distributors where they will not screw customers. And that's important to me. This year, Arduino started to give back to the community. We donated a few thousand dollars to a bunch of open-source projects that are important for us, like Creative Commons. We donated money to the Free Software Foundation, to Processing. We use a wiki to run the web site, which is made by one guy in Canada. We gave him $2,500. So in a way, we spent about $25,000 at the beginning of the year to donate back to projects, and we're going to spend another $25K the second part of the year to donate equipment to schools and to people who request it. So buying an original product generates a chain of good. And we would like people to at least know that if they're buying a clone of Arduino, they are doing it knowing that they are doing it. They can buy this Chinese Fanduino. There's the Fanduino. You buy it. You know it's a fake one, so it means you're not interested in helping the good. I'm okay with that. So the Hall of Shame is really only for people who like to trick people.

Osborn: Thanks for the clarification. I think people using that name are taking credit for a lot of work that you did. I'm a little curious where the name "Arduino" came from.

Banzi: Well, when we started working on Arduino, it was temporarily called Wiring-lite, but obviously, we didn't want to use that name, because our project turned into a separate project that was redeveloped from scratch, both hardware and software. We only reused the name of the functions because we wanted to migrate the work I did with the students on Wiring, but we just redeveloped everything from scratch. We wanted to give it a proper name.

In the town of Ivrea, where we are working, a lot of things are called Arduino-something, because Arduino used to be the first king of Italy in the year 1000, or he was kind of the self-proclaimed king of Italy. So we were at this bar where we used to go get drinks, and I thought, "Maybe, yeah, maybe we just call it that, and we can change the name later on." So we just went with "Arduino," and it worked and we kept it, and now it's fun.

There are a lot of people who have a lot of weird theories about that because "ino" in Italian is a suffix you use when you want to make something small and it's used also in nicknames. So something that ends in "ino" tends to be small, and so people thought that "Arduino" was a contraction of "small hardware"—"hardware" and "ino"—"hardwarino." So the theories are endless. I keep hearing new theories. But effectively, it was just that we needed a name.

I was sitting in front of the computer with some files open and I was on the phone with the PCB manufacturer, and he said, "Look, either you send me the files by 12:30 so that we can process them and send them to print on film so that we can start the manufacturing process, or you're going to slip and you're going to get all these files in another week's time." And my friend David had a class starting in Malmo that needed those PCBs.

So I said, "Okay, don't worry. I'll get it to you in fifteen minutes."

So I put the phone down. I said, "David, we have to find a name." And so we looked at the screen, and I thought, "You know what?"

I said, "David, let's call it Arduino like we talked about at the bar. Then we can change it later." So I put "Arduino" on the board. Then I sent the e-mail and that was it. A few weeks ago, I even found an invoice that this guy gave me for the first three hundred PCBs. It was funny for me to find the invoice for the very first batch. We used the blank PCBs to assemble it for ourselves to use in class. I used to keep a few of these PCBs in my bag, so when I met somebody, I would say to them, "Take this PCB. Go to this web site. You can find all this information and then build it yourself."

Osborn: At this point, those are collector's editions.

Banzi: I guess if there were a market for that, it would be a collector's edition.

Osborn: So people are putting Arduinos or some spinoff of one with Arduino software on it in just about everything these days. The projects are endless. I've seen heart-rate monitors. I've seen autonomous RC cars. What are some of the interesting things you've seen people do with the Arduino platform?

Banzi: I try to divide the interesting users of Arduino into two main areas. There are the ones that are in a way exciting, fun, and inspiring but maybe not going to change the world. Then there's another category, which is the areas where the Arduino is used in a less exciting way, but it really becomes a building block for something bigger. So if you look at most of the open-source 3D printers, such as the original MakerBot,[8] or the current Ultimaker,[9] and most of the RepRaps,[10] they use Arduino as the motherboard. Or if they designed their own board, it's an extension of the Arduino board. So it became the enabler for 3D printers. When they made an open-source laser cutter, they used Arduino. Or when they made an open-source drone platform, like Chris Anderson[11] is using, they used Arduino for a long time as their basic development platform, because they could bring in beginners to work on the product and then grow them to become experts in the process.

So in the end, the interesting uses are where the Arduino becomes the building block of something else, and then people build upon it to build another product. So it creates this nice stack of open-source hardware and software technologies that enable the maker movement. They enable innovation. They enable a lot of different areas. Some people build this PCR machine,[12] which is one of the machines you use when you do a DNA analysis to amplify the DNA samples. It is all based on Arduino, all open-source ideas. So there are a number of exciting platforms that are based on Arduino. Those for me are the least visible to the end user, but they are the ones where Arduino has become substantial. It has become one of the building blocks of the maker movement.

Then obviously, you have more people—some people use it as a basis for making the ArduSat, which is this open-source satellite platform, designed to be put in space, and then even high schools can hook it up and run their own experiments inside the satellite. Again, every time you take a complex thing like space and satellites, and you make it simple, open source, available to anybody, then you get a lot of innovation.

---

[8]www.makerbot.com
[9]www.ultimaker.com
[10]http://reprap.org/wiki/Main_Page
[11]http://diydrones.com
[12]http://openpcr.org

Osborn: Is the ArduSat a spinoff or part of the CubeSat thing?

Banzi: It is a CubeSat satellite based on a little Arduino that comes with a bunch of sensors. So basically, you can buy the development platform, you can prepare the experiment on the ground, and then you can basically get access to the satellite, upload it, and you run your experiment on the Arduino on the satellite, which to me is quite exciting as an achievement.

Osborn: I have one question for myself. Why the offset pin configuration for the shield? Was that just an accident, or is it something intentional?

Banzi: It was an accident. When we developed the first Arduino, I made a mistake. Originally, the layout was much more boring. It was just a rectangle. Then David gave it the shape you see now. Then I was adjusting the layout and preparing for manufacturing, and we made this stupid offset, and then we sent it out to production. Then we started to base all the other designs on that one before somebody actually realized it. We probably reached a few thousand boards or something before we realized it was off, because somebody tried to use a regular prototyping board to put it on top. It was weird, because back in those days, a thousand boards seemed like a huge number. Then in 2006, which was probably the second year when Arduino was actually really happening as a project, we ended up hitting ten thousand official Arduino boards. At the time I was like, "Wow."

Phil Torrone wrote a blog post on *MAKE* saying, "Arduino hits 10,000." You can understand how silly we were back then, and how naïve we were, and how this was very far removed from the maker movement as you see it now, but hitting ten thousand for an open-source hardware platform like ours was an achievement. To us, ten thousand was already like a huge amount of people, and we didn't want to force the people who started to make shields for Arduino to throw them away. Now looking back at ten thousand boards as a piece of news is funny, but it shows you the growth of the movement.

Osborn: I love the fact that something that was unintentional ends up being so ingrained into the platform now. There have been, I'm guessing millions of Arduino or Arduino-compatible devices, and they all have this quirk, but we now we know the history of it. It's pretty funny.

Banzi: Then at some point, Limor Fried told me, "Don't worry about it. Actually, this quirk forces people to plug the shield into the Arduino the right way." It's like when you key a connector and make it only work when plugged in one way.

Osborn: So when your shield is rotated one hundred eighty degrees, it won't plug in.

Banzi: I guess that, in a way, was the justification I needed to feel less bad.

Osborn: I don't think you have any reason to feel bad at this point.

Banzi: Well, we got some heat for that on some blogs, and some people tend to comment using fairly strong language.

Osborn: I'm sure people accuse you of doing it on purpose, of making it incompatible for profit and all that stuff, but whatever. Your success speaks for itself, and it's open source, if somebody wanted to fix it and make it themselves, they could do that.

Banzi: That is true.

Osborn: What are the plans for the future? I know you're launching new boards. I know there's the Arduino Due that has the ARM processor. I don't know if you have plans to make more ARM boards or if you are just focusing more on software. What are the ideas for the future that we can talk about?

Banzi: We have been releasing a number of pieces of hardware, and there is this tendency from the market to ask for more powerful products, but effectively, the issue is not the more powerful products. You can do amazing work with less powerful hardware if you have the right tools. I want to concentrate in the future on the tools. Make them better. Develop the environment. Make it much more integrated with the web site. Make the Arduino development environment a tool that gets together all the different aspects of what a maker does—the software, the hardware, the digital part—in a way the fabrication part, try to figure out ways you can combine all these things, so that one Arduino project contains all these elements.

I guess that is a lot of work. I think it's interesting because I believe there is a lot of growth that we can do with Arduino by keeping the hardware the same and just inventing new tools that make it easier and easier or let you squeeze more out of the tools you have already, which I think is probably important for the future. The world doesn't need a lot more hardware. It needs better ways to use the hardware you have. Also, in general, I would like to extend the work Arduino has to new technologies. Arduino has become known for making more complex technologies simpler, available to a larger audience. I think that this paradigm extends to a lot of other aspects of technology where we could work.

Osborn: For most people wanting to learn about microcontroller programming and electronics an eight-bit AVR is more than enough to learn what they need to on it. You don't need a 4-Core ARM chip to teach somebody basic programming skills.

Well, I learned a lot about Arduino. I'm really glad you took the time to do this because I think many people know what an Arduino is, but they may not know the story behind it, and I think it's a good story.

Index

Get the eBook for only $10!

> Now you can take the weightless companion with you anywhere, anytime. Your purchase of this book entitles you to 3 electronic versions for only $10.

This Apress title will prove so indispensible that you'll want to carry it with you everywhere, which is why we are offering the eBook in 3 formats for only $10 if you have already purchased the print book.

Convenient and fully searchable, the PDF version enables you to easily find and copy code—or perform examples by quickly toggling between instructions and   applications. The MOBI format is ideal for your Kindle, while the ePUB can be utilized on a variety of mobile devices.

Go to www.apress.com/promo/tendollars to purchase your companion eBook.

Apress®
THE EXPERT'S VOICE™

Other Apress Business Titles You Will Find Useful

Lobbyists at Work
Leech
978-1-4302-4560-5

Lawyers at Work
Cosslett
978-1-4302-4503-2

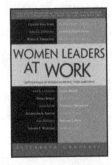

Women Leaders at Work
Ghaffari
978-1-4302-3729-7

Inventors at Work
Stern
978-1-4302-4506-3

CIOs at Work
Yourdon
978-1-4302-3554-5

Advertisers at Work
Tuten
978-1-4302-3828-7

Venture Capitalists at Work
Shah/Shah
978-1-4302-3837-9

CTOs at Work
Donaldson/Siegel/Donaldson
978-1-4302-3593-4

European Founders at Work
Santos
978-1-4302-3906-2

Available at www.apress.com